WORKING
IN THE
LIGHT

DAILY REFLECTIONS

STARSHA DAWN

BALBOA.
PRESS
A DIVISION OF HAY HOUSE

Scripture taken from the King James Version of the Bible.

Balboa Press books may be ordered through booksellers or by contacting:

Balboa Press
A Division of Hay House
1663 Liberty Drive
Bloomington, IN 47403
www.balboapress.com
1 (877) 407-4847

Because of the dynamic nature of the Internet, any web addresses or links contained in
this book may have changed since publication and may no longer be valid. The views
expressed in this work are solely those of the author and do not necessarily reflect the
views of the publisher, and the publisher hereby disclaims any responsibility for them.

The author of this book does not dispense medical advice or prescribe the use of any
technique as a form of treatment for physical, emotional, or medical problems without the
advice of a physician, either directly or indirectly. The intent of the author is only to offer
information of a general nature to help you in your quest for emotional and spiritual well-
being. In the event you use any of the information in this book for yourself, which is your
constitutional right, the author and the publisher assume no responsibility for your actions.

Any people depicted in stock imagery provided by Thinkstock are models,
and such images are being used for illustrative purposes only.
Certain stock imagery © Thinkstock.

Print information available on the last page.

ISBN: 978-1-5043-9277-8 (sc)
ISBN: 978-1-5043-9278-5 (hc)
ISBN: 978-1-5043-9279-2 (e)

Library of Congress Control Number: 2017918443

Balboa Press rev. date: 12/07/2017

Contents

My great thanks and appreciation go out to Kimberly Clayton for her efforts to help me find locations and shoot photos that would complement book pages, as well as her encouragement to complete the project.

My profound thanks go out to Judith Wilson, my friend and editor who worked along with me for 25 years to find my voice, style, and words to express my thoughts in 366 stories for each day of the year.

Judith and Kim, I salute you! Thank you!

Introduction

Where two or more are gathered ...

I invite you to join with me on a lightworker mission to heal the earth and heal ourselves. Let us work in God's light on a project for each day of the calendar year. Our duty as stewards of the earth is to take care of it, cleanse its wounds, and help it to rise to a higher state as we all rise in our spirituality and our love. I use the concept of directing God's light to a situation, actually seeing in my mind what a better world looks like. Sometimes I call God "Spirit." When you see that word, translate it to God, Buddha, Lord, Jesus, Universe—whatever is your way. Maybe you send prayers. My friend chants in Hawaiian. Whatever your spiritual practice, let us all be lightworkers working to envision a new and better world.

I invite you to spend a few minutes on each day's topic in whatever way you choose as we work together on our mission. Together, our focus can help our earth to move into a new age of peace and a time when the lion will truly lie down with the lamb. I see signs of this coming new world all around, so I have included a couple pages every month to remind us that even when the news seems dark, behind the headlines are many beautiful people doing wonderful things to help the earth rise. Other pages are for our own personal growth, and still others express our gratitude for being alive and working on this mission.

Lightworkers, will you join me?

KIMBERLY CLAYTON

Walking the Path Together

January gets its name from the ancient god Janus, who has two faces—one looking forward and the other looking backward. To start off this new year, take a cue from Janus. First turn around and gaze back along the path you followed this past year. Have you moved forward from where you started? Do you see obstacles you have overcome? Lessons you've learned? Have you grown in understanding?

Perhaps there have been crises and pain, separations and difficulties, endings and beginnings. These were the hilly and rocky parts of the path. Aren't you relieved you've crossed through those badlands?

Now, like Janus, look forward to this brand-new year. A new part of the path spreads before you. Do you embrace it with eagerness, or do you worry about the hills and rocks that might be there?

You need not fear. You are not alone. There are kindred souls whose paths cross yours, some even merging with your path. Your teachers and guides are close at hand. Your higher self goes with you, and your obedient subconscious too.

Let us join hands and set off together on the journey of this new year. United, we strengthen and comfort each other. United, we aid and heal the earth. Let us enjoy this adventure of Spirit's making, this step toward forever.

January 2

Log On

Today, let's borrow a term from the computer field and "log on." We are going to the real World Wide Web. Today, we all have the same code name: lightworker. Let's type it in and see what comes up on the screen:

L i g h t w o r k e r (enter)

Welcome! You have joined the Network of Light. Click here to join our projection zone.

Click.

Unite with us today and picture a tightly woven World Wide Web of light—our combined light—as we each ask Spirit within us to pour light down through us and then out to link with the World Wide Web of lightworkers. See the planet aglow, revving up its vibration, casting off its darkness and debris. Hold this light with us every day.

We link awhile and then click on the High-Self Chat Room.

Welcome, most beloved! I am your High Self, the I Am within you. Do you have a question?

Go ahead and type in your question, knowing you will be answered in Spirit's time. Keep this website address in your heart and log on often.

Brightly Wrapped Packages

There you are in a new setting, a place you've never been before. It may be on a plane, at a shopping mall, in a new job or school, or even in a new town where you've just moved. Does the newness and strangeness bother you? Do you feel a little uneasy meeting new people or being alone in a crowd? This need not happen if you can trust that Spirit has presented you with a new adventure.

You can turn anxiety into excitement and pleasure if you can see the new situation as a brightly wrapped package. What could be inside? Could there be a smile, a kind word, a pleasant conversation? Could you be receiving a new idea, accepting an offer of assistance, or sharing a laugh?

Everywhere you go, there are interesting people just waiting to be discovered. There might even be a new friend in the crowd or a fellow lightworker. What a wonderful adventure awaits you. What marvelous gifts Spirit leaves here and there for you. But most of these gifts are wrapped, and their contents concealed. You must do your part to discover the gifts. So go ahead—pull off the wrappings and open the boxes. Treasures await inside.

Pushing Your Buttons

There you sit with emotions wounded, telling your best friend the sad story of how you are being terribly mistreated. You describe the affronts, believing your friend will reply, "Oh, you poor thing! How terribly you've been abused!"

But instead, when you pause for breath, your friend gives you a puzzled look and says, "Well, I really don't see why you are so upset. It doesn't seem so bad to me."

You stare at your friend in disbelief, thinking, *Has she lost her mind? Can't she see how horrible these events were?*

Your friend continues, "Perhaps you are reacting too strongly. Maybe this situation has pushed one of your buttons."

There is the key. If people who know and love you can't see why you should be so upset at a situation, perhaps it is time for a review of your buttons. We all have some triggers from past experiences. Perhaps a jealousy button, a fear button, a rejection button. We all tend to read meaning into situations from nonverbal as well as ambiguous verbal cues. Might we be seeing a lack of a prompt response to a request as a rejection because we were rejected before? Might we see an act of careless inattention as a deliberate affront because of something that happened in our past?

If there is a current situation that produces an unreasonably strong reaction, perhaps a button has been pushed. The realization that this has happened allows us to remove the automatic responses from the past and reevaluate the situation on its own merits. Has anything pushed your buttons lately?

The Copper-Bottom Pot

You are standing at the sink with a large job to do. In your hand is a copper-bottom pot that has a thick crust of burnt-on black grease. You have a scrubbing pad in your hand, and you begin.

Rub, rub, rub, scrub, scrub, scrub, puff, puff, rub, rub, rub, puff, puff, rub. You pause to wipe the sweat from your brow. Your fingers are turning to soapy prunes. But as you wash off the soap to take a look, you are discouraged to see you have made very little headway with the pot.

You ready yourself for a second assault. You widen your stance, get a death grip on the pot, and resume your task with a vigor bordering on mania. You throw your shoulders and hips into the scrubbing dance. Another rinse, and you are just starting to see a tiny section of the shiny copper emerging in all its glory, taunting you to scrub some more.

What is this copper-bottom pot? It is us—encrusted with erroneous ways, untruths, and attitudes of the lower self. Our mission in this lifetime is to work with vigor and determination to scrub the pot clean until our iridescent light emerges in all its glory.

Already the little spots we've cleaned glow and attract people, and we, likewise, are attracted to the bright spots in others. Let us remember today that those people we see on the news or meet in person who seem all covered in grime have that same glorious glow underneath.

January 6

One Million Times

Have you ever found a person in your life who truly loves you, no matter what? This could be a parent, spouse, friend, teacher—anyone you could be sure of. Think of this person now. Immerse yourself in the feeling you get when you think about the interactions between you and this person and the trust you have in this person, and then answer these questions: Do you believe this person always has your best interests at heart? Do you trust this person with your secrets, your pain, and your joy? Do you feel a cozy security thinking about the bond with this person?

Feel those feelings. Do they feel wonderful? Are you smiling just thinking about this relationship?

Now, put on your imagination cap. Try to imagine a love that is one million times stronger than this person's love for you. Turn up the volume on love until it is off the dial. Does your imagination show you how all-encompassing and powerful this love is? This is God's love for us. It is beyond our wildest attempts to comprehend.

Can you imagine the pleasure of trusting your special person magnified one million times? Can you find the security and relief of trusting God's love enough to turn over all the outcomes of all the situations in your life to God?

Wrapping Yourself with Light

There are many people meditating these days, and that is great. But for meditation to serve your highest purpose, it is wise to protect yourself as you enter into an altered state. If your goal is to link with other lightworkers to project thoughts and prayers and light to people and situations, and if your goal is also to receive inspiration, healing, and guidance from masters, angels, and your own higher self, then you must make sure you are open only to the highest levels and closed to beings who function at low levels of enlightenment. To prevent low-level beings from contacting you, I offer the technique I have used since I began meditating in the '70s.

When I sit to meditate, the first thing I do is visualize the white light of Spirit wrapping around my body, beginning below my feet and wrapping around and around about a foot or so out from the body to encompass my astral body too. I am creating a cocoon of light, closed at the bottom and solidly wrapped to the crown of my head. At the crown, I picture the cocoon narrowing to a little stem of light. I declare silently but firmly that I am now wrapped with light and open to contact only from the highest levels and only with permission of my High Self who directs this meditation. Now I am ready to receive only the highest contact for my highest good. How about trying it yourself when you meditate today?

Staying Wrapped with Light

When you will yourself to be wrapped in a cocoon of light, you are within a shield that protects you from the world's negativity. And you have established a link to your higher self's guidance, so your intuitions can come now from the highest source. It is good to keep yourself protected all the time, not just in meditation.

So I invite you to wrap yourself with light when you wake up each day. But here's the issue: when you express negativity, you break the cocoon of light. That's okay; just revisualize it and rededicate yourself to keeping the link with your higher self and the light cocoon intact. It only takes me about two seconds now to wrap myself in the cocoon of light, and, believe me, I know when I have broken it. It is often when I have just called some driver an idiot in my thoughts. And, oh, there is one more thing to do before reestablishing the light cocoon: I must change my negative thought. In my example, I acknowledge that the driver's behavior was reckless, but the driver is a divine child of God, just like me. I apologize in my mind to this divine being, then acknowledge that my anger was a natural reaction to almost being killed, and l let the anger flow out of me. Then I can get back into my cocoon of light. I hope you will do the same.

UBWHOUR

Hmm. Another cryptic license plate in front of me on the road. I love to try to figure these out. Let's see if I can get it before that car disappears. Okay. The UBW Hour. I wonder if that is a radio station? No, can't be. U must be you. Okay. What is BWHOUR? Hmm. BW—bewitching hour? Hmm. Are they witches? But that doesn't go with U in front of it. As I rack my brain, I get a little closer as we pull up to a light. I give the license plate a hard look and discover that its owner had put little strips of red tape underneath groups of letters to delineate the words for the uncomprehending.

If you haven't figured it out by now, here's what it says: You Be Who You Are.

Now I smile and laugh at myself for being dense. And then I let the beauty of the message sink in. This person is encouraging me along my way, letting me know it is okay to be myself, no matter how different I am.

Thank you, fellow traveler, for providing this loving blessing from Spirit. So I pass it along to you too, Dear Reader:

U B WHO U R!

January 10

Thy Will Be Done

Surrender is not a popular word. In the minds of many, it signals defeat. But is it really?

Surrender is letting go of the need to control everything. It is realizing that God is and should be in control. When the master Jesus taught us to pray, "Thy will be done," he showed us the proper relationship between our mortal self and our higher self, which I honor by calling it the High Self. Our goal is to become one with that spark of God that should be directing our lives, and to learn to desire the highest result.

"Thy will be done" releases us from worry and fear, from anger over outcomes we did not prefer based on our limited physical-plane wisdom. It does not relieve us of the obligation to try our best, to work at our tasks, to set the stage for the manifestation of good. But when our part is done and we await results, we can rest easily knowing all is in God's hands.

Let go of your will. Turn it over to Spirit's will. Experience relief and joy.

January 11

Martha and Mary

When Jesus came to dine at the house of the sisters, Martha and Mary (Luke 10), Martha busied herself with the meal while Mary sat at his feet and listened to his words. Martha was so caught up in her traditional hostess role that she missed the point of the visit, which was the sharing of thoughts. She was showing Jesus a well-run house and an elaborate meal, as she had been taught.

I think of Mary and Martha whenever a guest from out of town is coming to stay with me, especially if they have not been to my house before. When I hear that someone is coming, my Martha side kicks in. I look around the house with a critical eye. *This room is messy. I have to move this furniture around. What food shall I buy?* I become a product of my childhood training to show off an orderly house and plan for every physical need. (*Soft pillows or hard? I wonder which is right.*) This can lead to a level of panic in which I can mull over the pillows or the salad dressings for days on end. If I can get a grip on this Martha side, I can resurrect the Mary side, the part that is eager to share conversations with my friend, eager to drink in the pleasures of the visit and the visitor, without being too worried about the house and the food.

Yet if I go too much over to the Mary side, there will be no food and no clean sheets. So I must balance Martha and Mary—get ready but be ready to have fun, to sit and talk and let the dirty dishes wait. I'm working on it. You may have this problem, or you may be the visitor to someone who has it. Let's see what we can do to be the best of both Martha and Mary.

Signs of the New Age: Innovative Solutions

Garbage has become our monster. There is so much we have run out of places to put it. Barges are hauling it long distances from cities to the last few rural places that need the income enough to accept it, and these are getting full too.

Long ago, I heard of an inventor thinking outside the box to solve this problem. Back in 2003, a magazine reported that someone had come up with a way to turn garbage piles into oil, using a simple method of pressure cooking it in a specially designed machine. The oil was then useful for running that same machine. The excess oil was used to run other equipment. At that time, a chicken-processing plant was trying out the method with good results.

Although this inventive method did not catch on, it is still an example of someone using creativity to invent a way out of a problem. There are so many problems, and we surely need many innovative solutions. So, today, let's focus on these brilliant people who can see beyond a problem to its possible solution. Let us envision these innovators receiving needed funding to do their research, and let us see some good results happening too. And let us also envision the world's massive garbage dumps melting away and being replaced with lovely landscapes.

The Wisdom to Know the Difference

The serenity prayer says:

> God, grant me the serenity to accept the things I cannot change,
> The courage to change the things I can,
> And the wisdom to know the difference.

This last line is a very important one. Look at it again. Many heartaches are the result of banging our heads against a wall, trying to change things or people that we have no power to change. Is it possible to change another person by wishing for it, demanding it, or manipulating it? No. The only result is resentment and resistance on the part of that other person and frustration for us.

Who is the only person we can change? We know the answer—ourselves. Can a change in us bring a change in the other person? Maybe, but that's not the point.

Make it a project today to look at one *small* thing about another that you want to see changed. Now what can you do about your attitude toward that situation? Can you surrender and admit you are powerless to force or manipulate a change? Can you honestly tell the other person how you feel, avoiding the word "you" and sticking to "I feel"? Can you put it into perspective? Is it a small thing? Will it kill you if it continues? Can you detach, go on with your life, send peace and love, and let go of the outcome?

If you can, then you are truly wise enough "to know the difference."

January 14

They Have No Country

Here I was once again watching the Olympics, like I do every time. I just love to see the opening ceremony where the athletes all march in, each group behind the flag of their nation. It makes me so glad to see so many nations marching together in peace, so many young people smiling, no matter what the politics are in their countries.

Well, in 2016, I got to see for the first time an amazing sight. The Olympic Committee became aware that there were athletes who had fled their war-torn countries and were living in refugee camps. They had no flag, no country. So the Committee decided to let them march behind the flag of the Olympic rings. There they were, waving and smiling just like all the other athletes, so proud and happy that they had fulfilled their dreams of being in the Olympics.

To me, this is a sign that our world is showing more empathy and compassion. Gradually, we are moving to a higher level of light. Today, let us join together to thank all those people everywhere who are working in the light, helping their fellow humans, no matter where they are from. And let us also send light to all those who have fled their countries, to uplift their hope that they will find a home at last.

Choose Your Future

All our thoughts, words, and deeds have an impact, not only on others but especially on ourselves. We create our future by our attitudes and actions in the present.

Martin Luther King said, "All life is interrelated, all humanity part of one process. And to the degree that I harm my brother, to that extent I am harming myself."

Once everyone on earth comes to understand the truth of this concept, then our race can finally break free from the hatreds and conflicts that have bound us to the third dimension. Together, let us project this thought to all our brothers and sisters incarnated in physical bodies: "Do unto others as you would have them do unto you, for what you do unto another, you truly do unto yourself. Choose by your actions and attitudes the kind of future you want to create for yourself."

January 16

Using Your Word for the Year

In the December 28 and 29 pages (skip ahead to read them), I talked about my picking a theme word for the next year, something I wanted to work on with my personality or spiritual development, something I was not good at and wanted to become better at. Perhaps you decided to pick a word for yourself. So now what will you do with your word to make it into a project for this year?

When a word comes to me for the next year, I always react by thinking, *Oh no, not that word!* And that's how I know it's the right word. it is always something I don't want to face.

If you have your word, I suggest you meditate or journal or discuss with a spiritual friend why this word has come to you. Ask them what their reaction is to the word for themselves and how they see this word in relation to you. That will be the start. Ask to be guided to learn more about the word and to receive situations that will help you practice the art of doing things differently, based on your study of the word.

Expressing your intentions to learn and grow in this area will draw opportunities to you to learn more about yourself through studying your word.

January 17

Trapped in the Elevator

So you're standing in the elevator, and in comes someone with enough perfume on to knock you dead. Oh no! Thirty-six more floors to go! You try to hold your breath, but you only last for seventeen floors. In desperation, you gasp, but the renewal of the killer scent leaves you coughing and your eyes watering. When the elevator opens, you run toward the relief of good air.

Whew! Are we ever guilty of coming on strong like cheap perfume? Do we ever trap someone into breathing an unpleasant scent for thirty-six floors? Does anyone ever run from us, glad to get away?

Think back to the days before we began our quest. If we had heard stories of karma, channeling, the New Age, and so on, wouldn't we have felt trapped and assaulted?

Sometimes we can get so excited we forget that another person might feel frightened or assaulted by our views. Easy does it. Remember the old 50s commercial, "A little dab'll do ya." Well, a little dab of Spirit will certainly be enough for many people. Let's strive to speak of our beliefs only to those willing to hear. Perhaps if we wait, a question will come on a topic the other person wants to discuss. Let's wear our perfume lightly so that the other will say, "What's that interesting perfume you have on?" And if, Dear Reader, you don't have New Age beliefs, would you try to think kindly of those who do and of our mutual desire to heal the earth?

January 18

Using Cosmic Law

Learning to use cosmic law in our daily life seems quite hard at first. What about all these laws: oneness, equality, cause and effect, give and take, noninterference, example, attraction, sacrifice? What of the law that encompasses all others, given by the master Jesus, "Love God and love one another"? How do they all fit in? Which one relates to what I am doing and saying this day, this moment?

Relax. We have learned many different things already in just this one life. They all proved to be difficult at the beginning. The alphabet, reading, multiplication tables, tying our shoes, learning to walk and talk, to ride a bike, and later to drive. All were so hard when we faced them for the first time. But think of them all now. They have been learned so well their use has become automatic. No longer do we have to focus conscious attention on placing one foot in front of the other or writing a letter or driving a car.

How did we learn to do them all? Practice! Little successes and even the mistakes helped us to learn. So take it easy. Don't be anxious. When in doubt, stop and ask, "What would a great master teacher do in this situation?" If you still don't know, don't worry. Turn it over to your High Self's guidance, and eventually the answer will come.

The Talking Stick

I spent a weekend with a group of about fifty people who share my passion for improving the culture of the nation's nursing homes. We are each so eager to tell our stories to each other that we could become a cacophony of voices speaking all at once. But we have adopted a method of interacting that solves the problem and also solves the opposite problem of encouraging the quieter, shyer ones to contribute their wisdom.

We have borrowed from our Native American brothers and sisters the practice of the talking stick. We actually use some object—a stick, big spoon, pen, even a can of corn nuts—and go around our quite large circle clockwise. Only the person with the stick can talk. There is no rebuttal or even discussion. Each other person gives attention and listens with respect. This creates a safe space for viewpoints to be expressed without threat of challenge. It is a gorgeous tool for getting to know each other, for brainstorming, for interpreting a common theme that has been set before us.

If you find yourself in a group discussing something this week, even a small one, I suggest you consider introducing the respectful concept of the talking stick.

January 20

Changing the Bottom Line

Some corporations have been making changes to become more conscious of the environment, to treat their employees better, and to make a good product or perform a good service at a fair price. Let's send our thanks to those companies who are leading the way in this awakening. Bless you. You have come to understand that you share responsibility for the earth, your employees, and your community.

But what about those companies who are not trying, who see the bottom line strictly in terms of profits? I've heard and read about various companies saying they can't make these good changes because their stockholders won't tolerate any lessening of profit in the short run, even for long-term gains, even for noble reasons.

I think many stockholders are, in fact, spiritually motivated in many aspects of their lives. They recycle, they donate to good causes, they don't litter, they pray for others. But they may not be spiritually motivated when it comes to their MONEY.

So let's direct our attention to stockholders and to companies today. Let's see them waking up to realize that it is beneficial for a corporation to be a good steward of the earth and kind to its employees. Let's visualize dissolving their resistance as they awaken to their responsibilities toward the earth and to each other. Let's visualize companies being inspired to join the movement toward goodness as they realize good stewards can also be profitable companies.

And, if you feel inspired, write to a company doing poorly and ask them to change to benefit the earth we all share, and write to a company doing good to thank them.

Letting the Answer Come

Do you ever get stumped in figuring out how to fix something that is working poorly in your home? I surely do. Do you ever lose things around the house and frantically go room to room searching for them? I do that too.

Once I realize that I am not getting anywhere with my own ideas or searches, I stop trying and sit quietly, waiting for the answer to come. After a couple minutes, when I have calmed myself enough to be open to other realms, I get a strong and sudden hunch of what to do. I jump right up and follow the hunch, and almost 100 percent of the time, the hunch is right. These hunches I get are very specific and are things I have not thought of on my own, such as when my keys had fallen off the nightstand to the floor and accidentally got kicked under the bed.

So I ask you, do you frustrate yourself with problems that seem unfixable or with lost items in the house? I think that frantic pursuit of the fix makes us too anxious to find the right answer. I suggest the next time this happens to you, give up fussing and sit quietly, asking for an answer and letting it come.

The Tower of Babble

Hear the voices, all talking at once. "Come to me. I'll show you your past lives." "Buy this magic talisman—have power over others." "Come hear me channel beings from other planets." "Let me show you how to find your inner child." "Come do a fire walk, sweat lodge, mindfulness retreat, shamanic journey ..."

On and on, in newsletters and magazines, on bulletin boards at health food stores and crystal shops, vendors are selling products of the New Age. So many people! So many books! So many promises! The voices cry out loudly, trying to attract our attention. So much noise—a veritable Tower of Babel, or as we could call it, a Tower of Babble.

Many people have found a piece of Truth, something that has worked for them, and they are eager to give it to the rest of us. People are excited over their discoveries, and they want us to join them on their path. Some just want to exploit this for financial gain. How do we pick the right teacher? How do we know we are on the right path?

Spirit often sends us messages through outward means when we are deaf to the still, small voice within. It's okay to learn from others as long as we retain our powers of discernment. If we are exploring paths, let's put on our judgment caps and ask some questions:

1. Is this teaching consistent with the golden rule and with our duty to love God and love one another?
2. Does this path promise power over others? If so, reject it. Cosmic law does not permit interference with the free will of others.
3. Does some teacher charge an unreasonably high fee? If so, they may be more interested in material prosperity for themselves than spiritual development of others. The highest teachers only ask a "love offering" to allow the participants to follow their own guidance on how much to give.

When in Doubt, Don't

When I was young and first encountered thoughts new to me—reincarnation, the Edgar Cayce materials, Hinduism's teaching that we are all part of God—I was eager to tell others what I had found. But I soon found myself stung by criticism and rebuffed by aggressive disbelief wrapped in sarcasm. I learned to be silent to everyone about what I believed. Yet I knew there might be some people who would share my excitement and want to further investigate these new thoughts. So I decided I must be patient and listen to a go-ahead signal from another person before I revealed myself. I wonder if you are having the same struggle—knowing when to speak and when to be silent?

Jesus knew when he was questioned by Caiaphas and then by Pilate that they were not eager for his truth. So he kept his silence, even though he had preached to many crowds.

So I watch and wait too. But I live my life as true to myself as I can be. And sometimes someone will come to me and ask what my beliefs are. Then I can speak a little at first and more only if encouraged along. I do not need to "save" anyone with my words. Everyone is in Spirit's hands, not mine. If I'm in doubt whether I should speak, I don't. I invite you, for your own peace of mind, to follow this same guidance. When in doubt, don't.

January 24

The Appointment Book

Both my work life and personal life are filled with appointments: work meetings, teleconferences, medical appointments, dinner with a friend, going to a play, office luncheons, and so on. Every day has so much in it. I'm at the point where I'd never be at the right place at the right time if I didn't have my appointment book.

I was watching the TV show *Touched by an Angel*, and one of the angels said to the other that he was "assigned here tonight." Gee, so they have appointments too. It got me to thinking about real angels and what they are doing to help us all. They must be quite busy fulfilling requests for their help.

This made me think that I was not scheduling in my appointment book any time to spend in meditation, prayer, or inviting my angels to heal and help me. Well, I've got to fix that. My dear angels, I'd like to spend time with you each day to feel your love and thank you for your help. Could I please make an appointment with you today?

How about you, Dear Reader? Are there any special appointments you'd like to add to your book?

The Darkness and the Dawn

I often wonder how far I've come
From those old days I've known,
When I was young and ignorant
And underground, a seed un-grown.

It wasn't so long ago
I thought some thoughts that turned out untrue.
How many of these thoughts I think of now
Someday will I see as untrue too?

Where do I stand?

Somewhere in between where I was and will be.
And yet one thing I know I've learned:
To love the whole journey and not just its end
Is the key to peace for me.

To know all of life is beautiful,
Not just the parts I'd choose to see.
Yes, even those parts where my light was dim
Showed me something about the world and me.

Thank you, Spirit, for my path thus far.
Take my hand as I continue on.
Let me know you more and more.
Show me the darkness and the dawn.

January 26

Signs of the New Age: Kiddie Cars

I saw a video on Facebook about a good man who noticed that toddlers in wheelchairs were often shunned by other children. So he used his mechanical skills to turn electric kiddie cars into vehicles for use by these children. The video showed a child in a specially designed car being part of the gang, as giggling kids ran along with him.

The man customizes his vehicles for kids with particular needs. For one child who had trouble keeping her head up, he placed the accelerator in a pad behind her head, so she had to press back into it with her head to move forward. For a boy who was learning to strengthen his weak legs, the car was adjusted so it would only move if he stood up in it.

Let's bless the compassion of this good man as well as his innovation and creativity. Let us bless all good people who are seeing needs and stepping up to do what they can to make a difference. And let us envision people sharing their talents more and more, reaching out with their special talents to help others.

Aquarius—The Water Carrier

"This is the dawning of the _____ _____ _____ (sing it out)."

In my college days in the early 70s, the play *Hair* came to Broadway, and the song "Aquarius" was an anthem of the young people hoping for a New Age—the Age of Aquarius. In astronomy (not astrology), the earth and its solar system progress in a circle through the galaxy over twenty-five thousand years, going through each of the zodiac constellations for a little over two thousand years, in reverse of the order of the signs. The Piscean Age lasted from about the time of Jesus's birth till about the year 2000 or so. At the edge of each transition from one constellation to another, we are in between. In about 1960, the in-between time began as we prepared to slide into Aquarius.

We are at the edge of this New Age as our world gradually leaves behind war and aggression and begins to see us all as One. Signs we are moving upward are all around if you look for them in the midst of constant bad news. Even science is learning that we all affect each other, and we even affect the molecules themselves.

But what of Aquarius traits? Aquarians are the humanitarians—progressive, modern, creative, truth seeking, friendly, popular. Hey, if you are reading this book, this is a description of you. We are children of Aquarius. Let's send our light today to all those who share our path to greater spirituality. Let our union in light begin to heal us and heal our earth. Picture us, the humanitarians, reaching out our hands to all who need us, giving them hope for a bright future, for a New Age.

January 28

International Cooperation

What do the following countries have in common: Bolivia, Brazil, India, Ivory Coast, Mexico, Nigeria, Peru, the United States, Vietnam?

Stumped? These countries are scattered all over the world. What could possibly link them together? Well, I was eating nuts from a can of mixed nuts and found on the label that all these countries had contributed their nuts to what was in the can. Well, well. I looked anew at the nuts in my can. They are a sign of international cooperation, each country contributing something it does well.

If countries all over the world can cooperate like this, then I believe we are on the way to eventually becoming a world of friendly nations that can use their resources to contribute to a better world for us all. So today let's envision international cooperation expanding more and more, not just in nuts but in all things.

Faith in the Coming of Spring

In the northern climates at this time of year, many places are under a blanket of pure white snow. Yet in spite of the cold, lifeless appearance of the landscape, we believe with absolute certainty that the snow will leave the ground, to be replaced with the spring burst of color and warmth as nature comes back to life.

We have faith that this will happen because we have seen it happen year after year for as long as we have lived. We can remember last year's spring, and we are sure it will come again. This faith is different from wishing or hoping, because there is no doubt. We know nature will not let us down.

When we think in a larger time frame from life to life, and we think of those who are no longer with us in this life, let us capture that same sure, strong, undoubting faith that we will be reunited with those we love. For we know that the bond of love is stronger than the temporary absence caused by so-called death.

If you as a lightworker have achieved this faith, let those around you see it and feel the comforting strength of this faith whenever they are in doubt or feel that their loved one is lost. Let them feel your sureness that, just as spring comes again, so we are reunited with those who love us.

January 30

Into the Pool

How would you react if I told you that I was going to hoist you up on a crane and then drop you into a deep swimming pool? Would you feel afraid? Feel you were being unfairly treated or even punished?

On TV, I watched this very thing happen to a man, and he was just as happy as could be. For, you see, this was John Glenn, and he was undergoing training for his ride on the space shuttle. He was in full space suit and helmet, hoisted up about twelve feet and dropped. I guess it was a test of both the fit of his suit and his reaction to the rough splashdown.

It's funny, isn't it, that the same events can arouse such different emotions, depending on our expectations and attitudes? We may not be able to control what happens to us, but we can always control our response to it.

If we can trust that Spirit has a hand in our lifel, we can see each thing that happens to us as a chance to grow, to test our faith, to have an unexpected change that leads to something good. I believe all that I experience is part of my plan, and I am supposed to use these situations to learn, grow, and find new directions on my path. I try to stay alert to the possibilities.

For example, a traffic jam becomes an opportunity to think something over, to hear something interesting on the radio, to sing along to a favorite tune. If I can find the positive in things that at first seem negative, then I can be happy on my own terms and not just reacting to whatever happens around me. So how will you handle your expectations and attitudes today?

Lightwork—PTSD

Today, let us unite to project Spirit's light of healing to all those around the world who suffer from PTSD, post-traumatic stress disorder. This condition comes as an aftereffect of a great stressor. It could be from a rape, a terrible accident, a war, a tsunami, or any traumatic event. Those who have PTSD suffer terribly with emotions so strong that they can hardly cope. Some cannot cope, choosing instead to kill themselves.

So let us lightworkers send healing light that seeks every person with this condition. Let this light descend on them like a cozy blanket that makes them feel safe, relieved, loved, and understood. Envision them healing, their pain lessening, being able to return to life with happiness that they are no longer victims of this condition. And if you know someone who is going through the pain of PTSD, show them your kindness and love.

February 1

Seeing Auras

As we move into the higher vibration of the New Age, we will learn more and more to see auras. This regaining of one of our spiritual talents will cause a great change in society. Along with this ability to see the swirling colors and their changes will come the knowledge of their meaning. To a seer of auras, it will be obvious when a person is angry, distressed, lying, or thinking lower thoughts. We will see the colors change as the lie is told.

Ancient rulers often had a wise man or woman with them whenever they held court. Perhaps some of these advisors were seers of auras who could tell their king who was lying and who was trustworthy.

Just think of the things that will change as more and more of us begin to see dishonesty. Think of all the situations in which lying is part of the customary strategy. They can include lying in job interviews, on the witness stand, on the campaign trail, in commerce, and especially in everyday personal relationships.

Just think what kind of TV ads we may see in a future in which we recognize lies. Just think of the effects this would have on the jobs of a judge, police officer, counselor, executive, and parent. Daydream a scenario of the new way these interactions will unfold. Does your present pattern of interaction with others bear scrutiny by a seer of auras? Think it over.

The Orchestra

The audience crowds in and finds their seats. Their talking and laughing quiets as the orchestra files onto the stage. And then the orchestra begins to play the song that sounds the same for any orchestra in the world. This song is the song of tuning. The players warm their instruments by playing scales, adjusting the pitch with raucous disregard for every other player. Some practice the hardest parts they will play that night, and some test their high and low notes. This unintentional song always excites me, for it is a sign of the wonders to come.

Then the concert mistress or master comes on stage and plays one pure note. All those on stage cease their individual playing and adjust their pitch to this one in order to play in harmony.

This is the challenge for the lightworkers on earth now. We have spent years studying and practicing to play our instruments. We are now up on stage before the audience of mass consciousness. Our task is to cooperate in tuning our instruments to one pure note—the note of love.

When the tuning is complete and the musicians are waiting attentively, the conductor will arrive on stage to begin the symphony of truth, love, and light. Our song will resound throughout the cosmos, proclaiming us one planet, united in love.

February 3

Pain

Your head is pounding, or maybe it is your tooth, your knee, or some other part. Pain takes over your world for a few minutes, hours, or days when you become ill or your physical body goes out of tune. Pain is a reminder, a loud messenger that says, "Divert your attention to the physical. Take a look to see what is wrong and find out what to do about it." Pain is our red light that says, "Stop, look, and listen to the physical."

Sometimes pain is a sign of major spiritual growth while the physical body struggles to keep up with changes. I like to think of these as spiritual growing pains. They include tiredness, aches and pains, a minor sore throat, tension, irritability, and headaches. These growing pains are caused by old beliefs resisting the change to higher patterns. They often appear suddenly during or after struggling with a spiritual problem.

But at other times, it reminds us we have gone too long without taking care of the body, to change our schedule to accommodate the needs we have developed for rest, good food, exercise, and recreation.

Pain says, "Whoa! Slow down!" Whether it is a spiritual growing pain or a pain caused by neglect of the physical body or even an illness that is going around, pain is a signal that something needs to be addressed. Let's heed the call of pain when it comes and not try to conduct business as usual. Let's listen and be kind to our bodies. Soon we will be better than ever.

Trust but Verify

President Reagan's favorite Russian expression every time he met with Mikhail Gorbachev was *droverai no proverai*—trust but verify. This expression held true for his negotiations with the Soviet president, and it also holds true for our duty to verify material we receive spiritually. This applies to messages we receive directly in meditations, dreams, or other psychic means, and also to information we read or hear.

Trust is important too, for it cautions us not to be too quick to throw away spiritual guidance just because we may not understand it. It could be that this material is meant for a later time when we are ready.

If material we receive or hear from others violates Cosmic Law or appears inconsistent or on a low path, this should be discarded. But if the message is a dream that you left the stove on, by all means, check it out. If your stove is off, reexamine the dream for its symbolic references, such as (in this dream) you're burning up too much of your energy or just leaving something undone.

Messages, both our own and those of others, can come from higher or lower realms. Judge the message by saying, "Would an ascended master teacher such as Jesus be telling me this? Is it consistent with the golden rule?"

Trust but verify.

February 5

Robin Hood

Think of him for a moment—Robin Hood! He stole from the rich to give to the poor, a noble idea but implemented all wrong.

Let's turn this tale around to Spirit's way of operating. Let's concentrate today on the money that wealthy people have locked away out of fear of future need.

Let us connect with those holders of great wealth and affirm for them, "Fear not. Spirit will provide for you always. The money you hold is your opportunity to serve Spirit. This money must dance and flow, not be stuck like glue, for however much you choose to give, so much more will flow back to you."

Now, really see and feel the hearts of these people open up to this message. See them realizing the chance they have to help their fellow human beings and planet Earth by sending a flow of money on its way to do good. See it as a small brook flowing from each person, uniting and forming a river of flowing goodness. Thank you, Spirit, for opening our hearts and blessing us all with abundance.

KIMBERLE CLAYTON

The Bridge

When darkness comes
And pain is all around,
Like a bridge over troubled water
I will lay me down.

—"Bridge over Troubled Water" by Paul Simon

Do you have someone who will comfort you when you are sad and care for you when you are down and out? Do you have someone who will rejoice with you when you succeed and grieve with you when you have lost a battle?

Some of us are fortunate enough to have a real, live person who loves us this much, who understands and cares. If you do, realize that as much as this person loves you, God loves you so much more.

If you have no person who fulfills this role, you can go directly to Spirit, to Jesus or another master you follow, or to your High Self within. It happened to me some time ago that I was deep in grief, sobbing in my bed while trying to get to sleep. I was all alone with no one to comfort me. I cried and wailed and could not stop. In pure desperation, I called out to Jesus for help and comfort as the pain of this sorrow was too much to bear. All at once, love descended upon me, a blanket of pure love that I knew was from Him. I had no visions, no messages. But the feeling was so far beyond anything I have ever experienced as love, wildly beyond and too much for words to describe. I ceased crying, taken aback by the wonder of this blanket of love. I had never felt so good in my whole life. Not only wasn't I sad, I was elated with this fire hose blast of love. I was so comforted that I smiled and fell asleep.

I will never forget that feeling for the rest of my life. Just remembering it brings sweet tears of joy to my eyes, the kind of tears I sometimes cry when listening to beautiful classical music like the "Halleluiah" chorus.

When you are down, ask for Spirit's comfort and healing love and believe it will come. And project to all those who grieve and cry today that Spirit will come to them and heal them.

The Hershey's Kiss of Light

I drive a lot, and when I drive, I try to use some of my time to project light to other drivers. At first when I decided to do this, I would visualize each person in the car being surrounded by their own light cocoon, one at a time. But that didn't work, as the cars were going by too fast, and I'd miss a lot of folks. Then I tried to visualize all those cocoons going around everyone all at once, but I couldn't hold the image. Finally, I settled on the idea that I should wrap the whole car so that it would run well and get the occupants there, and the light would include everyone inside too.

But I still had trouble cramming a car into a long, narrow cocoon shape in my mind. Finally, while eating a Hershey's Kiss, it dawned on me that this shape, firmly implanted in my mind, was great for enclosing a car. Nice and big at the bottom with a cute little, stem into the etheric plane and sparkly all over. So here's what I do now. As each car goes by me in the opposite direction, I wrap it instantaneously in a Kiss. To keep my mind from wandering, I say a noise to indicate I've completed one car—like "bam" or "wham." That keeps me focused on doing it.

I'm just delighted with the picture that forms in my mind of all those giant Hershey's Kisses of light going down the highway. My mind wanders after a minute, but in that minute, I wrapped maybe fifty to a hundred cars. Won't you try it today?

Ode to Joy

At the opening ceremony of the 1998 Olympics in Japan, a wonderful event happened that foreshadows the world unity we shall achieve one day. A symphony conductor of Japanese parents who lives in the United States and who leads the Boston Symphony had the idea of uniting all five continents in singing the "Ode to Joy" from Beethoven's Ninth Symphony. Through a modern miracle of not only technology but also of cooperation, he assembled two thousand local singers in the stadium in Japan. On five large screens, he had five other choirs, live and interactive.

One was in the Great Hall of the United Nations in New York, one on the steps of the Sydney Opera House in Australia, one in Berlin, a city once divided but now reunited, one in South Africa composed of both black and white singers, and the last in Beijing, China.

All those singers in the stadium and those around the world followed the conductor and sang together, despite the distance, despite the time of day (3 a.m. in one location), despite language, politics, and cultural differences. Inspired, the audience in the stadium stood up and joined in spontaneously.

Unison, harmony, and joyful smiles filled the air—and not only where the choirs were located and among the athletes in the stadium. Throughout the world, people experienced this uplifting music through TV. The song's lyrics say all men are brothers. If we can sing of brotherhood/sisterhood together, we can unite this earth in love, peace, and healing. Hold with me the visualization of our unity growing stronger until we all stand together—every last one of us joining our voices in a chorus of love.

February 9

Life's Darker Colors

Even in tragedy, there is good. Spirit's purpose is fulfilled not only when there is peace and harmony but also when we are called to face challenges. Our purpose at these times is to find the lesson, to learn from the event. Often, I see people who claim to be religious blaming God or even cursing God when a family member gets cancer or is killed in a wreck. They seem amazed that all their good churchgoing has not resulted in protection from grief and tragedy.

They are wrong. We did not come to this earth to be protected from life's darker colors. We came to experience life in all its colors, to learn lessons, to pass tests, so we can become better and better persons. We cannot create a beautiful tapestry of our lives if it is composed only of shades of white. The darker colors are also an essential part of the tapestry. No one should be surprised that people die, some young, some in sudden circumstances, and that many suffer from all kinds of losses. That is part of the life on this planet and is our opportunity to practice some of the qualities of spirituality that we are here to learn. Tragedy is oh so sad and heart-wrenching. But it is not a mistake. Before we were born, we made a plan with our master teachers and guides—a plan that included the lessons we agreed to learn. And then we forgot it, since knowing would be cheating on our tests.

It makes no sense to pray to avoid parts of life that we expressly picked to experience in order to grow. It would only delay our learning of the lesson if this kind of prayer were answered with granting what we asked in ignorance of the full story of our life plan.

No, we were taught to pray, "Thy will be done." Instead of asking to have certain experiences taken away from us, we can instead ask to be comforted, strengthened, and given wisdom enough to endure all that life provides and to learn all the lessons that life teaches us.

The Kennedy Center Honors ...

Who is it this time? I thought as I sat down to watch the latest group of famous artists the Kennedy Center was honoring. As they were introduced, I recognized each name: Van Cliburn, Julie Andrews, Jack Nicholson, Pavarotti, and Quincy Jones. As each was honored for contributions they have made, their lives were summarized for us to see.

Well, it made me think. What if each of our lives took its turn on display? What if our accomplishments were known? For most people, there is not fame and public recognition. But everything each of us attains is an important, small step forward for the entire race called human.

So today, the Kennedy Center honors ... YOU!

We, the gathered lightworkers, join to honor you for all the things you have done, said, or even thought that enhanced our world. Thank you, thank you—our thanks go out to you.

All those who benefited from your kindness, your wisdom, your support, and your courage rise to tell their stories of how you affected them. Don't be too modest. Don't say, "No, not me. I've done nothing." We know better. If you have raised a child, helped a motorist with car trouble, held a door for someone struggling to get through; if you have done anything right and just and kind and wise, we salute each and every one of these accomplishments.

Today, think about the good things you have done, the good words you have spoken, and acknowledge our thanks for your contributions to raising the vibration of our world, thus benefiting us all.

Bravo! Brava! Well done!

February 11

Ten Thousand Ways

After ten thousand unsuccessful tries to develop a storage battery, Edison was known to have said that he didn't fail, he just found ten thousand ways that wouldn't work.

What profound spiritual beauty is contained in this simple comment! Edison, the inventive genius who told us, "Genius is 1 percent inspiration and 99 percent perspiration," shows us why he succeeded where so many others failed. He refused to give up. He trusted that the goal he sought was attainable, and all he had to do was find the right path to it. He truly had faith in what he was doing.

He was also wise enough to see all those unsuccessful attempts not as failures but as knowledge gained, paths explored. That knowledge helped him to refine his thinking and direct his efforts in the right direction.

When we think of Edison's stunning achievements—the phonograph, the lightbulb, the motion picture, and over a thousand other inventions—we seldom consider the enormous amount of work involved in each accomplishment. By his belief and through his determination, he willed into existence those many marvels. He made himself a ready and open vessel into which Spirit could put that all-important 1 percent inspiration.

Can we trust enough to keep going on our path, believing our goals are attainable and trusting that there is no failure unless we give up? Can we say with a smile, "I'm getting closer. I've just found ten thousand ways that won't work"?

February 12

Signs of the New Age: The Cultural Creatives

Two social scientists have been doing research on what is happening in the growing social movements in the United States. They have given the name "cultural creatives" to those individuals in America who have decided to participate in one or many of the social movements (*The Cultural Creatives*, Ray and Anderson 2000). The cultural creatives have come to believe in some of these: spiritual and emotional development movements, acceptance that we are each other's keeper and we need to help others, our stewardship of the world and the need to heal it, alternative healing methods, equality of men and women and all races, honoring elders, experiential learning, and natural foods. Holy cow! That sounds like me. Does it sound like you too?

The book says not only do we believe, but most of us are personally active in doing what we believe—recycling, feeding our kids better food, meditating, using alternative healing methods. But we are beyond just doing things for ourselves and our families. Many of us are doing things in groups, joining or starting movements. Our activism is bringing the issues before government and before the people themselves. We are changing the culture itself. But when questioned by the researchers in their study as to how many others in America are like us, we inevitably say just a few, less than 5 percent.

The authors have found that this is not true. Instead, they are finding that there are fifty million of us, almost a quarter of the whole United States! We are just not very good at finding each other, as we've been quiet so long and because the mainstream culture and its press does not find our stories interesting to put on the news. The mainstream group is called the Moderns by these authors. The Moderns are still clinging to the old dream of getting ahead, material success, competition, and so on. But even 70 percent of them are getting interested in ecology, which is the most agreed upon concern of us all.

Our culture is at an in-between place now, between old and new thought. Let's rejoice we are fifty million, and let's go about our affairs with a welcoming smile for those who will soon join us in creating a whole new beautiful world. It's just around the corner.

February 13

Saving That One

Today let's focus on what we can do to heal the earth. Most of us have heard the story of a man tossing stranded starfish back into the ocean. Another man came by and told him it was futile, as he could not save them all. Our hero tossed another in, saying that may be true, but he could save that one.

So today let's do our one little thing to make a positive change in the world. In our busy lives, we can still do one little thing, save one starfish. Now I know most of us don't encounter beached starfish, so what can we do? We could pick up a piece of trash from the sidewalk, or pay the waiter a little extra, or give a smile to a cashier, or shine the light of Spirit on the other drivers in traffic. You pick whatever you like, and imagine that what we do will spread to many millions, who will also take small actions to make the world a better place. Think of doing often some little things to save the world.

February 14

My Valentine

Valentine's Day: day of love.

A day when we celebrate the loves in our lives. This day has always made me think of the wonderful people I love. But to my surprise, I have found that I have been neglecting one very special person on this day.

And who is that? Myself, of course. In order to give and receive love from others, it is necessary for me to consider myself loveable and worthy of love. If I don't, I block some of that beautiful gift of love from getting inside to nourish my heart.

So today, before I think of the wonderful other people in my life, I will start with an expression of love for myself. "Beloved self, you are beautiful and wonderful. You are loveable just the way you are. You are a unique creation of God. You are a gift God has given to planet Earth. I love you. I cherish you. For always. I love you, my body. I love you, my mind. I love you, my emotions, my soul. You are my valentine."

February 15

Time-Motion Study

"Stop!" The researcher clicks the stopwatch off at the set time and records what her subjects are doing right then. Then more observing. Then "Stop!" Time again to measure what is going on.

Let's do our own time-motion study all day today. You are both the subject and the observer. Here's the research design: Every hour on the hour for all your waking hours today, stop what you are doing and ask yourself this question: are you doing something positive, neutral, or negative? Thinking counts here as well as actions. Score yourself plus one for each positive entry, minus one for each negative entry, and zero if your action is neutral.

For example: 7 a.m., brushing teeth (score +1 for taking care of yourself); 8 a.m., driving to work (so far seems to be neutral, but score based on both how courteously and safely you are driving and what you are thinking); 9 a.m., gossiping about a colleague's divorce (score -1) ... on to noon, eating lunch. Get specific. What item were you putting in your mouth when you noticed the time? Does it support a healthy body? (Score +1 for healthy, -1 for unhealthy.) Keep going as many times as you remember to call time all day (even if you don't exactly hit the hour on the hour).

Good luck. I hope you come in above zero. Wish me luck too!

Healers

Throughout our long eons of history as beings with physical bodies, we have had trouble with illnesses and injuries—not only physical but mental and emotional too. Always among our tribe, there have arisen people who have talent, desire, and knowledge as healers.

Let us give thanks today to our healers. They have kept the wisdom passed down through the ages, and they have fostered development of new healing techniques too. Think of people who have been healers in your life and thank them today for their dedication, their wisdom, and their love.

Let us unite to visualize together all past and present styles of healing coming together into a mammoth compendium of healing arts. Let us see those who practice Western, Eastern, and all forms of indigenous healing come together to share and enhance their arts through merging their best practices, old and new.

Healers visualize the person who comes before them as one whole being with all parts interrelated. Let us all, as receivers of healing arts, move forward and begin to use good techniques from all styles of healing with respect for all true healing arts, selecting those that are most productive for us at any given time.

Let us imagine the development of new ways of healing that will allow us to function with good health through our life spans. Last, let us visualize healing energy filling the air so that all people will receive healing light with their every breath.

Sparkles

I admit it. I play computer games. Mostly the adventure ones have me stuck in some old mansion, trying to figure what to do next. If I select the easy mode of a game, it shows me sparkles on areas in a room that I should check out. Very handy, those sparkles.

How I wish there would be sparkles in my life showing me things to check out. Well, in fact, there are sparkles if I think about it. If I enter a new situation, such as a party or a new vacation place, I find myself attracted to some things and not to others. This is the feeling version of sparkles. For example, I started a new job with many coworkers. When I looked around me on that first day, I found myself instantly attracted to one person, the switchboard operator. She wasn't looking at me and was busy answering phone calls and typing. Yet something about her was calling to me, like sparkles. Bottom line, I chatted with her, and we became good friends.

So today let's be open to finding the sparkles in our daily comings and goings. If you get that sparkly feeling about a bank teller, waiter, or anyone you come into contact with, take the opportunity to say hello and maybe give them a compliment. You may not get a friend out of it, but you may be causing a friendly encounter that gives you both a boost.

Vibrational Adjustment

Question: When is your favorite piece of beautiful music no longer
             beautiful and pleasing?
Answer: When it is played flat, sharp, or out of tune.

When a piano goes out of tune, the piano tuner comes with a set of tuning forks. These forks are permanently tuned to a series of perfect notes. Vibrating their note by striking them, the tuner uses the sensitivity of the ear to match the piano key to its correct pitch.

We too sometimes get out of tune physically, mentally, emotionally, or spiritually. Sometimes all that is needed for healing is a battery recharge of rest and refreshment. At other times, a specialized healer is called in to help restore our tuning. During this change from the third to fourth dimension, we can become flat or sharp as our vibration is raised and that of everyone on earth and the earth itself is raised.

The art of healing is that of putting us back in tune. You can help your own healing and balancing through the use of vibrations such as singing, chanting OM, reading poetry aloud, listening to sweet music (it is good to lie on the floor near the speakers and feel them vibrate with the notes), and looking at colors, especially the colors of nature. Lie on the earth, at the beach or on the grass. Absorb the vibration of earth to retune yourself to it, and give it back your own vibration, which is moving higher. This will help both you and the earth to raise your voices gradually and sweetly in singing a higher note of peace and love.

Four Gold Medals

Once again, amidst all the strife and turmoil in a seemingly hate-filled world, the 2002 Winter Olympics showed us why this world of ours will really succeed in learning to live together in peace. An astounding thing has happened in pairs' figure skating. Russians took the gold, and Canadians the silver medal. But the commentators and spectators thought the Canadians were better, as the Russians had made one major mistake in their jumps, which should have decreased their points.

Through tears, the young Canadians very graciously accepted the silver. Almost immediately, one of the judges—a French woman—admitted she had been pressured by her own federation to lean toward the Russians so that the Russian judge in ice dancing would lean toward the French pair later in the week.

This made front-page headlines in world newspapers and lead stories on many TV news shows. The poor silver medalists were interviewed over and over, and they were still able to maintain dignity, saying they had nothing against the Russian skaters and were glad to get a medal.

In a few days, the Olympic Committee leadership settled the matter with the International Skating Federation. They eliminated the scores of the French judge, which left the two pairs tied. The Canadians were awarded gold, as they justifiably should have been. The Russians got to keep their gold too. They were interviewed and said they were afraid to appear in a second medal ceremony, thinking the American audience would boo them for the dirty deal the judges had made.

I was privileged to see this beautiful piece of history—two Russians, two Canadians on the top of the podium together, two flags flying side by side, two anthems, four gold medals proudly held aloft to deafening cheers for them all and lots of hugging for each other.

In the midst of war, terrorism, and hate, events like this show us that justice can be done and wrongs righted. Whenever you worry about the state of this world, remember the four gold medals.

The New Driver

Only a few weeks after I passed my driver's test at age sixteen, I asked to borrow the family car on a Saturday morning. Pop (I always called my father Pop) threw me the keys, and I happily hurried to put on my coat and boots, as it was winter and there was fresh snow. As I ran to the car that was parked right in front of our house, I saw that a tire was flat. I turned around and ran right back to the house, yelling, "Pop, the tire is flat!" Pop, sitting watching TV, said, "You are a driver now. You must change the tire yourself." He calmly turned back to his basketball game.

My eyes widened, and I gulped with my new level of responsibility. But I was determined to do it. I went back outside, got the car manual, and read the procedure for changing a tire. Then I loosened the nuts, got the jack, and carefully placed it on the snow. I cranked the car wheel up off the ground and finished removing the nuts. Then I took off the wheel and moved the spare (a full-sized wheel) into position. Suddenly I was stopped cold. I lacked the arm strength to lift that heavy wheel up onto the five posts. I tried a few times, kneeling and grunting, but failed. I sat right down in the snow, frustrated and confused. I knew what to do but could not do it. I looked back at the house, only to see Pop now kneeling on the couch and watching me through the picture window. I felt even worse to disappoint him.

He shouted to me, "You can lift it with your feet." So I sat in the snow, put the wheel on my feet, and lifted with my ankles while steadying it onto the posts with both hands. It worked. I quickly got the tire up and on and replaced the nuts. I looked back again. Pop was still watching and now giving me a victory sign and a smile.

So too is Spirit watching, inspiring, giving needed guidance if we stop and listen, and applauding us when we make it. Whenever you are stuck, realize that Spirit is right there with you, pulling for you. Take strength in that. I do.

February 21

On the Phone

Of all the inventions of this modern society, my favorite one is the telephone. It brings my favorite people into a close and intimate conversation, no matter where they are, no matter how far. It has been a true and trusted link with loved ones whenever I've traveled among strangers.

Before it, we had letters—dear to the heart and substantial, to be read over and over and carried with us. But now we have instant two-way communication, a true sharing of heart to heart at the very moment that one is hurting or has exciting news to tell. I guess others must feel the same way, since I see so many people carrying cell phones around with them so they can make or receive a call at any moment they wish. True, many of those calls are about business matters, but still, the phone is available when we want to call a loved one. No longer need anyone feel alone, with a phone at their side.

But there is one phone call we can't make with a cell phone. It needs to be made more directly, from our mind and heart to the presence of Spirit. Let's make that call right now.

"Hello, my beloved Spirit. I've been feeling all alone until I called you. Let's talk. I could use some advice, some comforting, some sharing with you. It's so nice to be in touch with you again. Talk to me awhile." Then just listen …

Love Thine Enemy

The Bible tells us that it is easy to love those who love us; anyone can do that. But our divine duty is to go far beyond this to love those who hate us, hurt us, and war against us. Our mission is not only to forgive the injuries but to actually love the enemy.

By this, it is not meant that we must love the lower personality self that is persecuting or hurting us. But beyond the small self, we must look above to the High Self that is present in each and every person. If we can always greet that High Self in love, no matter what the outward personality is doing, or how hateful and destructive are the actions of this person, then we can finally, once and for all, break a pattern of hatred for hatred, hurt for hurt, that has cursed us and condemned us to war after war and crime after crime all throughout our existence in physical bodies.

Think of the most abusive, hateful lunatic in our history. Think of what the lower self of this person has done. Now, address the High Self of this person in love. Can you say, "High Self of _____, I greet you in love and recognize you as a divine, spiritual being. I forgive you." Try it.

February 23

Afraid to Go

Somewhere in this world, right at this moment, there are people in the process of passing from this life to the next, but they are afraid to go. Let us unite with these brothers and sisters to ease their way. Join with me in surrounding them with light and love of Spirit, letting them know there is nothing to fear.

"Beloved sisters and brothers, be free to go into your new adventure. It is all right to let go and cross over into the next dimension. Where you are going is beautiful beyond imagining. Turn toward it with joy. Do not worry about those you are leaving behind. They are in the hands of Spirit, who will strengthen and comfort them.

"Open your eyes to your new life that lies before you. See who comes to greet you and lead you forward. There is no death, for you or for anyone. You are immortal, a divine child of God. Take a breath and then release your body. Move upward into the light. May peace be with you always."

Signs of the New Age: The Tool Library

Berkeley, California, has a tool library. Their public library system provides over five thousand tools to lend out for three days to anyone with a library card. It looks more like a garage than a library. And it has tool librarians who give advice about what tools are needed and how to use them. Wow! What a great idea!

In past decades, most people who needed a tool had a neighbor who seemed to have everything. Well, those days are mostly gone in today's society. We often don't know our neighbors, and those neighbors don't often have a full set of tools.

So the Berkeley library system saw a need—people who wanted to fix up their homes who didn't have the expensive tools they needed and who didn't have a wise neighbor to tell them what to do. The tool library has actually become the wise neighbor of the community.

Not only saws and drills but forty-foot ladders and cement mixers are lent out to eager citizens. Way to go, Berkeley! You are an example of thinking out of the box, of recognizing an unmet community need and fulfilling it as a public service. Lightworkers, let us today applaud all those who are using the divine characteristic of imagination to see new solutions to problems and new ways to serve each other.

February 25

Fear of Statistics

Every day, I hear through the media another disheartening statistic: many marriages fail, a large percentage of new small businesses fail, smoking on the rise among teens, and so on. I seldom hear a positive statistic, so I'm basically bombarded with these dire reports masquerading as absolute truth. I believe that since I strive to do God's will, and I strive to progress along a spiritual path, my guides, angels, teachers, and High Self are all working hard to protect me and to communicate with me about what direction I should head on my path. So I've decided not to let statistics prevent me from doing things I want to do. Instead, I call forth Spirit's guidance and protection as I go on my way.

I invite you to join me in removing yourself from worry about statistics. Rates of success and failure tell us very little for ourselves. For instance, no matter what the odds are for business failure, your new business will either succeed or fail. That is, you personally will be either 100 percent or 0 percent, not somewhere in between. Or, if you are having surgery, it doesn't matter that 40 percent of the people with that type of surgery die; you will either be 100 percent alive or 100 percent dead. Statistics, even if they are true, don't tell us which group we will be in. So just plan to be on the side you like, and ask Spirit to take care of you and put you in the right group. Trust Spirit to lift you over obstacles that stymie others. Don't let fear of statistics keep you glued to your seat, unable to take a bold leap. When any worry crosses your mind, blow it out with your breath and breathe in Spirit's blessings.

February 26

The Faucet

"But I'm not sensitive enough to know how I affect others. I get myself in trouble because I don't know how he will view my words and actions. I'm just not good at communicating."

I heard these words recently from a friend. These words are not only a perception of how things seem to be, but they are also a powerful, negative command to our subconscious. The command tells our subconscious to make sure the flow of wisdom from our High Self is shut off in the area we feel we are incapable of learning.

All we need to know we can receive from our divine High Self if we just permit the flow. When we think of an area in which we feel we are a failure, let us think of our current inability as a faucet that we long ago have turned off. It is waiting to be turned on again. Let us turn the negative decrees we have been making into positive ones.

When we turn on a faucet, we can use it as a reminder to lovingly address our subconscious. "I am open to receiving guidance and wisdom from my High Self in all things." Ask your High Self to help you picture the flow of water as a flow of spiritual light that enlightens you with the wisdom to do all things.

Spiritual Fire

The light pouring upon the earth has been slowly increasing all through the dawning of the Age of Aquarius these past few decades. This is a time of marks and signs by which we are to recognize the dawning of the new age.

All those years of preparation, prayer, and projections by so many united as one have caused a mighty chain reaction. The very molecules of all physical substance on earth are now starting to vibrate faster and become more refined. Consciousness has reached the flashover point. That is the point when a beginning fire suddenly develops enough power to literally flash over and consume everything in its path. Our arising higher can no longer be delayed. The light within us is becoming so bright that it can no longer be ignored. We are starting to see it in each other.

See it now, our return to spiritual fire. Thus, we regain our heritage, our powers, our wisdom, our oneness as children of God. All the animals, plants, and elements are becoming uplifted and purified. Help us hold the fire of Spirit strong and steady as it cleanses and changes the earth and all of its people.

Hold Everything—I've Got a Cat on Me

Cat lovers know this is true. We can be intensely working on a project, doing the monthly bill paying, balancing the checkbook, or whatever, and suddenly the cat of the house decides we are worthy of being sat upon. Without a moment's thought of rejection, and without any consideration of the human's busyness, this confident four-legged being strides over, jumps on, and turns around several times, looking for the best spot.

So what does the human do? Essentially stop everything, put down the project, and start petting the cat. After all, cats only come when they have time for us and everything else can wait.

Then suddenly the visitation is over. Without so much as a word of thanks, the cat simply leaps off, finished with you and moving on to other important affairs.

Is there a lesson for humans here? Could we perhaps learn to react to life's sudden, unexpected opportunities as a cat lover reacts to being graced with the presence of the cat? Can we say, "Okay, I'll put aside my plans and take advantage of this opportunity"? Can we even be grateful for the surprising interruption? Can we learn to say, "Hold everything—I've got a cat on me"?

February 29

The Great Leap Forward

Today is the day when an extra day is added to the calendar so that human time and sun time can be realigned. Since this day happens only once every four years, let us take the opportunity today to look back to your life four years ago.

Where were you four years ago? What were you doing? More importantly, what were you thinking and how were you acting? When you look back on that time and compare it with who you are now, are you pleased? Have there been some accomplishments, some growth in these four years? Give thanks to Spirit that you can see a progression. Even if you tend to be negative toward your accomplishments, I'll bet you do indeed see some progress. Be glad that you are moving forward on your spiritual path.

Now look back to that same period four years ago and try to remember what you were hearing and seeing on the evening news. Have there been positive changes in the nations? Have the peoples of the earth begun to come together and to realize they are one? Ignore the many negative events and look behind their flash for the upward trend. I'll bet if you try hard enough, you can see the upward movements. We can all rejoice both in our personal progress in our thoughts, words, and deeds and in the progress of the nations of the earth.

We are moving rapidly from the old age into the New Age. Now think ahead to the next February 29, four years from now. Visualize the new wonders you will see in yourself and on planet Earth.

March 1

The Drug Trade

Let us direct our united light today into an area of great darkness upon our planet. Let us concentrate on all our brothers and sisters who participate in the business of growing, transporting, and selling illegal drugs.

This group of people lives in the darkness. In their hearts, they have replaced Spirit with love of money. Let us unite to strongly project the love of Spirit to all of them so that they can feel the connection with Spirit and with us, their family.

Let us see in our minds an image of drug traffickers and street dealers surrounded by white light. Let us watch the scene unfold as these people, our beloved family members, begin to feel the light. Let us see them finally realizing the harm they are causing to others and to themselves. And let us rejoice as they turn away from the drug trade in disgust.

As the biblical father rushed out to embrace the prodigal son while the son was still far off, let us embrace these brothers and sisters as they turn around and head for home.

Ode to My Body

I give you thanks, my physical self,
For you carry me through my tasks.
You are my strong and faithful servant,
Often ignored, often insulted.

You, my beautiful body,
Allow me to live and learn in this world.
You are the temple of my being,
And I respect and cherish you.

I shall be kind and loving toward you.
I shall treat you with respect.
As you show me your needs for rest, good food, and exercise,
I shall acknowledge you and take care of you.

I shall treat you as a mother treats her child,
Gently encouraging but not demanding,
Lovingly caring for you,
Being happy to take time for you,
Being glad you are mine.

Help me to do all the things I need to do.
Help me to live in harmony on this earth.
Support me and care for me as I care for you.
Thank you, my body, my gift of life.

I love you.

Learning to Be Free

In recent times, we have seen marvelous fruits of the New Age in the actions of the people in many countries to cast off dictatorships. The people in these countries have spent so many years in struggle and suffering, yearning above all else to be free. Now some of these nations are experiencing their first breaths of freedom. They are as newborn children to this new freedom.

We can assist in many ways as the yearning to be free is exchanged for learning to be free. Casting off oppressive government is a wonderful step but only a first step. Let us help by affirming for the people of these nations that their steps into the light of freedom be filled with enlightenment. Let there be no revenge on the oppressors. Let the people be filled with love and guided by patience and forgiveness. Let them feel their freedom as a right, but one that demands righteous and responsible actions.

Businesses and democracies are rushing in to help troubled nations establish the economic and political supports of freedom. Support these efforts in your heart. Join in if you feel led. But above all, hold the image of spiritual government developing in these newly free countries.

United Light

Jesus promised us that all the things he did we would also do, and even greater things would we do. That promise has always thrilled me and pointed me toward that goal. But I often wondered how we would be able to do things greater than he had done in healing lepers, raising the dead, and even resurrecting his own slain body. To learn to do any of Jesus's miracles, even turning water to wine, seems impossible. But I trust his promise. I believe that it doesn't matter that I do not know how to do these things. They will be gifted to me by Spirit when I become a purer vessel.

But what indeed could be miracles even greater than these, and why could we do more than he? I believe one miracle will be the healing of the environmental pollution of the planet, another surely will be enough food for all, and yet another will be true love among all people. And how will these be done? By the multiplied power of our united light as we, by the millions and billions, project together for these goals and also do our part to fulfill our plan.

I believe it.
Believe with me.
Project with me.
Grow with me in the light.
Unite with me.
Act out your part.

We shall succeed!

Are You a Gusher?

Are you a gusher? That is what they call an oil well as it first rushes up to the surface and spurts powerfully, high into the air. When we first become filled with the light of Spirit, we gush forth with unbridled joy and zeal. We want to shout out and tell the world of our great discovery.

Well, what happens to that oil well when it gushes forth? Everyone gets out of the way and runs for cover. Is that the effect we are having on others? Is the awesome power and zeal of our spirituality knocking people down and causing them to turn and run for cover?

In the New Testament, Stephen was an early convert to Christianity who was martyred for gushing forth his new spirituality to people who did not wish to hear. Sometimes we must realize that not everyone is ready to hear us and that we must work in the silence with them, giving them respect for wherever they are and whatever they believe at present.

For the oil well to become productive, it must be capped and regulated to produce a manageable flow that can be channeled to waiting vessels. Let us also regulate our zeal and cap our gusher to better serve Spirit.

Signs of the New Age: The Natural Step

Dr. Karl-Henrick Robért, a Swedish physician and cancer researcher, had tired of seeing so much cancer. It became obvious to him that the world had to get together to work toward ending the practices that were causing many of the cancers. The environmental debate was fragmented, with people focusing too narrowly on things like car exhaust or tobacco. He felt he had to do something about it. So he created the Natural Step.

He came up with a set of four principles:

- reducing and recycling all mineral and fossil fuels
- reusing and recycling all man-made substances
- stopping depletion of nature
- promoting worldwide justice for all people

What a manifesto that is!

And it is not just a document sitting on a shelf. Many industries are buying into these truths as they see the future of their own companies move close to the edge of collapse as we drown in garbage and use natural resources until there is nothing left, contaminating soil, air, and water until it can no longer sustain industry or even life itself.

Let's add our support as lightworkers. Check out the Natural Step and learn more, so you can tell others. Envision a new, clean, sustainable, beautiful world. Let companies know we insist on this. Thank a company that has gotten started. Goad a laggard to start!

Zeal

Zeal, that old biblical word. What is it really? The *New American Webster Handy College Dictionary* says it is "fervent ardor, eagerness, enthusiasm, diligence," and ardor is, "passion, fiery heat." Is there anything in your spiritual path, your mission, that moves you to fiery heat? It is that very heat that has the power to propel us forward to complete our missions against all odds, no matter what the obstacles.

So let's concentrate today on one thing in our life's work that passionately moves us, or ought to. It should be a goal not yet achieved, a path not yet walked, or even the very direction and probable future of your current path. For example, if your path now includes the raising of children, that should move you to proceed passionately with all enthusiasm to do your very best with these divine beings in your care. Whatever your role and mission is, concentrate on it. If you are feeling some heat but not enough to call it zeal, then maybe you need your level of enthusiasm turned up to high.

I'll tell you how I do it. I get myself around enthusiastic people who feel and believe as I do. I immerse myself in the enthusiasm of others until it fans the flame back into my embers, causing me to roar forth into flames once more. After a dose of group zeal, I am once again ready to return to my daily normal life with the eagerness and diligence to take the next step along my path.

So I invite you today to take a break to fan the flames of your zeal. Get in touch with a person or group that lights your fire. Let them work their magic on you and then boldly and enthusiastically lunge forward on your path.

March 8

Please Help Me

"Please help me." These three little words do not come easily to us all. For some of us, they seem to be saying, "I can't make it on my own," or, "I don't have what it takes to do this alone."

We don't need to feel bad or ashamed to ask for help when we genuinely need it. We are all here to help each other through the rough spots. We are not meant to do it all alone. The act of recognizing the need for help and actually asking for it opens us up to receive a gift given by another. It deepens a bond between two people when they share a rough spot or a hard task because they care about each other.

Louise Hay said, "It is being strong to ask for help when you need it." At first, that seems a strange contradiction, as we usually think it signifies weakness to admit we need help. But it really is a strength—the strength of knowing one's limits, of accepting the responsibility to take care of ourselves by *not* doing tasks too hard for us to do alone, and the courage to be vulnerable by asking for help.

Open your heart to receiving a gift of help from another. Thank the giver for their kindness and love. Accept their gift with enjoyment and gratitude, not guilt, because being a grateful receiver allows the giver to feel the joy of being useful. In return, you can pass on the gift by using your special talents to help that person or another.

Personality Traits

Please complete the following sentences:

The French are _____.

Mexicans are _____.

Old people are _____.

Teenagers are _____.

Asians are _____.

Lawyers are _____.

Now look over your answers. Did you fill in any personality traits that you associate with these groups of people? I used to. Really, the best answers to each of these are answers such as, "all different," "human beings," "children of God," "fascinating," "part of my family."

Just as I see change in my own attitudes and those of my friends as we grow and evolve, I can assume people are changing all over the country and probably over much of the world. In any group, there has always been great diversity of personality. And because we are evolving, there is even more so.

So I've decided to clean out my mental filing cabinet to get rid of stereotypes that I have used for groups. Stereotypes only keep us apart. When we label a group, we think we know something about the individuals in that group, but we don't.

I invite you to do the same kind of stereotype house cleaning of your mind. The more we see each other as individual manifestations of divine Spirit, the better off our world will be.

A Little Bit at a Time, We Grow

I've been having some trouble lately. You see, a part of me that is more childish has resurfaced. I haven't seen it for a long time and was hoping it was gone. This is a part that has low self-esteem and believes I'm not good enough. This part has experienced rejection and believes that people are scary beings who will reject me again.

So what can I do about this? I guess I had better have a talk with this part of me, this wounded inner child. Please listen in.

"Hello, darling child. I'm sorry to see you sad and scared. I know those hurts we have suffered were deeply painful. But we've changed so much. We've grown. I don't think the world is such a scary place anymore. Look at what I see: I smile, and people smile back. Not always but a lot. I say hello, and they say hello. Not always but usually. So many nice folks say so many nice things to us nowadays. People hug us. We laugh with others and have fun. But you know what? Not everyone is going to be nice to us. Some will even reject us. That doesn't mean we are not worthy of love. I know we are. We are Spirit's divine child—a being of light. When you get scared, look for that light deep inside and then look at other folks and see their light. We are one in Spirit."

There, we feel better now. Do you, Dear Reader, have anything to say today to a scared or sad or angry part of yourself?

Passing the Test

The word "integrity" is defined by *Webster* as "fidelity to moral principles; honesty." It is related to the word "integrate," which means to form into a whole. The test of personal integrity is to discard one's separate public and private faces in favor of acting as one whole being. This means making honest and upright decisions whether or not anyone else sees or knows.

As we go through each day, we make decisions about our words and actions. Do we remain true to our higher selves and principles when no one is watching? Or do we succumb to small instances of lying, cheating, or stealing?

In reality, our every thought, word, and action is watched by our High Self and teachers and is felt unconsciously by the whole world. Our quiet, private acts of honesty, justice, and compassion mark us as lightworkers. Truly, there are no small areas in which we can feel free to deviate from cosmic law. In fact, these private moments are times when we are challenged and tested in our heart of hearts. Which do we choose, integrity or deception?

I watched a good friend as she discovered a store had not charged her enough for her purchases. Without hesitation, she turned around and returned to the store to pay the small amount she owed. The merchant was so surprised and pleased to discover an honest person, he rewarded her with a piece of candy.

That reward was symbolic of the greater reward Spirit grants to those who pass the test of integrity. That one small act of honesty makes our world a better place for us all. Let us ensure that all our actions this day, large and small, pass the test of integrity.

Dedicated to Judith Wilson.

March 12

The Dance of the Whales

They glide seemingly effortlessly through the water, breaking the surface now and then for a quick breath. Then down they plunge again into the ocean they love. As I watch with delight at the beauty and music of their dance, I suddenly realize they are beings of two worlds. Their bodies, curved and sleek, are designed for a life in water, but they have lungs, not gills, and must breathe the air up above.

So are we beings of two worlds, with bodies designed for third-dimensional earth living and spirits and minds designed for a higher plane, a life unencumbered by bodily form. Yet, here we are, body and spirit linked as one.

What can we learn from our cousins, the whales? They have learned to live in two worlds at once in a harmony that shows their mastery of being two in one—air and water.

We often see our two-in-one nature as a struggle instead of a harmonious dance. But today let us dance between earth and higher realms with ease and joy. Let us celebrate being in two worlds as our cousins the whales do.

Window Washing

Squeak, squeak, squeak—you are cleaning a window. It had a few specks of dirt on it, but now it is perfectly clean. A neighbor comes by and remarks, "Um, I see you have a very sparkly window there, but there are several others that are quite dirty. Yet every time I see you, you are cleaning just this one, over and over, and letting the others go."

Pretty peculiar, huh? We'd never do that, clean one and let the others go. Well, let's use that analogy on our thoughts. We, being good lightworkers, have developed certain practices. Maybe you are a vegetarian. Maybe you help the homeless. Maybe you are a Boy Scout leader or a volunteer in a church or some other organization. Maybe you give blood. Maybe you meditate, exercise, journal, do tai chi. Maybe you recycle.

Usually we have a favorite set of things to do, and we do them repeatedly till they are quite polished. Today let's look at another facet of our lives, one that we don't consider a favorite, a goal we often ignore. Perhaps it is speaking the truth, turning negative thoughts into positive ones, letting ourselves rest and play, seeking help and support from others, making amends, learning and practicing good boundaries in relationships, or many others. Pick one facet that you don't spend much time polishing and concentrate on it for a minute—a full minute. Do any ideas come to you about something to be done? Does this area need an attitude adjustment? How about just for today, you take that action, adjust that attitude, clean that dirty window?

March 14

Signs of the New Age: A Holistic Doctor

I clicked the remote to public TV, and there was a lecture on by an MD named Christiane Northrup. I had not heard of her, nor had I often seen an MD doing a lecture, so I listened awhile. Wow! Was I ever bowled over by her! She has written a book on holistic health and was describing her treatment philosophy that is detailed in the book.

She actually said, right there on TV, a member of the medical establishment, that body and mind are inseparable. She detailed her own personal health regimen as including massage and meditation. She also said, "We are born with an incredible sense of who we are, and then we are talked out of it."

She gets it! She understands! She is not afraid of complementary healing methods. And, you know, besides speaking well and making sense, she glowed with health and strength.

I applaud you, Dr. Northrup. Thank you for being open to things you were not taught in school. Thank you for standing as a pioneer among doctors. I'll bet you don't refer to your patient as "that gallbladder in 114."

I am hopeful that people like you will help Western medicine and Eastern healing merge into the holistic healing we need in this New Age.

March 15

Lighting the Beam of Love

Think today about a person you have loved purely and selflessly. This could be a spouse, a child, a friend. This love makes the world go around, so the song says. I believe it is the most beautiful thing we humans can do, to love purely without expectations of someone giving back to us. Enjoy the warm feeling that the thought of loving this person brings to you.

Yet Jesus taught us that we should love others as He loves us. That means all others, not just one or a few special persons. Can we even imagine loving everyone? Our boss, the tax collector, Hitler, Judas, people we just don't care for or who are even our enemies. Just for this moment, how about we try to feel this love? First feel it for your special loved one. Picture them in front of you and direct this love like a beam of light to encompass them in a soft glow. Picture them responding to that beam of light with a smile at being so loved.

Now hold that image, that beaming of light, and expand your beam to surround your neighborhood, your city, your workplace or school, your nation, and then the whole globe. It is before you now, the planet Earth. Shining your love to everyone here, because everyone here is, like you, a child of God. See them feeling the beam and letting in the love. Let all people of the world be loved and feel what that feels like. Let them feel they are children of God and see them then shining a beam of love on everyone, until the whole planet lights up with love.

March 16

Is There a Should on Your Back?

Is there a project that you have been putting off? It could be large or small; it could be starting something or finishing something. I'll bet you can name one right now. We are all busy, and we all procrastinate in one area or another. But this act of procrastination has a harmful side effect: we pick up the burden of the task and carry it around with us as a "should."

Today, take a look at one task that you have put off. Begin by dealing with it in thought. First decide, is this project really worth doing? Ask yourself, "Is this a project or task that I have selected to do, or is it something that childhood experiences have taught me that I should do?"

For instance, suppose your burden is that you think you should organize your photos into albums. Who decided on that "should"? You or society or your parents? If the task is one that you never really intended to do, don't carry it on your back anymore as a should. Let it drop to the ground and be forgotten.

But, if the task is one you really want to do, one that would make your life more organized, neater, more peaceful, then change your "I should" to "I will. I am beginning it." Clear a space in your calendar, *do it*, and get it off your back. Give thanks for the lessons this task has taught you and feel the relief of completion.

You Are What You Eat

Our dietary preferences are very firmly formed by the end of our school years. That is why it is important to give our children a foundation of healthy eating early on. Some parents may try hard, only to find their schools are working against them by providing a processed, refined carb, and high-sugar menu of fries, burgers, pizza, hot dogs, ice cream, no fruit, no salad, and so on.

Long ago, I read an article about a school that was introducing classes for kids in world cultures and cuisines and actually providing the international foods they were studying in the cafeteria. That is cool. And I have a friend who has been trying for years to improve menus in the schools in her area, with some success. So I know change is happening, but it is changing too slowly.

Today, let's send our encouraging thoughts to those who feed our children in schools. Let them be inspired to look critically at their menus and replace some of the worst items with something healthier. Even replacing white bread with whole grain bread is a start. The problem is the children have already developed the cravings for the unhealthy foods, and they won't want to change. So the menu planners and cooks need to do it as a project, discussing with the families and the children what is going on and why. They need to find ways to generate enthusiasm in the children to try out samples of healthier food choices that are not now on the menu and see what they like. Oh, and by the way, there are those machines that dispense candy, soda, and chips. There are better things to put in vending machines. Some schools are having discussions with vendors about items for their vending machines.

So let us envision this healthy trend catching on all over the country in all our schools.

The Golden Sphere

Today, let's focus our attention on an international situation of hatred and strife. Pick a specific situation and gently bring the scene before you, as if you were hovering over that part of the globe. Now see, just below you but still hovering in the air, a large sphere of golden liquid light. This sphere is surrounded by a gently swirling energy field, violet in color.

The gold represents all the divine energies needed to reprogram the situation. Within the sphere of liquid light are all decrees, cosmic principles, and spiritual patterns now being set into motion to bring a perfect spiritual resolution to the situation. The violet energy field is the transmutation flame needed to purify and transmute all existing patterns of error.

See the energies of the gold sphere beaming down on the area, like sunbeams shining on the land. See all areas of erroneous thinking and actions rising as dark, wispy clouds into the violet energy, there being transformed and changed to violet and then returning to the situation.

Keep your thoughts focused on the light and away from imagining what earthly actions need to be taken in this situation. Let Spirit's pure light do its work unhindered. Feel the power of the light as it gently lifts and purifies the areas of darkness, turning a problem zone into a paradise.

The Day He Forgot to Fly

Have you ever heard of the Flying Wallendas? They were the family famous for daredevil tightrope-walking stunts. The father of this family was internationally acclaimed for such thrilling stunts as walking on a tightrope across Niagara Falls and between some extremely tall New York City skyscrapers. But one day during a relatively routine stunt in Mexico City, he lost his balance and fell to his death.

A reporter interviewed his widow, and she said she felt something was wrong when her husband awakened that fateful day, as he told her he must go and check on the apparatus. She said he had never questioned the work of his sons, who always set up the tightrope. In fact, he had never even mentioned the apparatus at all.

Maybe Mr. Wallenda fell because he lost his focus on his goal—the end of the walk—and began to worry about the danger and the apparatus. Can we learn a lesson from this fatal error? When we set out on our path, we must trust that Spirit will help us get there. We must keep our focus on our goal rather than worrying about the details. Examine your focus. Are you concentrating on your goals or worrying about the process of getting there?

March 20

Pisces—The Fish

Here are two fish swimming in opposite directions. This sign of Pisces reminds me of people who can't seem to make up their minds. They are so busy considering all sides of an issue that they can't pick a side and go with it. They say, "On the one hand … and on the other hand …" And long lectures come in those dots. Do you know someone who can't make up their mind? If so, let's send them strength and conviction to break their logjam and finally take action.

On the good side, astrology books list Pisces traits as sensitive, compassionate, accepting, imaginative, and helpful. Let's embrace these good Pisces traits today. Let's try today to be all of those good things. But let's also not allow sensitive to become oversensitive, and let's not allow imaginative to become dreamy and unable to act. Let's dream of a better world and do one act of kindness today to help that better world come about.

Path Maintenance

We are each walking our own path toward a higher consciousness. Those who have gone before us on the journey have helped to carve the path from the tangled brambles and dark thicket of ignorance and lower mortal errors. We can thank them for what they have left behind, a space to walk and guideposts to show the direction.

Now it is our turn. As each of us walks, let us be mindful of those who will follow along behind us. We are each responsible for a segment of people who resonate closely with our own notes. They could be people who have some common element, such as a shared ethnic or religious heritage, a shared profession, people whose family backgrounds are similar. These people are our special responsibility. They look to us, hoping we are leaving behind markers for them to follow.

Let us look at our path. Is it dark? Then set forth lamps of everlasting flame to light the way. Are there rocks or other debris on the path? Clear them aside.

How? How do we leave lights and markers? How do we clear the debris? By making right choices, by holding steadfastly to the light above all mortal ways, by touching others with love and kindness, by doing what is needed. See the path made better by your having walked it.

March 22

Messages

How does Spirit guide us as to what we should do, what we should change, and what are the next steps on our path? I envision my angels, guides, and my own higher self around me, trying to get messages through and largely having a hard time because I don't hear them. "Yoo-hoo! Hello! We are trying to tell you something."

That is what I believe they are actually doing, but I also believe that they guide us through many other ways. I find guidance from reading something, hearing a sentence said on a TV show, something a person says to me, and so on. How do I sort the messages from all the other stimuli of a day? I find that, for me, when something is a message, my attention suddenly is riveted to it with a bolt of recognition that hits my body. *That is for me.* Or, *Gee, I need that message.* Or, *Wow, that is a great idea I didn't think of.*

Often, I find messages in what a person says to me. And very often, it is unexpected, something that person would not characteristically say. It could be a hotel clerk, a waitress, a plumber fixing my sink, suddenly saying something that seems odd coming from them. I have come to know these are messages from Spirit, given by people who don't even know they are Spirit's conduit.

For example, I was working full-time in a nursing home and going for a master's degree, one course at a time at a university fifty miles away. I often worked very late to make up the hours I was in class. One night I was charting at 10 p.m., and the barber suddenly said to me, "You look exhausted. Why don't you go on leave from work and finish full-time?" He never said that sort of thing, and I hardly knew him other than saying hello. I felt the shock of recognition that he was speaking a message, unknown to him, about the next step that I should take on my path. And take it I did. And it led me, step by step, through a whole series of further messages and steps all the way through many years.

I hope you are getting messages and realizing that they are, indeed, messages for you, delivered by Spirit's many messengers.

Aries—The Ram

What comes to mind when I say, "Ram"? To me, it signifies the clash of two rams running forward to smack their horns in battle. Can we find some good quality to claim for ourselves in this Aries trait? Well, many changes in our society, like women's suffrage, had many battles, push back, and defeats before succeeding.

I've studied how Susan B. Anthony would travel by train all over the nation, making speeches about the need for women to have the right to vote. She experienced so much hatred that often people threw tomatoes at her as she descended from the train.

She persisted, she pushed, she rammed the thoughts home that women were equal to men and should be able to vote. This went directly against society's norm of women being subservient to men. The use of the ram quality has often been necessary when righteous causes meet up with violent resistance from the unenlightened masses. In the end, Susan B. Anthony and her many brave colleagues succeeded. Women in the United States have the vote, and Susan is honored on the dollar coin.

Today, let us honor the Aries ram quality and thank those who use it to make society better.

March 24

I Await in Joyful Hope

I learned this affirmation in church, "I await in joyful hope for your coming, O Lord." What does it mean to await joyfully? It means trusting that what you are waiting for will really and truly come. That is where the joyful part comes in. We cannot wait with joy unless we are sure, unless we can count on it.

What does this joyful waiting have to do with me? Am I waiting for anything in my life? To heal? To grow? To achieve a goal? These things take time. Time to become someone new. Time to awaken to our High Self and fully realize that magnificent connection.

Can I await with joyful hope today? To do that, I must remove anything that is blocking Spirit's process from unfolding in its own time, like the unfolding of the petals of a flower.

Let's look within ourselves. Are we waiting for these good things joyfully? If impatience is in the way, throw it aside. If doubt is in the way, cast it off. If envy of the pace of others is blocking your joy, kick it aside. We are moving at exactly the right pace for us, and we are awaiting joyfully now. Yes, we are enjoying the present and the process as well as the prospects for the future.

Lay Down Worries

So many people tell me they are worried—about their children, about finances, about health, about the world. They mull over the wars, pollution, whether we will get hit with a meteor. On and on, worries piled up on top of more worries.

Having so strong a worried reaction to events can ruin your day. Today let's do double duty as lightworkers. Step one. For today let's let go of worries about things we can't fix, like the world. Instead, let us ask Spirit to carry this problem for us. Let it go. See it migrating into the hands of God. Take a breath and be free of it.

Step two. Let's project this thought to our fellow humans: "Lay down your worries upon God. Let them go. If there is something you need to fix, work on that. All others now migrate to God's hands." For you and me and all of us, enjoy being free and easy today.

March 26

Peeling off the Labels

As I was struggling one day recently to get the price label off a mug, I was frustrated by how stuck it was. With all the persistence I could muster, I tried to scrape off the label with my thumbnail. Finally, I gave up, having succeeded only in scraping off a few tiny pieces and leaving the rest as stuck as before.

The higher meaning of this escaped me until a few days later. I was reading a story about how people of different faiths pray. One person said he thought everything we do in life is prayer, but it is often a prayer of the negative—thinking dark and pessimistic thoughts instead of a positive, affirming prayer that would lift us. He added that whatever we hold in our minds is what we bring into the world.

All at once, my mind related this statement to the names we call ourselves in our own minds—our labels. I truly believe that this person is right. What we think, we create. I've seen it in people around me. On the negative side, I've seen people who labeled their own life bad and labeled each day a struggle. Those thoughts show in their faces, in their frown lines and downcast looks, and in their bodies, which do not stand tall but rather look bent and crumpled. And I've seen the positive side too, in people who label their lives as good and themselves as blessed children of God. Their optimism and joy shine in their eyes and their smiles. Their walk is light and free, and they appear almost ready to leap up and fly. I think the labels in their heads have created the differences in those faces and bodies.

Hmmm. What labels do I have? Well, they seem to be a mixed bag, some positive and some positively awful. I want to get rid of some of these, the ones that are dragging me down. But as I decide this, I realize that the worst ones are stuck tight and fast, like the price label on my mug. Okay. Now I know—this will take persistence. I vow to pick off those negative labels by challenging and rejecting them each time I use one on myself. I'll say, "Whoa, there! Stop! That is not true, and it is *not* me! Then I shall reverse those nasty words and create the new affirming label I want to use instead. Here is my new label: "I am a Child of God, and I am good. I can do anything with Spirit's help."

What's yours?

Swept Away

Do you remember Jim Jones? I've been thinking about him and how he mesmerized his followers into committing suicide with him. He was a powerful personality who must have had a kind of charisma. Here was a man who was certain of the rightness of his viewpoints. There are many of these powerful leaders. They seem to attract a following of ultra-devoted disciples who have this trait in common: they are willing to let another person think for them. The followers are swept away by the grandeur of the leader and the viewpoint.

So today let us unite to project light to disciples and followers of charismatic leaders of all types—religious, political, cultural. People, hear us, your sisters and brothers. We cry out to you that you are divine children of God. You need no one to tell you what to think and what to do. Hear your own voice of Spirit within. Decide for yourselves what your path shall be. Judge your leaders, day by day, sentence by sentence. Judge them against cosmic laws and the golden rule, which is love God and love one another. Big danger signs are leaders who demand control over your money and how you live your life. Another big danger sign is a leader who is male telling female followers that God wants them to have sex with him. That is not spiritual at all. Don't allow yourself to be fooled or used. Do not ever throw away your money or your life at the decree of another. Do not set anyone on a pedestal, thinking that only this person is connected to the divine. You all are divine.

March 28

People Are Not Stoves

When I was young, I learned an important rule, as I imagine many of you did. It was this: when the burner of an electric stove turns red, it will burn your flesh. That is an absolute lesson, and I learned it very well. Never, never, never will I place my hand on a stove's red burner. Oh sure, my mom had told me to stay back, as the stove would burn me. But I had to find out the hard way. Yep, it burns! As children, we learn things so often from what we experience.

The trouble is, when we relate to other people, sometimes we have a bad experience. Then the rule-maker part of our mind kicks in and says, "Never, never, never do that again because _____ will happen."

Well, that learning of rules gets us into trouble when we apply the absolute command of "Never do that again" to personal relationships. If we make it our rule to never try again, we take away our flexibility to try things with other people or just try again when we are more mature.

For example, have you ever had a bad romance? Broken up? Did your rule-maker kick in then to command you to not have another romance. Maybe you had a bad response when you made a speech in third grade or got rejected in high school when you asked someone to dance. Or maybe at work you were betrayed by a friend. If we make absolute rules out of these bad outcomes, we diminish our lives. This is because we may be obeying our old rule instead of making our decisions in the moment when we have an opportunity to try again.

I've been guilty of making absolute rules, but I am working on trying to reconsider rules to see if they still make sense today. Absolute rules like not touching red stove burners are necessary, but people are not stoves. And one person is not the same as another person who hurt you in the past.

Do you have any rules you need to look at again?

Lightwork—Refugees

We turn our lightworker attention today to helping all those people who have fled their countries. They have left behind their homes, possessions, and their lives as a result of war or disaster. Now they grieve losses while living in tent camps, standing in line for food and water, living outside in heat and cold, and being dependent for all they need to live. And some have not even found a camp to welcome them.

Let us turn our combined light of Spirit on these people and on those kind souls who try to serve them through organizations such as the UN or Red Cross, or other humanitarian groups. Bless you all, the servers and the served, the givers and the receivers. We feel for you, and we send you light to give you hope and courage and comfort. We envision those who live in camps finding new homes or being able to return to their former homes. And we thank you, workers. What you do echoes the biblical passage in which Jesus says, "What you do to the least of these, you do to me."

March 30

Speaking the Word

In the beginning was the Word …
—John 1:1

Speaking the word is a powerful exercise in which we give substance to thought and cocreate our future.

How do you speak the word?

Do any of these sound familiar: I can't; I won't; I'm worried; I'm depressed; I'm stupid?

Are you creating a future in which these states of darkness are called forth by your speaking of them and giving power to them?

Today let us examine our words. Let us substitute words of light, faith, and love for our habitual words of dread and negativity.

Today is spring cleaning day for our word closet. Step back and listen to yourself. Our words create our world. What does your world look like?

Your Best Friend

Let a friend who knows you
Help you to see your own reality,
Help you to grasp it like a diamond
And turn it over, revealing its facets.

Let a friend who loves you
Hold your hand and help you open your closet
To examine the scary monsters within.
"Look, this one is so tiny, not a threat at all."
"Look, this one is a mechanical doll
With a big key in the back.
It was wound up long ago and is still running.
It speaks no truth."

Let a friend who respects you
Be a safe haven in times of trouble and pain,
A place where you can rest,
Knowing you are loved and things will work out in the end.

Let a friend who believes in you
Encourage you onward in your path
And celebrate with you all your triumphs.

Let a friend who appreciates you
Tell you that who you are right now
Is a beautiful person,
Growing day by day into a magnificent being.

Who is this friend who knows, loves, respects, believes in, and appreciates you?
Your High Self is that friend, always there, always loving, always ready to help.
Hold out your hand to your best friend. And if you have a loved one who models
this divine love on earth, be doubly grateful to feel the love of Spirit manifested
in a human being.

Spiritual Government

When asked to decide the fate of Jesus, Pontius Pilate first tried to pass the buck by sending him to Herod. But Herod only sent him back. Since Pilate was afraid of the wrath of the mob, he washed his hands of the affair, saying, "I am innocent of the blood of this just man ..." (Matthew 27:24).

Today, Pilate would be known as middle management, caught between the angry mob and the policies of his superior, Julius Caesar. Today, he might have said, "It's not my problem. That is someone else's job; I only work here."

Government today functions little better than in Pilate's time. Within agencies, employees and managers fight turf battles and take no personal responsibility to do the right thing. They pass the buck, hoping someone else will do the deciding and take the responsibility. Democratic governments are at least a step forward from Caesar's rule of dictatorship. But government by man-made laws is only an intermediate step toward the government of cosmic law and spiritual love.

Let us visualize the governing process moving to higher levels of divine law—levels of caring for all humans, for the animal and plant kingdoms, for the earth itself. Let us visualize the dawning of wisdom to make decisions based on stewardship of the earth, not abuse of the planet. Let us see leaders arising who are bold in making right decisions based on divine love without fear of political consequences. Let the thought of reelection take second place to governing rightly. Let those who govern say, "This *is* my responsibility."

Determination

Ray Bradbury is one of the most admired science fiction authors of all time. I've read many of his books and greatly enjoyed them. An article I read said that, when he was young and trying to start out as an author, he received 150 rejection letters from publishers. Gee, it must have taken a lot of determination on his part to keep trying in spite of so many rejections. I imagine that he might have even questioned the worth of his manuscripts. But even if he did, he kept it up until finally he got someone to publish his first work. Good for him. If he had given up, millions would have missed out on the pleasure of reading his wonderful stories.

Today, let's think about our level of determination, not to sell a book but to keep ourselves going in our beliefs that we are stewards of the earth and lightworkers who are helping to lift the planet into a golden age of peace and love. If you find that your ideas or values are questioned or rejected, remember you have many companions on this journey. Walk away from rejections without letting them shake your confidence.

If you are doing okay and not getting rejection, then turn your thoughts to those who are struggling and send them light and love to carry on.

April 3

In the Hands of the Carpenter

Today we are going on a field trip. Everyone into the bus—we are going to the carpenter's shop.

There, we've arrived. "Hello, Mr. Carpenter. Could we look around your shop and watch you work?"

"Sure, come right in."

"Oh look, on the table—what a beautiful carved bowl, and there, a lovely candlestick, turned on the lathe. Come over here. Look—here is the supply of fresh-cut wood, still with bark. How dull it looks, how uninteresting next to these beautiful works of art."

Come, let us watch the carpenter work. To a partially finished piece, he sets his hand. Carving, chipping, sanding, sweat on his brow, laboring to find the perfection within the unfinished wood. He now stops to get another tool, and we stand, looking at this piece of wood, gripped in a vise and covered with a few shavings.

"Hello, folks," says the wood.

"Oh my gosh, we didn't know you could talk! Tell us about yourself."

"Well, I've been having a bad time. I feel so hemmed in. I've really been dealt a blow. My emotions are rubbed raw. I'm not what I used to be. Matters are out of my hands."

From the rear of the shop, the carpenter interrupts, "Don't worry. They all say that when I'm working on them. They don't understand what I'm doing, and when I try to explain, they don't listen. I say to them, 'Which would you rather be—a piece of rough, unfinished wood or a lovely work of art?'"

At that, the wood says directly to you, "Which would you rather be?"

The Judas Spirit

Are you under attack? Does someone hate you, curse you, abuse you, even though you have done no wrong? Sometimes the dark aspects of another person can arise against the High Self they feel in you. When this happens, they are acting in the Judas spirit. Judas is symbolic of the mortal, low side of consciousness. The real Judas plotted against Jesus. Symbolically, Judas is the part that fights against the light of Spirit.

Step back from responding personally to the attack. Instead, consider it as symbolic of this person's lower self fighting the light of their own High Self. The battle is really being waged within this other person; you are just a visible reminder to this person of their need to accept Spirit as ruler of their life.

At these times of attack, hold on to your spiritual light. Visualize light and peace surrounding the attacker. Place this person in the hands of their higher power, bless them, and withdraw from the conflict. Refuse to accept abuse. Let go of the issue, knowing your part is completed for now and Spirit is guiding the outcome.

April 5

Online

There is a new day dawning for those on spiritual paths everywhere. Thanks to the new mass medium, the internet, and to other communications advances, such as video conferencing, the ability to create and self-publish our own ideas, newsletters, web pages, and chat rooms, the world is at last meeting itself mind to mind and truly becoming the global village of tomorrow. Now the power to communicate has been placed in the hands of not just the elite who run TV, newspapers, and magazines but in the hands of nearly everyone. I know many spiritual seekers have mixed feelings about these new tools, but for today, let's look at and give thanks for the bright side. These communication tools are just that, tools. Like dynamite, they can be used for enlightened or dark purposes. So don't malign the tool just because some people have chosen to use it for darkness. We all have free will to use tools in any way we wish, with the resultant consequences.

For today, let us give thanks for this new important power in the hands of all of us. Rejoice with me that school children can work on projects together even though they live in different countries, that people can keep in touch, share ideas, support each other. Let's join the crowd and put our spirituality online!

Freedom

Throughout the darkest times in our history, through oppression and torture and slavery, there have stood the kind and courageous few who have been a help to those in need. One shining example has been the Underground Railroad, that blessed network of God's conspirators who banded together to help runaway slaves make the journey from the South's plantations to the North's freedom. Ah, freedom, that divine right that burns hot and bright in us all, that moves people to travel dangerous paths to achieve—freedom!

Let's link into the vibration of those who risked their own lives in that dark time to help strangers because it was the right thing to do. Thank you. Thank you. You have brightened our world with your courage and faith. You have shown us there never is any excuse to tolerate the enslavement, torture, or murder of anyone.

May your legacy burn bright always, and may those who are oppressed reach out their hands in need and find others like you who help them on their path to freedom.

April 7

Spring Forward, Fall Back

Just like that old phrase that jogs our memory about daylight saving time, so goes our spiritual progress. Today, let's be kind to ourselves as we review our progress. Let's not expect a straight line of ever upward movement. Instead, let's realize there is nothing wrong with our stops and starts, our glow of spiritual high followed by a bit of a retreat into today's problems.

Do you make a habit of cutting yourself down with insults whenever you are not perfect? For today, watch for that trend and head it off at the pass. If you evaluate a word or action, keep your appraisal tuned to the event and don't tell yourself you were stupid. You are not. You are a spiritual being, temporarily confined to a physical existence on a planet of great temptation.

Forgive yourself if you goof now and then. And while you are at it, forgive others too. Then let it go as a lesson you have learned.

Singing a New Song

As we grow spiritually, we eventually move toward a higher vibration and make it part of ourselves. It has a counterpoint—namely de-crystallization of the lower vibration. In order to become greater, we must let go of the lesser and let it dissolve. Think of it as a note of music, the vibrational expression of what is. Everything has a note, a song that is its essence, as does each person. When a higher note begins to manifest, it is dissonant with the current note. Like a soprano shattering a glass with a note, our higher vibration de-crystallizes the lower one we were clinging to. This is the nature of life—constant upward evolution of all, with the current note being replaced by ever higher, purer notes. At these times, there can be discomfort but only if we cling to the old self, the old note. When you find yourself between two versions of yourself, old and new, have the faith to let go of the previous you and grasp the new. Sing your new song with a glad heart. Accept who you have become.

April 9

Signs of the New Age: The Cheerleader

There she was, physically fit and slim, perched on the shoulders of her cheerleading team in her hot pink, sparkly little tennis dress. *Great legs*, I thought in admiration. At the end of the cheer, she leaped down from their shoulders into a full split. *Good gravy*, I thought. *I've never seen that done before. What an athlete! How flexible, how fit she is!*

So what—a cheerleader is fit. Big deal. How is that a sign of the new age? Well, the part I didn't tell you is that she has white hair and is over seventy years old, as is her entire team!

Ponder that. I don't know about you, but I don't even know anyone in my middle-aged group of friends who can do a split, even slowly. But to leap off people's shoulders into a split? No way.

I'm truly inspired. Old isn't decrepit anymore. Sure, it can be, but it surely isn't a sentence of doom and disability to be seventy anymore. Wow, am I ever glad!

Let's all take the vow to keep our spirits up as we add years to our lives. Let's promise ourselves never to stop doing things, never to let an outdated picture of old age inside our heads slow us down. And then let's get up off our butts and exercise!

Paralyzed by Perfection

I have a confession to make. I have a great deal of difficulty filing my paperwork. It's not so much that I'm lazy and don't like to do it, although I admit that is true. No, it's something else. When I set out to do the task of filing, I take the big box of papers I've been meaning to file (usually weighing as much as a small child), and I gingerly pick out an item. If it is something that already has a file folder in my cabinet, I'm okay. I put the item into the folder and move on. But when I get to an item that doesn't have a folder, I stand there, paralyzed, not knowing what to name the new folder. For instance, I was paralyzed for at least an hour wondering what to call the file for my car. Would it be "Car," "Auto," "Pontiac," or "Grand Am"? All of these seemed like good choices to me, but each choice would put that file in a very different part of the cabinet. I just sat there in a quandary until I finally forced myself to pick one. This has happened over and over with many papers I have had to file.

Finally, I consulted a friend who keeps her desk and files at work ultra-neat and put away. I told her my sad story, and she said I should stop trying to get the perfect name and just pick a name for the file and put the papers away. Wow! A lightbulb went on in my mind. Of course! It was my perfectionism that was paralyzing me and preventing me from doing this simple task that others do with no difficulty. So I listened to her, stopped fooling around, and just picked something. It's a relief to let go of that bit of perfectionism. I truly hope you don't have the perfection paralysis too. Do you?

April 11

Cats and Dogs

There has been a commercial on TV for the American Society for Prevention of Cruelty to Animals (ASPCA). It is so terrible that I can't watch it without crying. I quickly find the remote and change the channel. It shows poor abused, beaten, and starved cats and dogs, looking closely into the camera with terrified or despairing expressions.

So many of us love these animals and keep them in our houses as pets and family members. How very sad and angry it makes me to think that these dear souls who depend on us for food and shelter and their very lives could be abandoned or treated so badly that they are injured or killed. We owe it to these precious ones that bring us so much joy to pray together for their health and safety.

We project our light and love to these dear animals, and we project a firm command to abusers: stop it! You do not deserve to be near an animal. Either care for them properly or give them to another kinder person.

And if you are so moved, do something to support the rescue of our furry friends.

One Nation

A democratic nation is a group of people who have made some agreements to give up some of their individual choices in order to act in the world as one united entity for the highest good of all. What we give up is that we agree to be governed by representatives whom we have elected to serve our best interests.

So let us turn our thoughts and prayers today to all those who govern our nation. We link together to send our united light and love to the national government. We see the capital aglow with the light of truth, justice, mercy, and divine love. We see all darkness dissolved, all dishonesty cast aside, all personal desires for power over others laid to rest. We see those who govern truly inspired to fulfill a divine mission to take good care of the people, to do what is right and true, to live up to the highest spiritual ideals.

We see dissension replaced with cooperation, coordination, and harmony. We see the united light of those who govern our nation as building a spiritual government of beauty, peace, plenty, justice, mercy. Please hold this vision until it manifests as real: one nation, under God, with liberty and justice for all.

Sometimes You Just Need a Little Nap

We surely live in a hustle, bustle world, don't we? There's so much to do that it reminds me of poor Alice in Wonderland who was running as fast as she could just to stay in the same place. We have forgotten a slower style of life.

For some, there never was a slower time. But for me, I remember the 1950s when I was a little child. There was so much time, especially during the summer, that I could sit on a curb for an hour watching ants transport a little piece of carrot back to the nest. Or sometimes I would gaze at a squirrel or pop the little bubbles of tar on the street on a very hot day.

I wasn't scheduled. No child was. If you missed that slow and free time, you missed something great. Along with play came a lovely sleepiness in midday. It was time for a cozy little nap. I never wanted to stop and nap, but the custom was enforced by my mother. First I read, but soon I fell asleep.

Well, today we are in need of acknowledging that sometimes we just need a little nap. It's okay. It is a custom in many countries to take a nap—adults and children alike. So today, give yourself a break. If you can, take a little nap. (If you can't do it today, try to do it soon.) You deserve to be good to yourself. Keep the little nap in your tool kit of nice things that you deserve to do for yourself any day that you like.

Ping-Pong in Space

Do you think you could play Ping-Pong on the space station? At first, I thought, *Of course not.* Ping-Pong depends on gravity. The ball is hit, arcs up, and then gravity brings it down to bounce on the table. So then I thought, *Hmm, maybe I could think out of the box, actually out of the earth.* And I started to giggle. Because I now could envision two astronauts hanging in the air, and one hits the ball. That not only causes the ball to streak forward, but it also causes the astronaut to spin around or maybe go upside down like a cartwheel (yes, I know there is no upside down in space—just work with me here). Then the next person hits the ball, and both the ball and the astronaut go flying in different directions. Wouldn't that be fun to watch?

What is my point? Well, besides having a giggle imagining this scene, let us look at our thinking about anything that we think is impossible for ourselves. Those are in-the-box thoughts. Can we envision adapting that impossible situation into something that indeed is possible? Sure, for Ping-Pong in space, we had to let go of tables and gravity bounces, but it is still sort of Ping-Pong.

This concept of adapting old ways into new is how we change the earth, how we bring it higher. We need to forget what things are like now and forget our attitude that things won't change. Things will change. The earth will get better, countries will treat their people better, problems in the ecology of the earth will get better, maybe not exactly the same as when there were hardly any people on earth but better and different. We don't even have to envision exactly how things will get better or what they will look like later. We just have to believe and work on it however we can and envision a wonderful earth. If we can play Ping-Pong in space, we can do anything!

April 15

Render unto God

This date is widely known in the United States as Tax Day. It is the deadline to give the government its share of our incomes. And the government makes sure that it collects its share. But what of our obligation to God? Jesus discussed this in Luke 21:25 when he answered those sent by the chief priests, "Render, therefore, to Caesar the things that are Caesar's and to God the things that are God's."

If you have devoted your time to study, your heart to your High Self, and your life to serve Spirit, have you also remembered your income? Could you give a portion of it back to God?

Examine your feelings about your money. Is it really yours or do you just have the use of it, loaned to you by Spirit? Do you fear poverty? Do you try to amass money but never feel secure? Turn instead to the security of Spirit.

If you will step out in faith and promise God a portion of your income, your reward will be great. Claim your right to prosperity by rendering unto God what is God's. That which you give will be returned unto you a hundredfold.

Healing the News

Today is a special assignment day. Lightworkers, let us unite in a project of healing global, national, and local conditions. This assignment is to watch the TV news today. As you watch, take part as lightworkers. Pick out one or more news stories that concern affairs that are in darkness, disease, conflict. These stories are not hard to find.

Let your High Self guide you to decree a proper, divine outcome of the situation or problem. Decree that Spirit's will is being done in the situation and that the healing taking place on the inner planes will soon manifest in outer changes.

I invite you to picture the situation of conflict and darkness being replaced with peace and light. Visualize your image replacing the image you have just seen on the TV. Picture the reporter breaking in with an update that details the amazing turnaround of events.

This special assignment is also a training exercise. It is not just for this day only. It is part of our mission to train ourselves to gradually and automatically make divine decrees and visualization whenever we see negatives presented on the news.

We are gifted through TV with knowledge of what is going on in our world. Let us take what is projected electronically to us and use our spiritual powers to heal the news.

Signs of the New Age—The Horse Whisperer

An article appeared in *USA Today* (8/28/97) about Monty Roberts, who has figured out a nonviolent method for taming a wild horse to accept saddle and rider. He has written a best-selling book about his technique. He says he listens to the horse and persuades the horse to accept the saddle.

This use of a psychic connection to the animal kingdom is part of our divine heritage but is a surprise to the Western world. This man shows respect for the animal, and it, in turn, complies with his wishes willingly. What a wonderful demonstration to all of us of a better way to live cooperatively with the animal kingdom.

Roberts says, "For centuries humans have said to horses, 'You do what I tell you or I'll hurt you.' I am saying that no one has the right to say 'you must' to an animal or another human." And is he ever gathering interest! The article says he is drawing crowds of over one thousand people in cities he has visited in which he demonstrates his technique. The rightness of his way strikes a chord in us all. "Yes, that's a better way!"

Thank you, Mr. Roberts. Let's join in projecting that humane methods like his become our predominant way of relating to our domestic animals.

Volunteers

The Red Cross, the Salvation Army, Big Brothers and Sisters, scout leaders, volunteer firefighters, neighbors who collect money for good causes, the group that crochets afghans for homeless people—today we celebrate the kindness of heart of all those who volunteer their time and talents to help others.

Volunteers, thank you! You are the lights of the world!

What would we do without you? Volunteers set a standard of pure altruism, divine love, for their fellow humans or animals and for the environment. They turn from self to others. They put aside their rest and recreation to be of service. They are a shining example of the golden rule.

If you are a volunteer, I thank you. Take a bow! You are wonderful.

As we go about our lives today, let us take the opportunity to pass on our thanks when we see a volunteer in action. They don't do it for reward, but how nice it is to be noticed and appreciated. So let them have your thanks and a pat on the back.

And if you aren't already volunteering to help others, consider becoming a volunteer today. Someone out there needs you.

April 19

India and Afghanistan

What do these two countries have in common? Nothing, I thought. One is in Asia, and one is in the Middle East. They do not share a border. And I have never heard anything about them having any connection. Until I read that some people in India have turned their compassion for the poor, war-torn people of Afghanistan into action. What are they doing? They are actually inviting and transporting some Afghan women to India to be trained to be installers of solar panels and then helping them to get solar power going in their own communities.

I thought that action was a wow! It was not the governments of either country that had collaborated. No, it was just citizens who took coordinated action to help another part of the world. And it is not only this project that uplifts me. Almost daily, I read of some other wonderful project happening between the people, bypassing governmental structures and reaching out, people to people.

Let us today be inspired by these healing projects. Let us bless all the efforts any citizens of anywhere are doing to help others or to help the animals, the atmosphere, the water. Let us send light to help them keep their determination going. And if you hear of a project in your country or anywhere else that moves your heart, connect with it and help it through your prayers and projections of its success, your donations, or even your actions. Envision the people stepping up to help each other, not letting anything stand in the way of peace and love.

April 20

Control Rods

In a nuclear reactor, there is a danger that the awesome power of splitting atoms will cause an explosion. In order to control this energy and produce a steady flow of power, rods of cadmium are interspersed among the nuclear fuel. They moderate the reaction, dampening the tendency for the reactor to spiral out of control and explode.

The earth is now facing a tremendous surge of spiritual power as it moves from the third toward the fourth dimension. The molecules of every substance are being quickened, which can cause distress.

As we surge forth into the fourth dimension, let us help the earth by visualizing the united power of the network of light pouring down from the top of the atmosphere straight through to the molten core of the earth. Let the steadying force of this united light act as a set of control rods. Together we stand firm in the serenity of the light and calm the gyrations and imbalances of the planet before they cause great damage. Picture all of us uniting now to keep the earth settled and on course as it revs up its power into the New Age.

April 21

Sudden Exits

No one knows the day or the hour when we or anyone else may be leaving this earth plane. Today we have a special project. Today we can work to bring more serenity to our relationships while we still can.

Think for a while about the people who are important in your life. If you or any of them were not here tomorrow, would something have been left unsaid between you? Who comes to mind when you think of this possibility? Maybe more than one? Whoever it is, is there something you want to tell them?

Well, you have a chance to say what is in your heart. Maybe this will mean making a phone call or writing a letter. Maybe it involves telling them you really love them or really appreciate something they did.

Maybe the person who came to mind is someone who has hurt you, upset you, or let you down. If this person made a sudden exit tomorrow, would you regret not saying something you needed to say? If so, tell this person. Make a plan to communicate as soon as you can, for your own peace. If it is not wise to communicate, write a letter that expresses your heart and don't mail it. Strange as it may seem, this can help give you peace.

I think I need to make a call right now. How about you?

KIMBERLY CLAYTON

Hug a Tree

Today, we have a special outdoor assignment. Yes, this is Hug a Tree Day. Oh no, how embarrassing! Do I have to go outside and let people see me embracing foliage? Cavorting with bushes? Winking at greenery?

Well, let's not go overboard. Today, give some thought to the plant kingdom and our relationship with it. This kingdom is vital to our physical life, providing food, oxygen, wood for shelter and furniture, even maple syrup. The plants help cure pollution, help hold the soil in place, and keep us cool on summer days. The flowers delight us with a brilliance and clarity of color we cannot duplicate with paint and canvas. This kingdom is productive, beautiful, and peaceful.

Let us thank this kingdom today and send it our love. See it quickening its vibratory rate to prepare for the New Age.

Let us share our auras with the plant kingdom. Go ahead, hug a tree. Are you too shy to be so forward with a stranger? Well then introduce yourself first as a lightworker. You will be welcomed. If you just can't do that, go lean on a tree.

April 23

Stress Break

My, we've been working hard at healing ourselves and saving the world. It's time for a stress break. Come with me—we're going to the beach. You don't need to pack or travel; just come with me in your mind …

There! We are now sitting at our favorite beach. Feel the wonderful, strong breeze. Hear the rhythmic crash of the waves. Smell the salt in the air. Breathing seems more vibrant now, as if divine energy is entering us at every in-breath. Gaze at the row upon row upon row of ever-moving white rollers of surf, as wave after wave encounters shallowness and tumbles over in greeting to the earth below. At the horizon, we see a few sailboats.

We look at the people to the left and right. Some are building sand castles, some are walking or jogging the surf line, some are swimming. And many are just sitting or lying down on towels.

Life has slowed down for us. We have left behind duties, schedules, traffic, even our usual clothes. Our feet caress the sand, feeling its coolness. It is enough here to just be, not do. Oh, we may do this or that while we are here, but whatever we are up to, it is part of being at the beach. Let's just sit for a few minutes and be. Feel stress leaving you as the waves lull your mind and body. Linger awhile till you get that feeling of serenity.

April 24

The Public You

I find myself in traffic behind an amazing person. How do I know this person is amazing? It's because her license plate is giving me the sweet and simple greeting of HELLO. Well, hello right back to you too! I feel buoyed up while stopped in traffic by this acknowledgment that this person knows another human being is behind her and she wants to greet me.

What I find so charming about this plate is that it is so unusual compared to the many vanity plates I've seen. What's different is that those plates that I've seen all have said something about the driver. I've seen names and nicknames, designations like BST-MOM, METS-FAN. I've seen car pride like SWT-RDE and RED-DVL. I've seen college plates. I've seen cryptic inside-joke plates that I never figure out. But all of these are saying something to the world about the driver, some tidbit telling the world who they are.

This person ahead of me actually wants to extend a hand of greeting to me! Wow! In some ridiculous way, I've personalized this license plate, as if she is actually greeting me. I feel special for a moment. How much our gestures to the world affect each other! Let's go out and about in public with a hello in our hearts and make someone feel special today.

April 25

Signs of the New Age: In-Class Massage

I was reading *Massage* magazine and came across an article about the Netherlands. They highlighted a school called Axelson's Gymnastiska Institute in Stockholm that has a training course for teachers in how to give massage and how to teach children to give massage to each other as part of their school day. The photo with the article shows two kids of preschool age working on two others who are on mats. They did a study and found that massaged children are calmer, fight less, concentrate more, and show more empathy. This school has trained over nine thousand teachers all over the country to integrate massage into all levels of education, from preschool through high school. Well, how about that? Kids who make massaging each other a small part of their day are learning to respect each other across race and class lines, and to be calmer in their whole daily lives, not just for the twenty-minute massage period. The kids just love massage and carry their techniques back home, massaging their parents.

A person interviewed for the article commented about the no-touch policy in US schools and said she is happy that in her country the attitude is very positive to touch. She added that children being touched appropriately gives them the knowledge to say no to inappropriate touch.

So let's today applaud this wonderful addition to schooling. Some US schools are already trying out the concept of teaching compassionate touch and massage, but the efforts are small and not nationwide. So, for today, let us envision all US schools becoming more aware of the great benefits of comforting touch, not only from teacher to child but from child to child.

The Automatic Door

We've all been in a situation where we've felt we were stopped, that opportunity was closed to us. It may have been that we lacked money to pursue a dream, or we lacked help or time or something else. We may have felt, *I might as well give up because that door is closed to me.*

When we are up against situations that feel impossible, and when we are sure there is no way to accomplish our goals, we set up a negative vibration. That vibration is set into motion by the power of our thinking, *This won't work. I can't do it.* We have now stopped Spirit from working on this situation because our negative decrees have stopped the flow of spiritual power from flowing through us.

Things are not always impossible just because we don't see the way to accomplish them right now. In order to counter our own thoughts of defeat and failure, let us see the situation as if we were walking through the parking lot of a grocery store. In America, we have a deep-seated trust that the door of a grocery store will open automatically but only as we reach the door.

Looking at that real grocery store door from afar, we see it is firmly closed and has no door handle. It could seem an impossible task to open that door. But we trust from long experience that the door will know when we have arrived on the threshold and will open for us.

Let us see our obstacle as one of those automatic doors. If it looks closed to us now, let us keep striding forward, taking the actions we can toward the goal. Let us hold in our mind the picture of that door opening for us just as we get there. Let us hand over our impossible task to Spirit, and let us realize that Spirit has the power to open that door.

Starsha Dawn

April 27

The Network of Light

Okay, lightworkers. I hope you've been practicing wrapping yourselves in light. Now it is time to work with others. First, take a breath and wrap yourself in light, leaving a little stem of light open from your crown to the highest etheric plane. The light comes in through that stem. Okay, you are filling up with light, and now it is time to give it to others.

Open your eyes and look around you. If anyone is present, ask Spirit to flow the light through you and out of you to wrap those other people. You can do it one by one, but it is faster to do everyone you see at once. Now close your eyes and picture yourself linking in light with all other lightworkers in and around this earth in the astral and etheric planes. See a spider web of inter-braided light encircling this whole planet in a grid of light. Hold this visualization until you actually feel the powerful connection. Now visualize all on earth being wrapped in light that comes to them from the grid. The whole earth now takes on the light inside and out and glows a brilliant white, like a beacon in the black velvet of space. Hold this picture and let the light lift us to a higher vibration.

As you come out of this meditation, will yourself to stay linked permanently to the Network of Light. As with the light wrap for yourself, negative thoughts dissolve the link, so whenever you think of it, reconnect. When I do this, I feel a power surge of connection that gives me goose bumps. But whatever you feel or don't feel, know that you have willed it, and Spirit has fulfilled it. We are one, linked in light.

Taurus—The Bull

What comes to mind when you hear that someone is a Taurus? "Oh, that explains why he is so stubborn." "I'll never get her to change her mind." Well, let's talk about the positive side of this Taurus quality. Instead of stubborn, let's say steadfast, strong, loyal. You know, "strong like a bull" is a well-known comedy line.

To be strong and steadfast means we can hold steady on our path in spite of ridicule. Those who developed something new usually were ridiculed by others. We can thank them for their steadfastness in ignoring negative comments and producing original thoughts, decisions, inventions, art forms, music styles, and so on. Those who fight to make good changes in the world must stay strong. They must take their new ideas and hold on as negative reactions pound them.

The Bible tells us that Noah was ridiculed as nuts and stupid for building a big boat on dry desert land. But he ignored them and kept on building. Maybe he had a bit of Taurus steadfastness.

Can we claim the strong Taurus spirit too?

Lash Yourself to the Mast

There are two types of sea stories I've heard in which the sailors needed to lash themselves to the main mast for safety. One instance is during an extremely severe storm when their physical strength will not allow them to hold on. The other is in Greek mythology when the ship of Odysseus was approaching the Sirens whose voices lure sailors off course and into permanent captivity.

Let's use both these metaphors today to give us a picture of tests of strength and will. Imagine yourself happily sailing your spiritual course when—*bang*—a hurricane hits. It is a storm of personal crisis, a test of your beliefs and strength of purpose. Whenever this hits, use Spirit's assistance to tie sturdy rope around you, connecting you securely to your main mast of Spirit. Or *bang*, an irresistible temptation hits. Help your willpower by lashing yourself tightly so that, no matter how weak your resolve, you cannot break the rope.

Let's use this visual picture to help ourselves and all others who are suffering through storms and temptations. See us firmly tied, secured in our faith, connected to our true strength, lashed to the mast.

April 30

Spin the Globe

We have a personal assignment today. We are in charge of projecting light to one special place on earth. We are, each one of us in our own minds, going to do a little exercise. Visualize the globe of the world. See it in front of you, sitting on a stand. Get that image firmly in mind. Now reach out your hand and give that globe a hard spin. Watch the blur of continents and oceans going around and around. Now while it is still spinning, reach out a finger and put it on the globe, stopping the motion.

Okay, look where your finger landed. Wherever it is, this place is your assignment. If you hit land, then see and feel light descending from Spirit through you and out your finger to that very spot on the real world. That country is receiving light. Let it flow for a while. Let Spirit decide how to use this light. Just let it touch the earth.

If you hit ocean, then your assignment is that ocean. See the light striking that spot on the ocean. See it lifting all the atoms to a higher vibration. Believe that what you are doing on this globe is affecting the real world. Your intention will make it true. Thank Spirit for letting you do lightwork for this place on earth.

May 1

Upside Down

I was working on one of my favorite pastimes, a jigsaw puzzle. I had already put into place the edge and all the easy pieces, and the puzzle was three-fourths done. But now I was stuck. I stared and stared at the pieces that were left, not seeing any place to put any of them. I even tried picking several of them up, one by one, and trying them here and there, looking for the one place where they fit. But still no luck. I sat, sipping herbal tea, and considered giving up. But then an idea emerged. I took my chair and put it at the opposite side of the table so I could study the puzzle upside down.

Now I could see things differently. Quickly, I picked up piece after piece and found where they went. Stripped of my usual view of the puzzle, I could see the shapes and colors in a different light, and the connections of the pieces to the spaces became clearer.

Perhaps this upside-down process can apply to other puzzles in my life, such as deciding what to do about situations that have me stumped. But how do I turn life upside down? Perhaps if I have an issue with another person, I could turn it around and pretend I am the other person and look at the situation through their eyes. Perhaps in situations involving decisions about my future, I could turn around and imagine myself in the future I might create. I could look back from this future and report on what this future looks like.

Perhaps when you are stuck, you could try turning things upside down.

Spiritual Jealousy

Do you know a fellow lightworker on a spiritual path? Are you fortunate enough to meditate with a group of fellow seekers? How wonderful to share the light and unite your power for Spirit!

When your spiritual companions tell you of their growth, their visions, insights, growing awareness, and powers, do you ever think to yourself, *Why them and not me? I've been at this awhile, and here this person is, new to it all and doing better than I am?*

Jesus talked of this type of jealousy in his parable of the workers who came later to work in the vineyard at harvest time (see Matthew 20). In this story, some men were hired and began working early in the day for an agreed-upon wage. When others joined in later and still later, the master of the vineyard granted each of them the same wage as those who started earlier—no more, no less.

Those who started earliest became jealous, thinking their wage should be more because they worked longer. But the master told them that they had agreed to their wage, and they should not be concerned with what he gave to the others.

Whenever we feel jealous or envious of the seemingly effortless and rapid development of spiritual talents in others who have come later to work in the vineyards, let us remember we cannot see the lifetimes of study and preparation we all have had. Rejoice with everyone who is growing in Spirit, for as one is lifted up, we all are lifted up too.

Jesus Wept

Jesus wept.
—John 11:35 King James Bible

This shortest verse of the Bible is awesome in its simplicity. Imagine Jesus, aware of his mission and his powers, strongly connected with God, yet still moved to sorrow and tears by the death of Lazarus, his friend. Imagine tears rolling down his cheeks, his head bowed, feeling the pain of sorrow.

If we had been there, wouldn't we have wanted to embrace him and comfort him? Wouldn't we have wanted to stand by him to let him know he was not alone? We can. For he has told us that what we do for each other, we do for him.

Think back to a time when you have wept and longed for comfort, but there was none. We all need each other's help to get through the rough spots of life. We all can act as comforters of those who weep.

Let us join our thoughts today and project to all those who grieve and weep. Let them know they are never alone. God is always there, and we, their brothers and sisters, are there too. Let us visualize sending them our love and compassion as if it were an embrace. If you are sad, join with us to receive the embrace of your spiritual family.

As you go about your affairs today, keep an eye out for signs of sorrow in those in your life. If you find it, offer your compassion. Whether by words, a touch, or a kind smile, let them feel God's embrace through you.

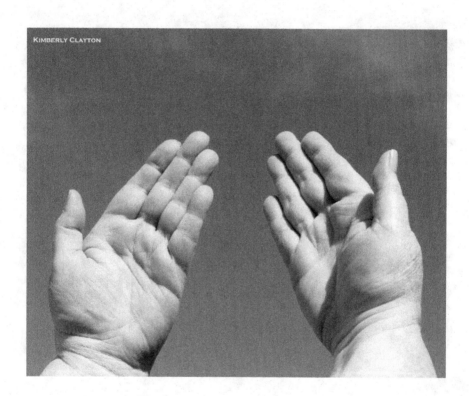

KIMBERLY CLAYTON

Hands

Look at your hands. They represent a point of physical contact with the earth plane. Through the hands, we as spiritual beings conduct many of our duties and affairs on this planet.

Whenever we use our hands, we channel ourselves through them. Our thoughts and emotions can crystallize into physical expression through our touch. How do you touch others? Is your I Am spirit coming through?

During the course of the day today, let us observe the many times we make physical contact through the hands. As we make those contacts, let us take advantage of the opportunity to unite with the aura of another human to share our I Am spirit. Be aware as you pat your son on the back, as you receive change at the store, as you hand a report to your boss, that you are in contact spiritually. Does someone accidentally touch your hand today? Be prepared to immediately direct peace and love through this accidental contact.

Are others radiating negatives to you through contact of the hands? Refuse it, shield yourself, and let the negatives bounce off. But return positive for negative, love for fear. Today, let your hands be healing, guiding, helping hands.

May 5

Love in Action

This is the time when the old way is being transformed into the New Age. It is the time when the lightworkers are beginning to demonstrate their talents and understanding in major visible ways. All the time taken for our spiritual birth into connection with our High Self, our growth through trials and tests, has produced the strength of will to set about doing our Father's business.

What an exciting time to see more and more lightworkers declaring themselves as such to the world at large. We are not doing this declaring by taking out newspaper ads saying, "Attention, I am a lightworker." No, we are declaring it through our very lives, our actions, our words whenever we display the golden rule in action, whenever we show divine love and kindness.

The importance of putting our love into action for the planet now is critical to our success in cocreating a better world of peace and love. Just *having* wisdom and divine love is not enough now. We must not hide our light under a bushel. We must boldly shine forth that light and show the world the spiritual self in action. Ready? Go!

Signs of the New Age: The Power of Money

As socially responsible investors we can make a difference.
When we invest in companies that value their employees and
their communities, we help promote the health of the economy
as well as the well-being of workers and their families.

— Amy Domini

I did not write the words above. I recently got them in the mail. They are in the annual shareholder report written by Amy Domini, the president of a socially responsible investment company, Domini Social Investments.

I'm pretty impressed with this company as they are very, very serious about using the power that comes from money to encourage big businesses to improve their commitment to their employees, to the environment, to quality in their products, to ceasing to buy from third world firms that use slave labor, and on and on. And they make money at it as well. Their report of fall, 2004, says that they introduced twenty-two shareholder resolutions just that year to some of the companies in the portfolio, and that eleven were "withdrawn when companies agreed to do what the resolution requested, or to meet us partway." They are out there, embarrassing companies into becoming better, since resolutions must be put on the ballot for the company's shareholder meetings. What power that is to bring to light otherwise hidden practices of companies. All shareholders can do it individually, but it is so much more visible when a big stock company requests the resolution be voted on. And, of course, we individual investors aren't aware of what practices the company is engaging in that should be changed.

Domini is not the only investment company doing this blessed mission. Let us salute them and other companies and individuals like them. They are taking the desires of the people for a clean planet, for fairness, for quality, for social responsibility and putting their mouth where their money is.

Let us salute these lightworker brothers and sisters and let us unite with them in light to send them strength and stamina to keep beating on the corporate doors to demand a higher way of doing business.

And as for us all, let us think for a minute—where is our money invested? Is it in places we would be proud to proclaim? If not, what are we waiting for to put our money where our heart is?

May 7

Signs of the New Age: Heart as the Bottom Line

In the investor's annual report from Domini that I mentioned yesterday, they highlight some companies in the portfolio that are doing marvelous things for their communities that show me the bottom line is not just profit, at least in these places. Here is some of what I learned:

- Dollar General. Their founder set up the Dollar General Literacy foundation to award grants for literacy and has set up in every store a learning center to help local people gain job skills.
- Hewlett-Packard. They give big bucks to worldwide charitable organizations and efforts. They run "i-communities" in poor neighborhoods in Houston and in Kuppam, India, and Mogalakwena, South Africa, that are initiatives for "increasing literacy, creating jobs, promoting entrepreneurship …"
- E.W. Scripps. They have a foundation that donated money to build a journalism school at a historically black university in Virginia. They support the Parity Project of the National Association of Hispanic Journalists, which aims to increase the percentage of Latino journalists in newsrooms.
- St. Paul Travelers (insurance). They sponsor a program that gives grants to neighborhood artists and activists to spend a year traveling to build skills to become leaders in their communities. They have a special focus on helping the large immigrant Hmong population (from Southeast Asia) in their local area.

Isn't all this news wonderful? Businesses are taking their responsibilities to heart, more and more. Let's bless these endeavors and others like them, and let's project light for many, many more.

Direct Attack

I was visiting a little town on the Chesapeake Bay. I stopped in a small market, and soon after me came a tall, loud man who greeted several other men in the store saying, "Is that your car with a massage therapy sticker?" Then he noticed me, a stranger, wearing a T-shirt with a message about massage therapy. He looked me in the eye and said, "Not another one of those massage kooks! We have enough of those kooks!" I was shocked at his direct hit of aggressive firepower. Blam! Right between the eyes! Have you ever been attacked like that by a total stranger? It shocked me to know that something I am and something I believe in was so unacceptable to this man that he had to fire off a shot at me.

Sometimes when Jesus went about preaching, he found himself in a town that could not accept him and what he stood for. So did the apostles. In those cases, they turned around and left.

And that's what I did. I got in my car and got out of there as fast as I could. I knew the vibes there were not harmonious to me. It does no good to stay on where we are despised. So if you ever find yourself under direct attack, don't fight back. Just turn around and leave. Find your peace and pleasure elsewhere.

But What If I Can't Leave?

"Fine for you to say on yesterday's page to just walk away from a direct attack, from places and people who are inharmonious to your values. But what if I can't leave? What if the place is something more permanent, like my job?"

Okay. Take a deep breath. Let's think this through. For all those who are in jobs that are painful to them, with people who attack them, let us project this message today.

Brothers and sisters under direct attack: First, take care of yourselves. No, sometimes you can't just up and quit. But you can meet attacks with silence, break your eye contact, and direct your attention elsewhere. Attackers love to get a rise out of their victims, and you take away their fun if you ignore them and refuse to play their game. It is a proven principle of psychology that your attention reinforces their behavior. If you withdraw your attention, they get nothing. Be aware they may try harder before they finally grow tired of you. So be strong in your resolve. You can weather the storm.

There is a second message too. This workplace may not be the right place for you. Maybe it is time to start creating a better life for yourself in some other setting. The pain of the situation can make you more ready to take a look at your options, to get needed training to do something else, to make your move in following your heart to a bright future.

May 10

Kindred Spirits

About an hour after the incident in which I was insulted for being a massage therapist, I found myself in a very different little town on the Chesapeake Bay. This place felt much more alive, more attuned with me. I decided to take the narrated cruise, and while I was buying my ticket, the boat's captain noticed the book in my hand, James Redfield's *The Tenth Insight*, sequel to *The Celestine Prophecy*. He just lit up and struck up a conversation, asking how far along I was and whether I had read the *Celestine Prophecy*. When I said that I had, he told me that he believed the insights in those books and that our growth into spiritual understanding and talents just must be true. I agreed and then realized Spirit had sent a kindred spirit into my path. Maybe it was to remind me I am not alone, that many travel the path I am on. I breathed a sigh of relief.

Kindred spirits will come to me if they can perceive our kinship. And those meetings can give me a boost of energy to keep on going forward.

So let's you and I start showing a taste of who we are so our kindred spirits can find us. And let us watch for the subtle signs in those we meet.

Homework

My neighborhood friend Bert had an older sister, Barbara. When I was in fifth grade, she was in tenth grade. I thought she was beautiful and grown-up and sweet. She was always nice to me when I came to ask if Bert could come out to play.

One warm spring day when I went to their house, Barbara was sitting on the porch doing her homework. While I was waiting for Bert to come out, I stood behind her and looked at her book. My eyes grew wide with horror! I felt my heart start to pound. Because, although I could read quite well, I couldn't make any sense of the words or pictures on the page. I asked her what this book was, and she said, "Biology."

Now I panicked and made some excuse and ran home and ran to my room. My future was over! I knew biology was a required course, and I knew I would never ever be smart enough to even understand what is was, let alone pass the course. I would fail high school. No college for me. My dreams collapsed, and I cried into my teddy bear.

Then Bert came by and told me Barbara wanted to talk to me. So I went back, red faced from crying and obviously upset. She got me to tell her what was wrong, and then she smiled broadly. She told me I had nothing to worry about, that I would understand all my high school classes when I got older. I had never thought of that. I could only envision myself as smart as I was right now. I knew I would get taller, but I never thought my brain would get smarter too.

But I trusted that she was right, and I calmed down. Thank you, Barbara, for putting things into perspective and making me realize I could grow both in body and mind and that I would be ready when high school came.

Such has been my path. I get frightened by new endeavors, but when I am ready, they turn out to be doable. Is that true for you too?

KIMBERLY CLAYTON

Statues on the Path

It's the heart afraid of breaking,
That never learns to dance.
It's the dream afraid of waking,
That never takes a chance.

—From the song "The Rose"

Whenever I hear this song, these words move me. Life is full of chances to take or not. Every fork in the path results in one road taken and another not taken. But there is a third choice too. We can sit right down and refuse to move in any direction.

Sometimes I meet people who have just sat down and refused to progress along their paths. They will not move on and grow up. They could be fifty and still dressing, thinking, and acting the same way they did at age eighteen. Even their hairstyles are from the past. Some are still hanging out in the bar scene. Some have been dating the same person for twenty or thirty years without committing. Some are doing odd jobs like they did in high school. They have become cobwebbed statues, stuck fast in the past and refusing to progress on their paths.

No matter how much anxiety there is in making choices and taking a chance at a fork in the path, we must move on. We are not made to stand still and become statues. Let us send blessings to those who are stuck and also send a wake-up call to them: "Hello in there, my friend. It's not too late. There is still time to step forth and walk down the next leg of your path. Go on, take a chance. You'll be glad when you see who you are after going around the next bend."

Being with a Moaner

When asked in a magazine interview what advice she would give, Katherine Hepburn, a woman I've always admired for her grit as well as her talent, said, "Don't moan. Being with a moaner is a bore." I typed up that comment and hung it up at my workplace so I could always be reminded of it.

We all have our problems, traumas, aches and pains, financial woes. But when the negatives dominate our thinking, our spirit cannot soar. We can slip over the line and become a moaner. Close your eyes for a moment and think over the last three conversations you have had. Picture that you are the other person, listening to you speak. What did you say? What was your tone of voice, body posture, and gesture? Keep an eye out for moaning behavior. Go ahead. Do this now. I'll wait ...

Okay, you're back. How did you do? For those of you who were fascinating, or inspiring, or upliftingly comedic, congratulations! You are a pleasure to be with! If you did not do so well, take heart; you are not alone. How did you come off? Were you moaning, complaining, sighing, or sarcastic, even a little? Were you boring yourself as you listened to you? Probably you are somewhere in between these two extremes, the fascinating and the boring.

So here's the assignment. Get ready for your next three conversations with different people (not just greetings but actual chats). Plan ahead to be positive and respectful of the other and even inspirational if you can. Then, while you are actually having these conversations, stand back and observe yourself as you interact. Are you pleased to be with you?

Look up to Your Children

Do you have children? If not, do you see children regularly, in your family or perhaps in your profession? At this time, the vibrational level of earth is rising into the fourth dimension. This acceleration has allowed very highly evolved children to incarnate on earth to help bring about the New Age.

Look at the children you know. See within them the high degree of spiritual evolvement most possess. If this child standing before you were sixty years old and an important personage, you would be honored and pleased to have him or her visit you. In many cases, the child before you *is* that important personage, that highly evolved master spirit you have been wanting to meet.

Give this child the respect she or he deserves, one spiritual being to another, equals in Spirit. Look up to him or her, not down.

Yes, you probably play a supervisory role in the development of this being. Yes, you have authority. Yes, the child misbehaves and has difficulties adjusting at times. Wouldn't you have difficulties adjusting to living with a primitive tribe?

Through it all, keep in mind this small person deserves the same respect you would grant to an adult, maybe more. Try silently projecting an attitude of respect to a child. Watch if your message is picked up by the child, enriching your relationship. Direct a special few minutes today to listening to a child's opinion ... just listening.

May 15

Disturbing the Seeds

Are you living in the future? Does it happen that, as daily events unfold, you are paying no attention because you are daydreaming about or, worse yet, worrying about the future? Be careful you don't miss out on life today while you wait for the life of tomorrow. The tasks and activities that form your day today are the plan you have chosen. Your work is part of your growth, but you must experience it in the now, not let it slip away unnoticed.

Continually peeping into the future is similar to a novice gardener who plants seeds in the spring. Every day, the gardener kneels and stares at the ground in impatience, waiting for sprouts. Often this gardener sticks a finger into the dirt, turning it over to try to spy the fragile growth below the surface. This is mauling the future, distorting and harming the natural progression of our seeds into shoots.

Let the future be. You are not in it yet. All you have is now, and you must not miss out on that moment of now while devoting your attention to fruits that are meant for later. The seeds of your future will burst forth in Spirit's own time. Just trust that they will.

Peace Is Personal

Some people pray for peace and wish for peace and long for peace—peace in the world and in their own lives and families. Let's consider today that peace is not a wish but a choice. Although we cannot single-handedly end all strife and save the world, we can work on making the choice for peace an attitude to live by in our little corner of life.

Some people have not experienced sweet peacefulness and have not seen serenity in the face of another. I have experienced peace. My spiritual path has brought me to a great deal of serenity. This is because of my faith that the universe is in good hands, that we are rising in spiritual consciousness over the centuries, and that *all* experiences that come to me can be used for growth.

When busy life gets me agitated, I go to the outdoors, to nature. My slice of nature is lush green woods and farmers' fields. Maybe yours is desert, ocean, or city park. I hope you feel what I feel in nature. It is the harmony of the cycles of life.

Today, let us choose to dwell in peace, to let loose of control a little. Show a peaceful smile to all. It is contagious. See peace, breathe peace, be peace.

May 17

Peace Is Global

Yesterday, we worked on finding our peace and showing it to others. Today, let us unite our peace-bringing talents into a global net of lightworkers. This net exists whether it is noticed or not.

This poor planet, our mother, is being terribly abused by her people, the very people who are supposed to be her stewards and not takers of all her gifts. Today we take in the thought of the permanent connection we have with all other lightworkers—each of us standing for peace in our little corner of the globe, hands connected in a glowing, pulsing web that sings with every beat of our hearts.

Peace on earth. Peace on earth. Peace on earth. We call you forth. Unite with us, all people. Grasp our outstretched hands. We call the lightworkers first—those who are ready to save the world. Even if you do not call yourself a lightworker, you are one if you work to save the earth. We unite. The web grows brighter, and the pulse of peace grows stronger. Insistently, the words call out to all the rest of us. We humans have the power to create peace on earth. We shall. Feel the pulse of global peace coming forth.

Peace on earth. Now. Now. Now. Now. Now.

Picking Lint

Is someone picking lint off you? What do I mean? My mom constantly evaluated my appearance, often commenting on my haircut, my clothing, and yes, even picking lint off me as I got dressed. I found this constant surveillance annoying. It gave me a feeling I wasn't performing up to her standards.

Today, let's think about this evaluation of others. Is someone doing this to you? Do you lint-pick someone else? If you are the pick-ee, take a breath today and send a prayer to the picker. Maybe their own lack of confidence is making them want to make you perfect.

If you are the picker, look at the emotional result for the person you are constantly evaluating and commenting on. Can you ease up? Can you hold the thought that lint picking can make people feel bad about themselves?

If you are neither picker nor pick-ee, then project light to those who are involved as givers or receivers of lint picking. Let our projected light show both parties that their self-esteem resides in the soul, not in the outward appearance.

May 19

Earthly Treasures

"You can't take it with you" was a popular saying when I was young. Let's look at that today. "It" means material possessions and money. "With you" acknowledges that we all pass on from this life, but we are going somewhere, not simply lying there dead.

I truly believe both parts of this sentence. We are immortal. There is no death to fear. You may not believe in reincarnation, as I do. But whether or not that is your belief, I think we all innately realize we do not simply end. That thought gives me great serenity, and I hope it does for you too.

As for the other part, earth's treasures are ephemeral; they cannot come along on the next part of our journey. Yet some people hold on so tightly to their earthly treasures, as if they were important.

The true treasures are our achievement of unconditional love and charity that will allow us to realize that money is a test. For those who have so much more than they need, let us today call out to them, "Don't flunk this test. Use your excess to benefit others. Ask for God's guidance so you can do the right thing. Bestow your largess on the world's need, as you really know that you can't take it with you."

Letter to God

Dear God,

You created me as a manifestation of yourself, a being of light who is immortal, who is connected in oneness to all the universe, who is love and peace. You have set me free to explore myself and to grow and evolve.

I give you great thanks for the magnificent gift of immortal life in many planes and places. I thank you for my free will and for the spiritual talents that are the heritage of us all.

I come before you now to ask for your help in removing some blockages to my living the life of peace and freedom you designed for me. I know the only thing that stands in my way is erroneous beliefs I have acquired that affect my ability to receive your constant flow of divine energy.

As a patient surrenders to the healing ministrations of a surgeon, so do I now surrender all my thoughts, beliefs, and feelings to your healing power. I believe you know better than I the nature of these blockages that stand in the way of my peace and vibrant life. But I will mention those that I am aware of to make the process concrete and so I can work with you. The blockages in my physical self are _____; in my emotional self are _____; in my mental self are _____; in my spiritual self are _____.

Dear God, please heal these and all other blockages and grant me abundant life that I may serve you always.

Your child,

_____

May 21

God's Reply

Dear _____,

I have heard your plea.

I knew your thoughts already, but you saying them has released you to receive my healing power and guidance.

Just relax and let me heal you and show you more of my love—a love beyond what you can imagine.

Wonders await you now that you have opened the door to me.

I love you as Myself,

God

Gemini—The Twins

Gemini is ruled by Mercury. In Greek mythology, Mercury was the messenger of the gods, sort of a flying bike messenger, hurrying back and forth delivering communications. Gemini traits include being curious about everything and flitting from this to that, often being talkative and on. They can be haphazard in their affairs due to their desire for quickness.

So let's look at our Gemini traits today. Do you know someone who is so talkative that no one can even get a word in? Although the talk can be fascinating, enough is enough. Do you know someone who can't stay still, balancing from foot to foot, rubbing their hands, sitting and getting up to sit somewhere else, leaving the room while you are trying to talk to them, as they got a sudden urge for a drink or decided to take the garbage out?

Let's today send our light to slow down those with too much Gemini (regardless of the month of their birth). We need to do this carefully, as these folks don't like slow and may even hate the concept. So we shall show them just a teeny bit. Let's project to them, "Take a breath, sit and listen for a minute or two, chew before swallowing, and stick to one small task until it is done, rather than flitting to ten other tasks, all of which get partially done."

So tell me, does any of this remind you of yourself, even just a little? Well, maybe you can take your own advice and try a little slowness, just for today. You may even enjoy it.

May 23

Decluttering

Let's look at the concept of decluttering—eliminating what is outdated and no longer needed. Sure, we can pretty easily do that with our clothing, giving some items away and throwing away ragged ones. But what about the clutter of old and outdated thoughts in our minds? Close your eyes for a moment and direct your gaze inward at your thoughts …

Did you find anything outdated, old-fashioned, or just plain wrong in there? Not as easy as clothing but very much needed, this decluttering of the mind.

Today, let's pick just one thought or opinion that we think might need decluttering. For me, it is saying I am too old to do this or that, things that I used to be able to do. For you, get your thought in mind. Maybe it is an opinion about yourself or about a loved one or about groups of other people.

Okay, I promise that I will stop saying or even letting myself think my outmoded thought. If I try, I will say to myself, "Stop. I am not having that opinion anymore. That thought is banished." Then I need to replace it with something better each time I try to think of it. Better for me would be, "Hmmm, maybe I can just do _____ (the thing that I thought I couldn't do)."

Will you give this a try? Say the wrong thought out loud. There, it's already sounding wrong. Tell it, "No more. I refuse you." Then say your replacement thought. What will your replacement thought be? Get it ready, as the outworn thought may sneak back in. You can do it!

Car Problem

I had to take my car to the shop. It wasn't running right, kept stalling, and had no pep on hills. The mechanic said, "You are out of alignment." It was pretty easy for that expert to get my car back into alignment.

But what if we are out of alignment with God's plans for us? How do we know? What do we do? Well, have you lost your pep on hills? Do you keep stalling out? That is, have you been giving up on trying to be a better person? Do you only do the best thing sometimes and stall out the rest? Do negative thoughts still lurk in your head, and do you give in to them sometimes?

Well, today let's resolve to get realigned with God. Let's ask for God's guidance as we go through our day. Let's look at all that happens as opportunities to make kind choices. Let's make sure that TV's negative images don't affect our viewpoints. Let's shine God's light into our lives so that not only our actions but our words and even our thoughts are in good alignment. And while we are at it, let's pray that others will take actions to fix their alignment too.

Learning by Example

I want to learn how to live by watching how others live. How can I learn from everyone and not just from the highest teachers? As I sit today in a restaurant, I can tune everyone out or I can tune in and listen to and observe people nearby. Even if I can't hear the words clearly, I can listen for tone of voice. Why do I want to do this? Because I am looking at higher or lower ways of interacting.

I can then think, *Hmmm, am I demonstrating this same tone or body language when I interact with friends or family?* I learn best by example—good things to emulate, bad ones to eliminate.

A wise man said, "If I am walking with two other men, each of them serve as my teacher. I will pick out good points of the one and imitate them, and the bad points of the other and correct them in myself." That was Confucius.

What will you learn the next time you observe other people?

What Are You Like?

Yesterday, we discussed learning by observing others. Today, let's take things a step further by observing ourselves. Record yourself reading a paragraph. Then listen to it as if listening to a stranger. Listen for the tone and pace. Listen to the loudness or softness, the hesitations. What do you learn from this about the way you sound to others?

Then go stand in front of a full-length mirror. Pretend it is not a mirror but a new person you are meeting. Look over this person. What does their demeanor, posture, and face say about this new person?

Did you find anything in the auditory and visual observations that you didn't like? I'm not talking about physical beauty or lack of it but how we present ourselves, our style. What is our first impression of who this person is that we are observing? Do we want to be friends with them? If you can't say yes, then perhaps you have found some things you can work on.

May 27

The Purest Love

Have you heard stories of faithful dogs whose masters passed away, and the dogs break loose and go to the cemetery and lie down on the grave? I've heard these stories. Or the dog whose owner goes off to war, and he spends time daily sitting by the window, watching, even if it is a whole year. Finally, the soldier comes home, and the dog jumps on him, wild with joy. I've seen this on TV.

What is this characteristic of dogs? This is pure, unconditional love. Today, let's look with respect and awe at the beautiful character of dog love. We can learn much from them about how we are to give unconditional love. If you are lucky enough to be living with a dog, then you are on the receiving end of unconditional love.

Can we be so pure? Can we forgive a slight or hurt without diminishing our love? Can we keep love alive when we are separated from our loved one?

Today, let us say thanks to the dogs for showing us the kind of love God has for us and the kind we should practice too. And let us strive to be as unconditionally loving as dogs are.

Summer Vacation

Are you planning a vacation this season? Do your plans involve travel to another city, state, or country? If so, you have a golden opportunity to implant higher vibrations into the places you visit.

When you are en route, driving or flying, direct attention to those on the road or those who share the airplane with you. Project light, peace, and safe travel to these brothers and sisters. Wherever you visit, get in touch with the outdoors. Touch things of nature, the ground, trees, sand, the rivers, lakes, ocean water. Deliberately place your vibration of light in these new places, decreeing that they quicken unto the higher vibrations of the New Age.

Smile at the people of these new places. In many travel situations, people are hurried, stressed, tired, and sometimes rude. Refuse to absorb these negatives. Radiate calmness, peace, vigor, and kindness. If your travel plans are bogged down in delays or dilemmas, see the opportunities in these challenges with humor and serenity. So what if you are delayed? Look for a pleasant sunset right in the airport if you are stuck there. So you are stuck in traffic. It gives more time to look closely at your location and project light to fellow travelers. Make your whole vacation a light vacation. Enjoy yourself.

May 29

Signs of the New Age: Shoot Not to Kill

Here is the actual first line of an article in my college alumni magazine, the *Penn Stater*, "The police and military enter a new age with a new mission: Shoot not to kill."

I always believed that if we could get to see the humanity in our enemies, there would be no wars. It sounds to me like the process is beginning. The article discusses a new organization formed recently at Penn State in cooperation with the Marine Corps and the Los Angeles Police Department. It is called the Institute for Nonlethal Defense Technologies. This center, the first of its kind in the world, has as its purpose the study of a range of technologies that will allow police and military personnel to stop attacks without killing the attackers. This institute is housed in Penn State's Applied Research Lab, which I remember from the Vietnam War days as a designer of torpedoes and other military technology. This site was often picketed by antiwar students. And now, such a new thought— to defend but not kill.

As one LA police lieutenant said in the article, they must often contend with violent attackers who are enraged or insane with drugs. The goal is to stop them, not kill them. And a soldier said that in Somalia, the military encountered the situation of the enemy using innocent bystanders as human shields. The soldiers wanted to have a means of stopping these enemies without killing the innocent.

Lightworkers, the tide is turning. Soon everyone will realize that people are not expendable, even those who are committing crimes or are violent due to drugs. They are still God's children, our brothers and sisters. Let us hold the light for those who protect us to turn to what the article calls "kinder, gentler weapons" as a first step to prepare for the day when we will need no weapons at all.

The Wild Man in the Woods

I attended a workshop in which we talked about aspects of ourselves that we have suppressed because we don't like them or are even ashamed of them. They asked us to picture these aspects of ourselves in meditation. It came to me that these aspects were like a wild man who had been living for years in the woods.

He appeared to me, lingering at the edge of the woods, watching me. He had long, matted hair and a bushy beard with bits of leaves and twigs in it. His clothes were dirty and ragged. He was very thin, and his dark eyes were sunken in beneath his furrowed brow. He continued to watch me with a bit of fear in his eyes, apparently afraid I would shoo him back into the woods.

Instead, I greeted this ragged, wandering part of myself as a long-lost brother. I went to him and put my arm around him, leading him into my yard and then my house. I fed him and washed his clothes while he bathed and shaved. Then we sat at my kitchen table, face-to-face at last.

He was my fears, resentments, arrogance, laziness, and many more qualities I know I have but have been unwilling to face. He told me his story of how he got to be a ragged wanderer, a story of being hurt and needing to lash out in return. After being unappreciated for his efforts, he gave up. I asked him to stay and show me the positive sides of himself: Fears turned into appropriate caution and restraint. Resentments and arrogance turned into rightful ways of standing up for himself in a loving manner. Laziness turned into a voice of moderation in caring for himself when he got too busy and needed to rest. He agreed to stay and speak his wisdom to me.

Do you have a wild man in the woods? Perhaps you can invite him in.

The Sailor

There I was, sitting in traffic on a hot and sticky day, weary from work and eager to get home. But the traffic was heavy and moved oh so slowly. I felt my spirits drop as I realized I must weather this traffic jam, stuck where I did not want to be, doing what I did not want to be doing.

Then Spirit granted me a breath of relief. I glanced up at a tractor trailer heaving puffs of smelly exhaust, and I noticed a hand-painted message on the back of the truck. It said, "Sailor on the Concrete Sea."

What a wonderful attitude that person has toward his work, I thought. I pictured him in sailor cap and black striped pirate shirt, humming a sailing tune as he journeyed on his concrete sea, turning his job into an adventure.

All at once, I realized my spirits were lifting, thanks to the unknowing gift of this joyful stranger who for a moment had become a companion on my journey.

Thank you, Spirit! Thank you, sailor! Sail on! Sail on!

Home at Last

Deep within us is a delightful place at the center of our being. It is a place of wonder and light, of harmony and peace. It is the spark of God, the divine love and light of our High Self. Always pure and perfect, it is our ever-ready refuge, a safe haven far from the noise and stress of modern life. Let us return now to this place, our center, our source.

Visualize it with me as we walk a gently curving garden path past the outer aspects of our personality and soul record for this life, past our previous experiences and our many relatives, friends, and loves. We let go of all those experiences as we go deeper within. We follow a gentle light glowing before us, a light that whispers, "Come within. Come back to me." We are far along the path now, and we notice around us peaceful forests and meadows, majestic mountains, and the deep blue waters of a lake. We hear birds singing and the rush of a gentle stream. The weather is perfect, and the sky so blue. We come to the meeting place where our beloved High Self awaits. Our heart quickens with joy at this reunion with our true self.

All cares drop away as our beloved takes our hand and walks with us along a path lined with flowers of rainbow hues and sweet scents. We stay awhile and enjoy this visit with our beloved. We feel the peace of being home, at last.

Heal the Earth

Today, all lightworkers unite in projecting healing light to bind the wounds of our earth. Visualize the healing of all pollution of the ground, the water, and the air—now!

The power of the light creates a pure new earth. See the very molecules of waste being transformed into pure energy.

Together, we call forth our power as cocreators to rebalance the physical earth. A chain reaction starts as one particle of divine light ignites the next.

See soil becoming healthy. See water becoming clear and pure. Breathe the light of your love into the air. Send this light outward to spread over the whole planet—to the depths of the oceans, to the peaks and valleys, to the heights of the atmosphere.

All is made new.
So be it in truth.

KIMBERLY CLAYTON

The Bud

"I'm still not perfect. I've tried so hard, and there is still so much to learn. It is taking so long."

I felt discouraged at the long road ahead, not really noticing that I had come a good distance already. Am I moving, or am I stuck? It feels like such a large responsibility to walk the path, to get it right, to keep moving in the right direction.

Then I heard something that helped me feel better: A woman named Elizabeth reading her letter to God and God's reply. God had said to her, "I am growing you."

Upon hearing that, a large weight dropped from my heart as I realized that this is not all my lonely responsibility. God is growing me. And like the growth of a bud into a flower, the unfolding of the petals takes time and has its own beauty.

So, I thought, *now I can be more patient with myself. I am in God's hands. My unfolding is assured, just like the bud into the flower. Even though I cannot see what is to unfold, it is all right because God sees, God knows.*

"Dear God, help me to trust in my own unfolding, to let go and let you grow me into your beautiful flower.

June 4

The Friend Ship

I've always been fascinated by the tall ships, which are large, three-masted sailing vessels. They look so graceful on TV, yet I had never actually seen one. Then one day in 1990, I read that a tall ship from Russia, the *Druzhba*, would be sailing into Baltimore's Inner Harbor and that people could go aboard.

So, naturally, I had to go see it. I arrived at the harbor early enough to see it sail in and dock, with each tier of the rigging in this 360-foot-long square rigger filled with sailors in dress whites. It was breathtaking to see it in its stately grandeur. As I was waiting to go aboard, I read the flyer being handed out. This ship was being used as a training vessel for seventy Russian and forty American Marine Academy cadets to learn to sail the Atlantic. The combined crew was under the guidance of fifty professional Russian crew members and some American instructors. This voyage was the first ever in which Russians and Americans worked together as crew mates.

As I went aboard, I was greeted by a scene of many young men and a few young women cadets all excitedly talking among themselves in celebration of sweet success of crossing the Atlantic from Odessa to Baltimore in a two-month voyage. They were not segregating themselves by nationality. No, they had become one crew. I asked one of them what the ship's name, *Druzhba*, meant, and he smiled at me and said, "Friendship."

Let us envision many more international exchanges happening all over the world, getting to know each other as we work together, until national boundaries melt into true friendships.

Peace, Utter Peace

If we want to unite to bring peace to this earth and heal its wounds, we must first become living examples of peace. Let's take some steps toward this goal today. First, conceive a picture of peace for yourself and peace for all the earth. Hold for a minute this picture of peacefulness. Now step into the picture and see peace, hear peace, think peace, touch peace.

Now let the beauty of peace break over you like a wave on the shore of your emotions. It rushes in, overtaking any other emotion, and overwhelms your heart. Breathe peace into your heart and dwell in this feeling of peace.

Now seek in your soul's memories any hurts, tribulation, angers, or wrongs that stand in the way of your being fully at peace. Let the wave of peace wash your soul clean of anything that prevents you from having peace, feeling peace.

Now, utter peace. Tell Spirit you are ready to be peace, to live peace—as a healing to yourself and a demonstration to the people of earth.

Immerse yourself in the total bliss of peace, utter peace.

Native Americans

Consider the contributions Native Americans have made to North America. Consider their deeply spiritual philosophy of oneness with all creation. Their philosophy taught them to see the presence of the Great Spirit in all creation— in the animals and the plants, the moon and the sun, the rain and the wind. It taught a reverence for the lower kingdoms as worthy of loving respect. Whenever they gathered plants for food, their custom was to leave the first one they found untouched so it could propagate itself. Native Americans were taught not to hunt more than they would use and to use all parts of the animal.

Their respectful attitude toward nature's gifts is an attitude sorely needed on earth today.

Let us see this attitude coming into great prominence this decade, above commerce and profit, above the desires of people for more and more cement, more buildings, more throwaway products. Let us see this beautiful philosophy spreading all over the world,

showing us how to care for the earth and how to move with its rhythms.

So Let It Be Written, So Let It Be Done

Whenever I think about the movie *The Ten Commandments*, I picture Yul Brynner as Pharaoh making this decree in his powerful masculine voice, "So let it be written; so let it be done." This is a potent spiritual decree that brings things into manifestation.

The first part, "So let it be written," makes concrete that which we want to see manifested. It names it; gives it the power of words, of sounds. Once this decree has made concrete our desire, then the second part, "so let it be done," automatically begins to manifest. In our role as cocreator with God, we are manifesting it in our future.

When you wish to make something manifest for you, do more than wish. Make the affirmation, "So let it be written." Speak it aloud, that which you wish to see. Write it down, hang it on the wall, look at it, read it aloud, acknowledge it, and feel it becoming real, day by day.

And don't stop there. Work on the second part, "so let it be done." Take the actions that come to you to be done. You may not know the whole plan all at once. But Spirit will give you step one. Take that step. Then you will be given step two and then step three. Do your part. Once you have completed all actions that need to be taken, await in joyful expectation for its manifestation.

Starsha Dawn

So What's Your Five-Year Plan?

There I was at a personal development workshop in which everyone was being asked about their plans and goals. The speaker said, "So what's your five-year plan? And ten and even twenty-year plan? Because, you know, without a plan, you'll never get anywhere."

The speaker then told the participants to write down a summary of their plans. At this point, I gulped in fright and looked around to see all the busy fingers writing and writing. And I sat there and thought to myself, *How different I am. I seem to be the only one without a plan.* This exercise shook me up. I felt like I was taking an essay test and did not know the answers, had not done my homework! *Oh boy! I'm in trouble now! I will get an F in five-year planning.* I thought and thought and could not come up with anything specific to say. Major milestones have passed for me. I already have an advanced degree. I already have the job of my dreams, my own home, great friends, and a great life. So I couldn't put down something like "graduate from college."

After the event, I realized that many years ago I made a monumental decision to take the planning for my life out of my own hands and turn it over to Spirit's direction. I performed the actual handing over in a personally designed ritual in the 1980s. I really felt my life change hands then. Now, my only "plan" is to seek Spirit's plan for me and to follow it to the best of my ability. What I'll be up to five years from now, or ten or twenty, no longer concerns me. I need only to work on what is before me now on my path without worrying about what is around the next bend.

This has given me freedom from worry about the future and a deep serenity. Since I made this move, my life has taken off like a rocket in wonderful directions I couldn't have imagined or planned. I'm so very glad I finally let go. How about you?

What Took Me So Long to Let Go?

Yesterday I shared about my turning over my future to Spirit in the eighties. I had wanted to become bold and brave and trusting enough to make this move for a long while. But I held back for about fifteen years out of fear of letting go of control. I wrestled with my thoughts all that time. I would say to myself, "Okay, what if I say, 'Here you go—take my life and do what you want with it,' and the answer comes back that I'm being assigned to do something I would hate to do?" I imagined all sorts of dire assignments that were not in tune with who I am, like being told to go into the Peace Corps to some poor country without indoor plumbing and full of bugs. What if I was ordered to live in the inner city and work at a shelter? I appreciate the folks who are doing these assignments, but I felt it would kill me. My mind kept running on and on—*what if, what if, what if* … I was frightening myself to the point of an anxiety attack, one that went on for fifteen years.

And then something I read took away my fear of letting go. I read that we start any action with faith, then find the strength, then fall in love with what we are to do, and then we are able to bring forth our mission. Oh, love! We will do what we love. That made perfect sense to me. Now I understood that we are naturally attuned to fall in love with our own true mission, since our mission is designed to match our vibe, to take advantage of our gifts in order to fulfill the contract we made before we got here. How silly of me to think Spirit would plan something I would hate. Spirit would only guide me toward what I love, not send me off in some crazy direction that doesn't fit me and would be painful for me.

Now I knew that I was finally ready, really ready, to take my life that I had been clutching tightly in my own hands all these years and open my hands, holding my life out as an offering to Spirit. And I did. If you have let your life go too, bless you. If you are clutching it, I hope you will find comfort and courage in these words.

June 10

How Did I Let Go?

For the past two days, I've been sharing my story of letting go of my life. So, to continue, when I finally found the courage to let go, I didn't know *how* to let go. I felt the need for a dramatic rite of passage, a ritual that would demonstrate my decision, my surrender. But I had no ready-made ritual that I knew of. I thought of how a man goes through the Catholic ritual to become a priest, part of which is done with him lying flat, face-down on the floor to demonstrate his obedience to the church. That was certainly dramatic, but it did not seem right for me.

I decided I needed to create my own personal letting-go ritual and really put my whole heart and soul into it. A favorite play of mine is *Jesus Christ Superstar.* I always loved how personally it described Jesus's emotions as he faced his final challenge of the cross. I would watch the video of this show or listen to the tape over and over, until I had memorized all the lyrics. I would sing this emotional music loudly, feeling like I was there with Jesus and the apostles. The most moving part of the play for me is not the Crucifixion but the night in Gethsemane when Jesus prays for God to take this cup away from him. But finally, receiving no reprieve, he gives in and surrenders his life to God.

So, in my ritual, I decided to surrender along with Jesus. I put on the DVD and sang the words along with him, cried tears at his sorrow, and really felt myself give up my life out of my own keeping. I knew that Jesus had been entrusted with the very difficult mission God needed of him, and that my own mission would be so much easier. And that, whatever it was, I would obey.

That was a dividing point of my life. With my surrender, I set my future free to unfold without my strangling it out of fear. And it has unfolded wonderfully well. From that point, my life has taken dramatic turns for the better, and I couldn't be happier with where I've been led. I'm in good hands now, better hands than mine, and I feel safe and secure.

So what about your five-year plan?

The Infant Earth

The earth is coming to the higher vibrations of the New Age as an infant. Think of the image of a stork bringing a baby. Instead of an infant human, see the earth globe instead. Instead of a white cloth being carried in the stork's bill, see it as metallic gold, the color of divine love, peace, and rest. Hold that image with me for a few moments.

This stork now lands in front of you and presents this baby to you. This new earth is an infant now, totally dependent on your loving attention and service. See yourself joyfully taking this infant earth into your arms and embracing it with the tender love you would feel for an infant.

All praises! The new earth is born! Please nurture it with love and help it to grow.

Talents We Don't Know We Have

I recently taught someone to play racquetball, my favorite sport. Although she had played tennis for years, she had never attempted racquetball. She was absolutely delighted to find that she could really hit the fast-moving ball and hit it hard enough to make a satisfying "swack" sound that made her smile. And I smiled too, joining her in the delight of finding out she had a talent she never realized she had.

The only way she could have ever found out was to gather the courage to attempt something new. She did it and was rewarded with a new joy.

What can I learn from this? There comes a time when reading about something new that intrigues me, or seeing it on TV, or hearing about it from a friend *must* be turned into attempting it if I wish to progress and learn.

How about you? Is there something you are good at that you don't know about yet? Something you've been wanting to do but haven't? Well, maybe this is the time to give it a try. You may find yourself the joyful new owner of a brand-new talent.

June 13

Drink the Sky

I'm going for a drive in the country. Come along with me. We are driving down a two-lane road in the flat farm country of Southern Maryland. It is June, and the weather is just perfect—seventy-two degrees with a nice wind and a blue sky with white, puffy clouds. We are passing wheat fields on the right with golden brown wheat as high as our knees. On the left are fields of corn as high as our hips. We are riding with the windows wide open, and the breeze is ruffling our hair. In this flat land, the sky is so big, so blue. We drink the sky. Ah, it is refreshing. We breathe the greens and golds of the crops and admire how the wheat ripples in the breeze.

Now we are on a bridge over a wide tributary of the Chesapeake Bay. On one shore is a marina filled with sailboats, with their white sails bobbing in the waves. Little whitecaps dance on the water. We decide to pull in at a waterfront restaurant. Now here we sit, out on the dock in the cool shade, sipping iced beverages and gazing contentedly at the sparkling water.

Peace overtakes us. This is a moment to remember. We tuck this beauty away in our memories so we can pull it out anytime we need a drink of blue sky, a breath of green fields.

Secondary Gains

Do you know someone who is accident prone? Or someone who always seems to get the short end of the stick? They seem to be under a black cloud of bad luck. I often feel sorry for folks I know for whom everything seems to go wrong all the time. It is like they have a sign hanging on them that says, "Kick Me." And life does, over and over. Birds poop on them. They hurry to work only to be stopped by a long train crossing the road. The baby they pick up promptly spits up on them. I always thought how unfortunate it was that life seemed to be so much worse for them than for me and for most of the other people I know.

Then someone told me about *secondary gains*. Those are benefits to be had from misfortune. In other words, if they are always a victim, they get pity from others. And sometimes others try to rescue them from their disasters.

I had never thought of this. It is an unconscious phenomenon. But it may be that being a victim is a comfortable, habitual role for these folks. And it attracts rescuers. So let's look at ourselves today. Could you be either a victim or a rescuer in any of your relationships? Either role is unhealthy. Let's strive to dwell in sunshine and not under a black cloud. Let's not milk our disasters for secondary gains of pity or rescue. And let's not automatically rescue these unfortunate victims. Instead, let's use our divine discernment to tell us when someone needs our help and when it would be better to butt out and let them solve their own problems.

A Thorn in Your Side

Do you have a thorn in your side? Is there someone in your life who irritates you? Let's look at this thorn in the side today. Often that person who is so annoying to you is unconsciously bringing a lesson to be learned.

Sometimes the annoyance comes from a trait this person has that is similar to a trait you have. For example, the person may be constantly complaining and whining. The person may be loud and interrupting people who are speaking. The person may be angry and dismissive, or have some other trait that deeply pushes your buttons.

Let's look at the lesson of the thorn today. If you have someone who is a real thorn in your side, look at the trait that bothers you. Then think about yourself. Do you ever do a small version of what this person is doing? Could you rein in this trait in yourself?

And lastly, send your good thoughts to the thorny person. If you can hold good thoughts instead of annoyance when you are face-to-face with the person, you may find that they begin to change. Surround them with Spirit's loving light and see them blossom from a thorn into a lovely rose.

June 16

Water Responsibility

Today, I sit by the sea. Looking at it, I realize that all streams and rivers flow into the sea. We depend on water to live. In our own bodies, our blood and cells are mostly water. Our organs work to deliver oxygen to the cells and carry waste away. But unlike our bodies, the earth's seas can't keep themselves clean of all we are throwing into them.

So today, let us concentrate on sending light to our fellow humans, so that they wake up and stop polluting the precious waters. "Hear us! Stop letting industrial and farm waste slide into the water. Stop cruise ship toilet dumping in the sea. Stop all the illegal and immoral pollution of our waters. It is our shared responsibility to take care of the waters of the world.

Envision all the seas, rivers, and lakes becoming clear of waste. Envision that dumping is over, everywhere in the world. Envision the waters sparkling clean. Politicians, you must guard the waters and stop the polluters who won't wake up.

And if there is a pollution problem in your area, please do what you can to end it. Together, we will wake up the world, and we will reclaim our clean waters.

Good Signs

"But how do you know we are entering a New Age of peace and healing?" my friend asked. "I can't see anything but increasing violence, drug problems, poverty, broken relationships—"

"Hold it," I interrupted gently, "or you'll dig yourself into a pit of despair. Yes, surely all those things are present, and many have been there for centuries. But it is time for us to recognize and acknowledge the signs of an increase in vibrational level, which brings good things."

"Well, what good things?" my friend continued. "I can't think of any."

"Okay, how about these? A young boy in New York decided to help the homeless. He has set up an organization, and many have joined him. He is an advanced soul, come to help us. A toy manufacturer (Dakin) ran an ad saying they refused to make war toys because they wouldn't want their kids to play with them. And I've heard several instances of people from different religions helping each other, such as the Catholic church that invited the people of a synagogue that was burned down to use the church for months while a new building was built.

"Look for these subtle signs that we are growing in Spirit. The negatives you spoke of are reactions to the increasing light. Don't hold them in your heart; just project light to those problems as they occur to you and keep your attention focused on the positive. As we do that together, we create the framework for the New Age."

Text

KIMBERLY CLAYTON

Crossing the River

Have you come to where a river crosses your path? Are you stopped on the bank, looking across, with fear overcoming your sense of adventure? Are you afraid to cross?

Sometimes we come upon an impasse. It demands we leap forth from slippery rock to slippery rock to get across. The river represents major change. Many of us are stopped at a river right now because we are afraid to take those leaps in faith. What if it is too slippery? What if I miss my footing and fall in?

But a voice whispers to us, "Don't fear. You can do it. You won't slip. I am your guardian angel, and I will stay with you. Hold my hand."

We can wait a lifetime on the bank of that river. Or we can muster our courage, take the hand of our guardian angel, and make that first leap. Go on! Get up your nerve and jump! And keep on leaping until you are across, safe at last in a peaceful valley. When you get across, you will have conquered a dark part of yourself that has kept you from progressing. It will be gone. Your courage will bring you closer to home.

Will you make that leap?

June 19

Whales and Dolphins

We share this beautiful planet with many wonderful creatures. Of all the animal kingdom, among the most intelligent are the whales and dolphins. With relative brain to body mass larger than ours, they are the enigmatic rulers of the watery three-quarters of the globe.

Let us commune with these denizens of the deep today. They deserve our thanks for their caring, loving attitude and interactions with humans, their desire to be near us and to help us at sea. Their altruism is a shining example of divine love of their fellow creatures.

Let us project light to those of our own species who kill whales and dolphins. Let the power of our united light force uplift the consciousness of these people. Soon they will feel repulsed at the mere thought of killing and eating or otherwise harming creatures of such high evolvement and intelligence. We now see the killing of these lovely and loving creatures ending, once and for all.

Together we project an apology to their kind on behalf of the erring members of our kind who have not only attacked them with weapons but have also polluted their ocean home.

Will You Marry Me?

Your beloved asks you, "Will you marry me?" Your High Self seeks you as the bridegroom seeks the bride. Turn your attention this day to your wedding plans. As we grow in light, we come closer to the glorious reuniting with our High Self. See this part of you as your fiancé. The two of you are committed to each other, so in love and eager for the day when you truly become one.

For today, think about your wedding to come. Compose a wedding invitation telling your family and friends of the joyous news that your true love and you are about to be wed.

Picture the wedding ceremony. Think of the joy this oneness will bring and the wonderful children of thoughts, words, and deeds this wedding will produce. Plan the rest of your life as the spouse of your higher power.

Hear wedding bells beckoning all to their own weddings. The whole planet prepares for the royal wedding when the bridegroom returns to earth. Already nations scurry to cast off old, worn-out garments and put on the bridal gown of purest white light.

Accept the engagement ring your beloved holds out to you and prepare for the joyous day.

June 21

Rugged Individualists

America has always prided itself as a nation of rugged individualists, jealously guarding our precious freedoms and insisting on doing things our own way. That attitude is in need of change today. Rugged individualism can be carried to extremes, such as the man who refused to leave his home at the base of Mt. St. Helens, which subsequently exploded, as he had been warned, killing him. That is not rugged individualism; that is just plain, stupid stubbornness. And it bears noting that in a case like this, the stubborn man was not thinking of the dangers to the emergency personnel who were trying to evacuate everyone while faced with his recalcitrance. That is too selfish.

In this dawning of a New Age, we must judge our responses using the concepts that we all are one, we are here to help each other, and what we do affects us all. There is a time to listen to reason and trade in swaggering, rigid independence for a community-oriented point of view.

If you are a rugged individualist, by all means guard your liberty and the right to be different. But stop before getting yourself killed through stubbornness.

Let us unite today in sending light to all those who confuse liberty and stupidity and ask that Spirit show them the proper responses of a reasonable adult who is co-responsible for this earth with all the rest of us.

The Most Beautiful Flower

Think for a minute, dear friend, of the most beautiful flower you have ever seen. Take your time. Close your eyes and ponder for a minute or so, as you need to feel comfortable that this one is really the one—the most beautiful flower to you. Don't be left-brained about it, checking off a list of flowers in your head. Be right-brained; relax and let a picture form of this flower ...

Okay, do you have that picture? Look closely inside your vision of the flower. Describe it to yourself: height, color, type of leaves, scent, if any. Hold its beauty and now add one thing. This flower is you—your true self. It has been planted in the fertile soil of your heart, and it has grown right up your spine and out the crown of your head. The bloom is about a foot higher than you are.

Now look around, and you will see that you are surrounded by a community of other people. All of them have gorgeous flowers growing out of the tops of their heads. Some people are aware of their flower. They also see your flower. These ones smile at you and nod in recognition and admiration of the beauty that you are. These are the lightworkers, awakened to their flower-ness, their divine beauty in Spirit's garden. Greet them with your smile. Enjoy their beauty and nod back at them.

Now look around some more. Most of the people-flowers do not notice their own flower or yours. They do not look at you, and they are busy with other thoughts. But you can see—each and every one of them also has a beautiful and breathtaking flower growing out of the top of their head. You cannot tell them or show them, as they are ignoring you. But you know the truth and know they will learn to see it better in time.

Give thanks that you can see the flowers. As far as you can see, the earth is full of the beautiful and colorful garden of people-flowers. You send a thought to the ones who do not see: Awaken, my sisters, my brothers! See the beauty that you are!

June 23

Even in Our Thoughts

Recent scientific experiments have proven the power of prayer to improve the medical outcome in carefully controlled experiments, even when the subject of the prayers was not aware people were praying for him or her. Other studies have shown we can influence the path of electrons by thinking.

So today, let's take up the challenge of monitoring our thoughts. If you find you have just thought a negative sentence, correct it right then. You can shout in thought or even out loud, "Cancel that! Stop!" Then take the next step. Replace the negative thought with a positive one.

I use this technique a lot, whenever I realize I just had a negative thought. For example, I am in traffic, and someone cuts me off, practically hitting me. Most often, I won't rise to the bait. But sometimes I do, thinking something like, *You moron! You stupid fool!* When that happens, I quickly shout (often out loud as long as the car windows are shut), "No! Stop! Cancel!" I'm talking to my subconscious, telling her not to record that thought, to back up the tape and delete it. I say something like, "I'm sorry for thinking that. You are a divine child of God, and I acknowledge that even though I don't like your behavior."

After practicing this thought monitoring for so many years, I find that I can usually hold the better thought right away. I think, "You almost hit me. Be careful, my brother, for yourself and for others. Please calm down and drive serenely." Then I think to myself, *Phew, that was a close one, but I didn't lash out. I passed that test!*

Good luck on passing your thought tests today.

My List of Little Things

On weekends, I often find I have many little things that need my attention. I say little, meaning limited in importance, not quickly accomplished. I do like driving around with my list of little things: a watch needs a battery, a recent purchase is defective and must be returned, my new shower curtain needs to be matched with rugs and towels of the right color (wow, it's hard to find that shade of sky blue), I need a little paint to touch up something, and, of course, I need refreshments along the way. So I toddle along, visiting this place and that, stopping for a snack or lunch. While I'm out, I remember five other things I need to do. I never actually get my list done, since it grows while I'm trying to finish it. I finally return home, having done half of it.

It seems that our modern life causes us to "need" many, many little things. I can waste the entire weekend trying to accomplish my never-ending list of these little things. But while making progress in these things, perhaps I'm missing some big things that didn't make it onto my list. Big things—things that are important to me, or things that are just for my own pleasure. Things like calling my long-lost cousin, writing my thoughts, reading something just for me. I could be resting from the work week instead of running myself ragged.

Hmmm, it seems these other things have gotten relegated to the back burner. My list has only the little things and not the big ones, maybe because most of the little things are more concrete, more visible. I can say to myself on Saturday morning, "Look, there's that item I need to return to the store," but I can't look around and see my need to take a nap or make a phone call, if I'm looking outward instead of inward.

Okay, I've got to fix this problem. Since I'm a list person, and I just love to cross off things when they are accomplished, I'm going to change my priorities and give my big things a place on my list. No, I won't stop doing those little things, since they need to get done, but I will deliberately add to the list some of my big things too.

How about you? Does your list need some revisions?

Puuuh

I am working on a body problem I've had for years. When (infrequently) I check in with my body's posture and muscles, I usually find I am holding some body parts tight, even though I am sitting and don't have a reason for the muscles to be engaged. I think this is part of our rush, rush world in which there is so much to do that it seems to our bodies that we are just about to run off and do something, so the muscles are ready.

So today let's do a little check-in and correction. Okay, notice your forehead. Is it holding tension? Tighten even more and then release it. When I do this, I do the release as a big drop of the muscle with the accompanying sound *puuuh* (not pronounced but just air). Scan your cheeks, mouth (a commonplace to hold tension), and neck. Tighten and release. Puuuh, puuuh, puuuh!

How about shoulders? Tighten—then drop them with a puuuh. Let's go to your hands. Are they relaxed? If not, tighten them into fists, puuuh them down, and shake them loose. What about your stomach? My mother told me to always hold it in, and apparently I've made this message part of my life. So tighten your stomach and then drop it with a big puuuh.

Moving on to your hips, thighs, calves, and finally toes. Squeeze them tight and then puuuh! Shake your feet loose. Now check any other parts that need to be puuuhed and do it. Now shake your whole body. You might want to stand up for this and let it go! Puuuh!

The Little Spider

While cleaning the kitchen counter, I came across a small spider. He climbed right onto my cloth before he noticed it was attached to me. *Well, I'll just take him outside*, I thought as I began walking toward the door. But he had other plans. He leaped boldly into the air, trailing a drag line of silk, and disappeared in an instant. "Well," I mused, "he just doesn't know what is good for him. I only wanted to put him out in the garden."

When you stop and think, there seems to be a similarity between the spider and us. Sometimes Spirit tries to present an opportunity for us to extricate ourselves from negative situations. But we see it as a threat to our status quo and stubbornly refuse to cooperate.

When you are faced with a challenge or an opportunity, do you react like our little spider?

The Law of Attraction

The cosmic law of attraction is similar to magnetism. As we live our lives in the light, our spiritual electromagnetic force attracts people. They will feel something positive coming from us and be drawn to what we have to give.

It is not necessary for us to lecture others or hand out literature about God. It is enough to live lives of light. As tests are passed and we move higher in our evolving consciousness, the High Self is freer to flow down into us more and more. This creates a new body, vibrating at a higher level, a body part way into the fourth dimension.

Just as great physical beauty attracts nearly everyone, our spiritual development creates a growing spiritual beauty that likewise attracts attention. Let us be conscious of the effect of our vibration on others. Let us strive for a spirituality in our daily life that attracts others. And let us concentrate on only those positive things we want to attract to ourselves—health, growth, prosperity, compassion, love.

Instagram Activist

Okay, I confess I have never been on Instagram, and I don't even know what it is. But I'm going to go there now to support something I admire. Sometimes I read *People* magazine. It seems that they are changing their old format of looking at fashion and who is dating whom. Not that those things have disappeared, but they have added something cool. What? They provide information about some Hollywood person who is doing something good for the world.

So what did I find about Instagram? Well, *People* reported about an actor in a show I like called *Grace and Frankie*. She is June Diane-Raphael, who plays Grace's daughter. She has partnered with friend, Sarah Silverman, and her husband, Paul Scheer, to start a new Instragram site called @TheBigHundred. The site gives followers daily suggestions for bite-size ways to make a difference in the world. She comments that with all the negatives in the news, this campaign gives people something positive to do.

Great idea. What I like to see is people who have fame and a following using their position in the world to entice people to think about helping the world. There are many others besides this actor who are deep into actions to help others. Good for them. Let's salute all those famous ones who are using their fame for good purpose instead of focusing on themselves. And if you feel moved, go check out what is going on at this Instagram site.

June 29

Payback

Many of us, myself included, have great difficulty accepting help from others. Are you one of those who loves to be the helper but hates being the one helped?

Somewhere in my growing up, I picked up the viewpoint that I must be sure to pay back anyone who does anything nice for me. I was taught to keep score of kindnesses and to be sure I was ahead or even—never, ever behind.

That is a limited viewpoint that actually demeans kindnesses by scoring them and then trying to keep the score even. As my life progresses, I'm learning that payback is Spirit's role, not mine. The Bible says that what I give will be returned to me, not just one for one but multiplied many times over. Who is giving back to me? Spirit, not the person to whom I gave. Since I believe that, then it is my duty to become a gracious and cheerful receiver of the kindnesses of others and not to demean the gifts I receive by plotting to pay them back so we are even. Spirit will see to it that abundant payment goes back to the giver.

As children of Spirit, we all deserve to receive whatever we need, and usually Spirit uses other people to fulfill our needs. So when someone does something nice for me, I plan to thank both the giver and Spirit and not put myself into a position of being indebted to my giver. That is not an easy thing for me to do, but I'm going to learn this new skill of being both a joyful giver and a joyful receiver. Will you join me?

June 30

Signs of the New Age: The Oasis of Peace

There's a village in Israel of Palestinian and Jewish Israelis who came there specifically and voluntarily to live together in peace. They got started on land donated from a Catholic monastery. The name of this village in Arabic is Wahat al Salam, in Hebrew it is Neve Shalom, and translated into English it is Oasis of Peace. Are you thinking, *This will never fly, as these people hate each other too much*? Well, let's see how it is doing.

The kids have become friends in a land where many Palestinians and Jews in close proximity do not ever speak to each other. Gradually, surrounding towns have heard of this place, and outside students are coming to their small school, where classes are jointly taught in Arabic and Hebrew by co-teachers. Three faiths are present: Muslim, Jewish, and Christian. It is the only mixed school in all Israel. Thirty families live there. And guess what? This village has existed for twenty years.

The town hosts two hundred groups a year for four-day workshops on learning to live in peace, facilitated by psychologists. Over twenty years, this has amounted to twenty thousand people. They often start by screaming at each other, but by day three, there comes a breakthrough, and they start talking to each other. The village has been nominated five times for the Nobel Peace Prize and has won similar prizes given by Japan, Germany, and Italy.

Now, I consider that truly newsworthy. Why haven't I heard of it for the past twenty years? Lightworkers, let us send light to this place and hold with them as they express Spirit's will. Bless you, brothers and sisters of the Oasis of Peace. May your wisdom and courage inspire this troubled nation of Israel to find its way to peace. And may our news reporters find more stories like this one to share with us and give us hope for the future.

July 1

Accentuate the Positive

It is time to let go of negative thinking and speaking. Often, we do this without even realizing it. Let's listen carefully to ourselves today and practice replacing negative expressions with positive affirmations.

In the recovery movement, they say, "Fake it till you make it." I asked a counselor friend of mine what good that could possibly do, to pretend I believe something or can do something that I cannot. She smiled at me and said that it may sound strange, but it actually works. For example, a person may be very shy, afraid of speaking up in gatherings. If she can find the courage to pretend that she is going to enjoy contributing to the conversation, she changes her emotional response to the forthcoming event. And if she gets to the gathering and really does contribute, she has added an actual positive experience to counteract that persistent negative voice telling her she cannot. But to get to that first step, that first change of behavior, it is very beneficial to "fake it," to visualize things happening much better than they ever have. If you are a good visualizer and can picture the scene you want to create fully, with sounds and even smells of the occasion, your subconscious can register the visualization with almost the strength of a real event.

So today, let us truly accentuate the positive, learning to drop old patterns and pick up better ones. Let us also use our visualizing powers together, seeing the healing of our earth and all of its lifeforms.

Come on in, the Water's Fine

Is there something new that you've been wanting to try, but you are putting it off because you are a little bit afraid? This could be scuba diving, learning to make speeches, furthering your education, changing your appearance, or anything that you wish you could do. If you've been just a little too timid to get it started, here is a visualization to try.

Think of the thing you want to achieve or change as the ocean. Now mentally take yourself on a trip to the beach. Start by seeing yourself taking off your shoes and walking on the shores of this new "something." Relax until you can feel comfortable being this close to it. Next, roll up your pants and walk in the surf, getting used to the temperature of the water on your feet and legs. Look around at the blue sky and feel the warm sun. "Hmm, this thing isn't so scary." Okay, when you feel ready, take off your clothes (I hope you remembered to wear your bathing suit underneath). Wade in further and get your suit wet. "Why, this is great. It doesn't seem scary at all from here."

Now take a deep breath and swim out into the "something." There, you've done it. Hold the visualization of enjoying swimming while you picture yourself taking the actions to get yourself started in this new endeavor.

Now all that is left to do is to let your new confidence flow into your conscious and subconscious. Soon, the time will come when you really jump in and start to swim in your new endeavor. Soon you'll be shouting to others, "Come on in, the water's fine."

Top Speed

What mechanical device goes the fastest?

The space shuttle in orbit.

****

What mechanical device has the slowest top speed?

The space shuttle, bound upright to its rockets, moving from its hangar to the launch pad.

Ironic, isn't it? I find a lesson in this fact, that the fastest is also the slowest. Different speeds for different needs. That tells me I can be different in varied situations. I can walk fast for exercise and walk slowly while looking at paintings in a museum. I can answer a question fast while playing a quiz game and answer very slowly when asked a deep philosophical question. I can progress fast in working a task when I'm in the mood and progress slowly when not in the mood. I can learn and grow fast one week and slowly the next.

And here's the key. I can be different and go at different speeds without self-recrimination. I don't have to be mad at myself for going slowly today. I don't have to expect a constant fast pace. I don't have to think ill of myself for not being in the mood.

And I can let others be free to go at their speed of the day without judgment.

I can be the space shuttle in space or the space shuttle on its way to the launch pad, and so can you. Whatever part of the journey I'm on today, it's all okay. I give myself permission to be fast or slow. And I give thanks to Spirit for the gains I make in moving along my path, no matter how fast or how slow. Can you give yourself this permission too?

Independence

Today is Independence Day in the United States, independence from being a colony of Great Britain. This is the day the United States was born as a nation. Let us use the theme of this day to explore the concept of independence in ourselves. I was raised by parents who greatly valued independence. I picked up the habit of thinking of myself as an independent woman.

I feistily guarded my independence, the boundaries that define "my way" and not "their way." I prided myself in being an independent thinker, with my own path and my own decisions about my values and choices.

But now I've grown older and have had time to think again. How independent am I, really? My food is grown and brought to the grocery store by others. My clothes and shoes likewise. The philosophy I have acquired "independently" mostly has come from my reading and digesting the thoughts of others.

So I am not as independent as I once thought. But neither am I dependent, although I depend on others for many things. I now will say I am interdependent—freely exchanging thought for thought, money for goods, love for love. One person cannot share a hug alone. This is the dance of life—my energy moving among others, living and growing. Where do you stand on the concept of independence?

The Open Hand

Let us examine a very important concept today, the love relationship. Let us look at our interactions with a person whom we greatly love. The purpose is to test ourselves on whether we are loving with divine love or whether we have slipped down into some negative mortal patterns. So consider this loved one for a few moments and answer these questions:

1. Have you placed any unreasonable demands on your loved one? Such as, "You must love me forever, you must always be there for me, you must not make any mistakes in loving me, you must always put me first over everything and everyone else."
2. Have you tried to exert control over your loved one's behavior, plans, use of time, attitudes, or appearance?
3. Have you interfered in the relationships between your loved one and other people?
4. Have you developed any resentments over communication failures or your loved one's behaviors?
5. Have you been keeping score of how much you do for her/him versus how much is being done for you?

If you had to answer yes to any of these, as most of us would, let us start the cleansing of these lower patterns. Visualize your loved one held in the palm of your hand. Now concentrate on opening your fingers and letting that relationship rest on your open hand, free of your clutching it with mortal demands and fears. Dedicate yourself to serving your High Self and let your High Self and your beloved's direct the relationship.

Rough Edges

We are all in the process of becoming. When we look around at each other, we become aware that there is error and imperfection—rough edges. Let us visualize the process of becoming as if we were living statues gradually and slowly being carved. Let's look at people who are acting in hurtful ways as equal spiritual beings but with more of the rough edges still there.

Can we also take this attitude toward our own failures? Can we see our missteps as knowledge gained, little pieces of the rough edges chipped off? Can we hold fast to the image of the spiritual beauty present within ourselves and others, and can we learn to separate the actions from the actors? Can we learn to see that deep inside we are all the same, children of God, living and learning and making many mistakes?

Can we learn to love the person but not the behavior? If we can learn to separate actions from actors, can we also learn to forgive those actions? Can we learn to see these actions as the rough edges of partially formed, beautiful children of God?

Starsha Dawn

July 7

Looking through the Screen Door

Swat! Darn mosquitos are eating me alive! Guess I'd better go into the screened patio. Boy, am I ever glad for those screens. They keep the bugs out but let the evening breeze in. I remember before I screened this place, I had to retreat inside every time the mosquitos buzzed around. Now I can stay outside all evening.

So what's this all about? Just this: As I go about my day, out in the world, there are so many annoyances, like negative talk, bad attitudes, mean-spirited criticism, ignorant bigotry. I want to shield myself from these assaults, but I don't want to cut myself off entirely from the world, retreating inside and refusing to interact.

So instead of building a wall or an impenetrable shield, my image of protection from all this negativity is a screen door. I am behind it, and I control what gets through the screen door. I can shut out the negatives but welcome in the positives, those words of encouragement and love, those kind glances and sweet smiles. I can open the door and welcome trusted friends inside. I can look through that screen door and decide what gets in and what stays out.

Try this image today when you are out in the world. See if it helps you to keep the mosquitos out.

Signs of the New Age: The Miracle of One

Here's a story that made the back pages of *People* magazine (7/3/00). There was a young man named Chad Pregrake who grew up swimming in and adoring the Mississippi River. As a child and a teen, he was always in the water, eventually becoming a professional clam diver. One day in the mid-1990s, he suddenly woke up to the fact that the great river had become a garbage dump. It was horribly strewn with cast-off mattresses, tires, even refrigerators, and literally millions of other cast-off items. The shoreline had turned from lovely into a dump.

Something hit him then, an idea that the river *must* be cleaned up *now* and that he personally must step up and begin this monumental task.

Well, we all know that this is a job too large for one, so large as to be laughable, even impossible. Did that stop him? No. It just gave him more zeal. He started in 1997 by getting grants to cover expenses. And then he went out every day in his boat and picked up trash. Isn't that silly? What could he do for this mighty river?

Did he make even a dent in this impossible task? I'd say so. In three years—hold onto your hats—this now twenty-five-year-old has cleaned up one thousand miles of the Mississippi *and* over four hundred miles of the adjoining Illinois River. He has pulled out eight hundred thousand pounds of trash from the water. By the time *People* found him, he was living in his houseboat, the *Miracle*, with a few friends who had joined his mission, and every day, they keep going and going.

What a role model you are for us all, Chad Pregrake! When we are faced with a tough mission, one that looks impossibly large, let's remember Chad and the miracle of one determined soul. If he could do that, we all can do *anything*!

Mission to China

When I was six, my favorite thing in good weather was digging in the dirt of the flowerbeds in my little backyard. One day, I learned that the world was round and that on the opposite side of the globe was China. Like many six-year-olds, I decided it would be a good idea to see China by digging a hole through the earth to the other side. I told my parents about my bold mission. They didn't try to talk me out of it or tell me it was impossible. They just went to the yard with their eager little explorer and pointed out a place where they said I could dig a hole as big as I liked.

I set off with my usual excavation equipment, the garden digger and my little bucket. I dug furiously with all the certainty of youth that at any moment my hole would break through to reveal China. After a long while, I had a hole as deep as my knee. I was tired but kept going. By midafternoon, I was hot and tired, and the hole was not much bigger. My zeal petered out, and I stopped.

I went in to report to my parents that I had reconsidered my mission and had changed my mind. I told them that since China was on the opposite side of the world, everything there would be upside down and that wouldn't be a good way to live. Besides, it might upset the Chinese people to see someone looking at them from America. I had not failed. I had reconsidered. And I happily went off to other endeavors.

In yesterday's story, I celebrated a young man who took on an impossible job of cleaning the Mississippi and who persevered and made astounding progress. Today, I celebrate a child's knowing when to give up—um ... that is, to reconsider.

Today, let us ask for Spirit's guidance so we can choose the way of balance between extremes, knowing when to hang on and when to let go. Thank you, Spirit, for showing us the point of balance, the middle way.

Little Bottles

When I was a child, I loved to play in the sink. Mom would let me put all sorts of cups and glasses and tubs and bottles into the sink and endlessly run the water. I would pour water over and over from bottle to bottle, glass to tub and back again, mesmerized by the simple pleasure of filling and emptying different-size containers. I especially liked little bottles, the smaller the better. To me, the bottles were fascinating, not the water that was inside.

Now that I'm grown, I still like little bottles, but now I like them because they hold the most exquisite perfumes. What I like now is on the inside and not the outside. I think that difference is a reminder that, as we grow up, we realize our treasures are on the inside. What is inside us and inside others is what is important to me, not what is on our outsides—our appearance, our age, our accent, our wrinkles.

When we pass people by, the first thing we look at is the outside—what they look like and sound like. Are we making judgments by these outside aspects? I admit things go through my mind (not much education, bad haircut, bad teeth, a little dirty—couldn't really be people I'd like to talk to). I do this automatically, and I'll bet most of you do it too. Well, it is time I stop doing that. I challenge both you and me today—let's look at strangers without that automatic evaluation. No matter what their outsides present to us, they are all divine, they are all treasured creations of Spirit, they all are unique. We don't know what they think, what they believe, what they do for others.

Let's think about every stranger we pass today, *I wonder what treasure is hidden inside.*

July 11

The Pyramid

I visited the Mayan pyramid at Chichen Itza in the Yucatan. It was over a hundred degrees with sticky humidity. Yet I knew I must climb it and meditate inside the room at its apex. With my heart pounding because of my fear of heights, I inched myself up, crawling up the very steep and narrow steps to the top. I went inside and sat on the dirt, trying to be oblivious to the tourists talking nearby. I closed my eyes, and, almost immediately, I had this vision. The pyramid had a flame coming out of its top, and that flame set the sky on fire. As I watched the sky burn from the center out toward the horizons, I saw that the burning sky was a fake sky, a piece of blue paper that had covered the real sky, which was now emerging behind it. The real sky was much bluer. I felt a charge of energy, and the thought came that this pyramid was a center of power. It was removing the illusion and showing us the reality behind the illusion.

Perhaps I was seeing the third dimension giving way to the fourth dimension, the new, higher-vibrating world to which we are headed. Join with me today and project your thoughts to all power centers on earth. Picture their vibrations helping to lift this planet to a higher dimension.

Ultimate Peace

Once again, we celebrate citizen actions to help the world. I heard of this project called Ultimate Peace. It is a project seeking to build a bridge of friendship by involving children of different faiths in the Middle East in sport, teaching Arabs and Jews in an Arab town in Israel to play ultimate Frisbee together. In gathering the children to interact with those of other faiths in this team sport, the project leaders are fostering mutual respect, nonviolence, and even friendships of Jews and Arabs together. And it's working. The children are laughing and having great fun, without thinking about who is from which religion.

If you would like to check out this project, go to their website: UltimatePeace.org. Endeavors like these are sprouting up in many places. Once people actually meet and interact with each other, they start to see each other as people, and some of the hatred of "the other" diminishes. The children, if given a chance, will lead us to stop hating and start respecting all others.

So, today, let's focus on children all over the world and especially in countries filled with hate and war. We project light to the children, and we project our hopes that they find the way to a world filled with respect and love.

Sitting There Long Enough

Sometimes my life seems superficial as I rush from task to task, appointment to appointment. It often takes an actual written appointment in my book to be with a friend for dinner. I never seem to be in a situation long enough to relax into it. I bounce like a beach ball in the wind, leaving only glancing blows as I bump into an event and roll on to the next. Many of my friends are this busy as well, which means that sometimes I don't get to see favorite friends for weeks or months, even when we live in the same city. That feels to me more like surviving than truly living.

I guess that's why I love the beach so very much. When I go there, I get to sit long enough to really feel the healing in the salt air, the warm sand, and the constant crash of the waves. I idly watch what people and seagulls are doing and finally retreat into my quiet self for refreshment and peace.

But since I can't be there very often, I must start taking time to sit and listen to my ocean waves CD or maybe meditate just long enough so that I can settle in and find myself again. Will you, if you are busy too, give yourself a little time by sitting there long enough to reclaim your own peace?

Connective Tissue among Souls

I had heard that my favorite singer, Barbra Streisand, had a new album out, called *Higher Ground*. Maybe you don't like her, but bear with me here. I'll get to a point.

Was I ever surprised at the tunes she chose to sing. I was thrilled! "Streisand has gone spiritual," I said aloud to myself as I read the lyrics to the songs. Instead of singing song after song about romance, she had chosen spiritually uplifting songs for this album. Her album notes said that she was sitting at the funeral of a friend, Virginia Clinton Kelly, Bill Clinton's mom. And she was inspired by a song sung there, "On Holy Ground." Here are Barbra's own words:

"It's hard for me to describe that electrifying moment. The music united us, invoking Virginia's essence and elevating our spirits with every note. I knew then that I had to sing this song, and others like it .... Music is the connective tissue among souls. Moreover, I believe it is incumbent upon each of us to put positive thoughts out there in the universe, where they can be free to do their good work."

Well, I certainly agree. She understands how much power there is in words set to music—the connective tissue among souls. I applaud her courage in putting together an album of uplifting spiritual songs, and I applaud the world for buying this CD. She has truly used her fame and selling power for good.

Let us be inspired by the music Spirit gives us and let us see singers and writers give us new, beautiful, and powerful spiritual music to light our way as we walk toward our destination of a healed world of peace, love, and harmony.

July 15

Ballooning

Today, let's go ballooning! Come on along—let's soar above the trees. We walk over to our balloon, brightly colored, lying on the ground, being filled with hot air. The air roars into the balloon, and now it is upright and ready to go. We get into the creaking wicker gondola, and soon we begin to gently rise.

As we rise, we feel our troubles fall from us. We feel energy surge as we look upward and feel Spirit's power here in the cool air.

Our balloon floats over the land, farm fields, small towns, woods, a city, a river, a lake. We feel ourselves uniting with the earth as a whole, an earth that is one land without boundaries or dividing lines. We feel the beating heart, the breath of the winds, the pulse of the earth as we bask in the sunshine and enjoy the view.

Spirit's energy fills us, and we send it down into all plants, animals, and people, down into the water, the dirt, the stones, and the mountains. Feel them all begin to hum with an increased vibration that sings, "Unity, harmony, peace."

When we gently return to earth, we can feel that electric hum of our planet arising in vibration to become a new heaven on a new earth.

Signs of the New Age: A Healing

I saw a wonderful sight on TV (*Sunday Morning*, 9/13/92). A woman whose parents had survived the Holocaust got together with a woman whose father was a Nazi SS officer. They talked and became friends. And together they held a small gathering for fourteen people—seven children of Holocaust survivors and seven children of Nazis.

Each person had a chance to talk at length about the terrible feelings and burdens they felt. The Jews told of their indoctrination by their parents into hatred of the Germans. The Germans told of the pain they felt the day they found out their fathers had committed the most horrible crimes of recent memory on this planet.

One German told of her great fear the Jews would kill her for her father's crimes. As she talked, she cried tears of healing release. And as she cried, a Jew came and held her.

These people, who have suffered from what happened in their parents' generation, now saw each other as individual human beings. It was a beautiful sight indeed.

Please project with me that if these two groups can meet in a healing expression of hearts, other groups can too. Concentrate on one such group that needs this healing and send this beacon of healing light to them. See their hard, protective crusts of hatred cracking and falling off, revealing and then healing the wounds within.

Just Do It

We are in the demonstration period that ushers in the New Age. What is that? It is the time when each of us graduates from being a student into a teacher, a thinker into a doer. It is our time to give back something concrete and real to this earth. Many of us have spent long years studying, finding ourselves, thinking, and deciding who we are. Now we must seize the day. It is time to act, to do, to demonstrate the High Self in action.

How do you want to do this? Your High Self knows. Just listen …

Ask what you are to do right now, and you will be shown. You may see a story on TV or read in the newspaper of a group doing good in some way. If you are moved, don't just sit there! Call them and join them!

If you see an opportunity to share your light in some way, don't procrastinate. Don't make excuses. Just do it!

Cancer—The Crab

Cancer is ruled by the moon, and Cancers are sometimes called moon children. To me, the moon is connected to emotions and moods. And, like the crab, there is a connection to being hard on the outside and soft on the inside.

This may be a good day to look at these Cancer traits in yourself or someone you know. Do you ever feel you can be hard on the outside? Do you ever think you must protect a soft emotional inside and not let people get too close or know all about you? Do you think someone you know comes off this way—hard to get to know, hard with their opinions and their words?

If it is you, maybe just for today guard against hardness in what you say and in your body language. Soften your posture, unfold your arms. If someone you know fits these traits, just for today say to yourself, "His hardness may be just a protection. Maybe she has been hurt. I think I can look past it today to see the person inside."

Emotional Overload

I attended a play and was moved by the story, so dramatic, a tale of such loss and noble sacrifice that the tears ran down my face. It led me to think about the actors who must enact strong emotions in their roles every day and twice on Sunday.

When we experience stressful emotions, chemicals shoot into our blood. For me as an attendee, I can calm down later and go about my life. But for the actor, the heavy emotions must have such a terrible effect on equilibrium that we hear stories of them being unable to cope. Some turn to drugs or alcohol, and some commit suicide. Some may even become addicted to being "on," finding little meaning in life except when on stage. And even if their performances do not include strong emotions, the repeated performing, being on over and over, must have a strong negative effect on them.

Let us send Spirit's light today to all those artists who act out emotions, whether through plays and movies or through musical performances. We surround you with serenity and thank you for your work that we so enjoy.

Actors and musicians, don't take your performances seriously. Keep a part of yourself shielded away from these strong emotions and realize they are only your roles, they are not you. Keep yourself safe from too much emotional overload. We send you this thought, "Peace, be still."

Open the Cages

I have been infuriated to hear of farm animals badly mistreated and abused. Some agribusinesses, to make more profit, have placed chickens and pigs in teeny, tiny cages so small they can't turn around! So, deprived of the use of their bodies and the social touch of their companions, these animals go mad. Most of them are put on antibiotics, as they are so debilitated that they are sick all the time.

Well, I am mad! I can imagine that if I were confined so severely, I would go mad too. But many people are insensitive to the fact that animals have emotions as well as physical needs. So these animals suffer terribly from this awful abuse.

And so I decree, and I hope you join me, "What you are doing is evil. Have a heart. Wake up and see the light and realize that you are committing a terrible error. Stop using these tiny cages—now!"

We are supposed to be the stewards of the earth. We must not accept cruel mistreatment of animals. Let us envision instead large enclosed meadows. Let us envision animals living the life they are supposed to live. Let us envision caretakers using kindness in their interactions with them. And yes, I know they will be killed to become our food. Envision their deaths being kind and quick.

And if you will, let politicians know that you demand they pass laws against the torture of animals in tiny cages. Sometimes I see the words "cage-free" on chicken products. Let's see all the meat being cage-free.

July 21

Horse and Buggy Days

There is way too much negative thinking on this planet. Whole groups form just to be against something. Wars are fought as people go against each other. Whiners and naysayers abound.

Lightworkers, it is up to us to show a better way by being *for* something. It is up to us to rise above negativity and obstacles instead of beating our heads on them. We must be the ones to accentuate the positive and be for the good. We can condemn actions, but we should not condemn people, as all people are children of God. Instead of being against wrong, let us walk toward our vision of a bright new day where these problems are solved and peace reigns.

We can think of ourselves as the first ones to drive cars at the turn of the twentieth century, when almost all others were horse and buggy drivers or just rode horses. Those drivers envisioned a future and stepped into it. They learned to drive and went out and drove with glee.

They did not go against the current practice. They did not lobby lawmakers to outlaw buggies. They just stood up for the future, and people noticed them, and many were attracted to join them. They created a new future. Holding fast to a better future works.

Do you see many horses and buggies today?

Pink Roses

I remember that day when my mother arrived home from the shopping trip. Such a smile on her face! Proudly and with a great flourish, she opened her bag and pulled out her treasure for me to see.

Oh! It was the most beautiful cardigan sweater I had ever seen, soft and snowy white with the loveliest hand-embroidered roses in several shades of pink, Mom's favorite color. I just stared at it in delight as she grinned and tried it on for me. I pictured myself wearing it when I grew enough for it to fit me, for I was only nine.

We were leaving that day on a weekend trip upstate to visit Mom's sister. Mom decided to wear her new treasure on the trip, because, even though the weather was a little warm, she couldn't bring herself to take it off. I spent much of that three-hour trip admiring that beautiful sweater from the back seat, drinking in the amazing shades of pink and reaching out to touch its softness now and then.

At last we arrived. My aunt, uncle, and cousins came pouring out of the house as our car pulled up. Then began the hubbub of everyone laughing, hugging, kissing, and talking to my parents and me, all at once. As we made our way inside, I glanced back at my mother and my aunt, walking arm in arm, smiling and talking. My aunt gazed at the sweater and said, "I just love that sweater. I've never seen such lovely pink roses." In a flash, Mom had the sweater off, placing it gently around her sister's shoulders. Knowing that her sister could not afford such a treasure, Mom said, "I'm glad you like it. I picked it out just for you."

Thanks, Mom. Now I know what love looks like. It is even more beautiful than those lovely pink roses.

July 23

Leo—The Lion

Quick, the first things that come to mind when I say "lion"? Go!

- -

Here are mine: king of the jungle, strong, mighty, ferocious.

Now, what comes to mind when I say, "What are Leos like?"

- -

Mine—loud, big ego, boastful, center of attention.

Funny, I named only negatives. People with Leo traits like these can wear us out with their needing to be the center of attention all the time. So let's check today: do we have any of these Leo negatives? If so, let's agree to moderate them today.

But what about the positives of lions? Maybe we all could use a little more strength and confidence. So today, let us give a lion's roar and go forth and do great things!

The Freedom of Surrender

All my life, my identity has been entangled in notions of strength and independence. Even as a child, my fierce response to a parent trying to help me was, "No! I want to do it myself!" It could have been tying a shoe, opening a jar—anything. I adamantly did not want help. I wanted independence and accomplishment in everything.

Now I am in my older years and find myself needing to let go of that identity. And it is hard to let go of that important aspect of my self-esteem. But frankly, that old attitude has been getting in my way lately. I have some arthritic problems now and a lot of pain when I walk far.

My attitude was causing me to just avoid places where there would be a lot of walking, which had diminished my enjoyment of life. Museums were out, hiking was a no, and any large building or someplace where I had to walk from the parking lot, I no longer could do.

Well, I pulled up to a big-box store needing several things. I just dreaded the pain it would cause. Right there next to where I had parked was one of those mobility shopping carts. I gulped. My identity was on the line. Who was I? What should I do? Well, I surrendered and climbed aboard. I drove that cart down every aisle, getting everything I wanted and being free of pain. I decided I did not care if people saw me as disabled or weak. I was finally free of something that no longer served me, but I was still me; I still had an identity, just not the same one.

So do you have any identity issues that no longer serve you? If so, can you let them go and be free?

July 25

Take Command

I've heard it said that our subconscious records and obeys whatever we say to it. I believe it. And that realization makes me shudder with dread. Oh, what have I said! All those negatives I've put into my poor subconscious. She is trying to create for me exactly whatever I've said. Whoa, Nellie! I think it is time to make a vow to cease putting anything negative in there and to clear out what is already there. Yep! This is my new resolution. Want to join me? Here's how I'm going to proceed:

First, I decree my High Self is now in charge of my subconscious. I gladly give over this control. "Beloved High Self, please eliminate all past negative orders from my dear subconscious. I didn't mean them. In the future, please filter out whatever I mistakenly decree that is negative. Cast aside those booboos. Thank you."

As for me, what is my part? I decree that I will strive to become aware of what I am saying, out loud and even just in my head. I will banish any booboos and replace them with positive decrees. I will strive to think over my automatic responses and pull them into my conscious evaluation, deciding what to keep and what to toss. "My beloved High Self and beloved subconscious, please send me clear perception so I can do this important work."

From this day on, I decree and command, "No negatives allowed!"

Who Are You?

Well, who are you? Write your answer here. I am

_____.

Did you say you are one of your roles? I am a police officer, a grandmother, a student, or some other role or profession? Yes, you have a degree of identity from your roles, but roles are impermanent. True, some may last decades and some for a lifetime. But actually, they are not *who you are*. They are things you do (your job), relationships you have (your family roles, membership in an organization), perhaps status you have gained (Olympic medalist). So who are you that is not tangled in a role? Who are you permanently? Try again.

I am

_____.

I was in a spiritual development workshop one weekend, and this question was asked of our small circle of attendees. I happened to be last. I heard each person in turn describe themselves according to a role. But after they all spoke, I said, "I am a child of God currently experiencing life on earth." The attendees looked at me, and then they nodded. "Yes, that's what I am too," one said.

Look again at what you wrote the second time. Does it get down to the core, to the answer? Who are you?

July 27

Lightwork—The Servers

Today, let us direct attention to people who serve us, usually for little pay or appreciation. I'm thinking of fast-food workers, convenience store cashiers, and others in similar jobs. Servers or service workers, we salute you! We need the services you provide, and we are grateful. I admit that when I am dining with a friend, I get so engrossed in our conversation that I do not pay much attention to servers, often not even making eye contact. Well, I am going to try to do much better than that.

Lightworkers, join with me to wish our servers good days with smiling customers, light loads, and better pay. Servers, if you are annoyed or exhausted, know that we, the lightworkers, see you, and we care.

And let us surround the servers we meet with God's light to help them brighten their day. If you are served today, look at the person, smile at them and greet them, and don't forget to give a good tip. And while we are at it, think of all the servers all over the world. Thank you, servers; you fulfill a needed role. Bless you.

Money for Strangers

I always had mixed feelings about people on street corners with signs saying they need money. I thought, *Why aren't they earning their money like I am?* I usually passed them by, rejecting their plea.

Then I spent time with a spiritual friend who understood more than I did. We would be riding in the car, and at the traffic light, she would dig out money for the person on the corner. We talked it over, and I expressed my negativity. She taught me that it is not our affair to judge people. She said that if Spirit places them in front of us, we should be kind and charitable. We should not think them undeserving or wonder if they will use the money to buy alcohol or drugs.

Everything in this world belongs to God. Our money is not truly ours alone. It is a tool to further our path to being better persons. I'll tell you, it took me quite a while to let go of my attitude. If you already give to people on the corners, bless you. If you are just not ready, think about it and maybe just give up the judgment of worthiness. Try giving to the next person you see.

Dedicated to Kim Clayton.

July 29

Weeding the Garden

As every gardener knows, weeding is hard work. We plant in the cool spring with joy and anticipation. But as our beautiful young seedlings begin to grow and mature, the uninvited garden crashers—the weeds—mysteriously show up, thrive, and threaten our flowers and vegetable crops. So, on a hot and humid summer day, most gardeners find themselves on bended knee, pulling and tugging, sweating with determination to rid their gardens of the ugly intruders.

As gardeners of our own spiritual development, we likewise plant the beautiful ideas of peace, truth, oneness, and love by which we plan to live our lives. But as we go along from day to day, we find some ugly weeds growing side by side with these beautiful thought flowers. They are resentments we have kept within ourselves, unwittingly nurturing them by refusing to let go of the hurts, to forgive, and to heal ourselves.

Today, let us take on the task of rooting out resentment. Think of something you are holding in your garden as a weed of resentment. Its roots will be tough and strong, yet, like any weed, it will yield to persistence and strength. Picture yourself kneeling in your garden, asking Spirit for strength, then pulling with all your might until it lets go of its grip. Victory! Toss it aside; it will trouble you no more.

Food and Water

One of the basic things the world needs before there will be peace and goodwill is good food and clean water. Through television and the internet, we are becoming more aware of how it looks to die of starvation in many countries. Yet, here in America, I've also seen footage of farmers dumping fruit and grain on the ground because the market price was too low.

We, the lightworkers, must unite in channeling Spirit's power of supply to direct adequate supply of food and water to every person on earth.

Let us replace in our heads the picture of starvation with another picture. See all those who need food and water receiving it; see the obstacles of war and greed melting away like snowbanks in the spring sunshine. We have enough for all. Let us see people deciding to help their neighbors. Let us see the land itself changing as its vibration increases to be able to support farming. Let us see polluted water being purified.

We now decree as one and hold fast to this decree: all our brothers and sisters have all the food and water they need all over the world.

Thank you, Spirit, for your abundance.

You Are Wonderful!

Today is "You Are Wonderful" Day. Oh, don't squirm. Don't look behind you to see if I mean someone else back there. Square up your shoulders and take it like a woman or man. Listen up. You … are … wonderful!

How do I know that for sure? I know who and what you are. You are a divine being, a spark of the light of Spirit. You are a child of God.

Please acknowledge yourself as divine. And smile at yourself and appreciate the magnificent work of art you are in all ways—in body, mind, and soul. You are spectacular, even better than a sunset or a rose. Lovely, lovely you! Just take that in for a moment. No negatives, no denying it. Just feel the truth of it.

Consider these words attributed to Marianne Williamson:

> We ask ourselves, "Who am I to be brilliant, gorgeous, talented, and fabulous?" Actually, who are you not to be? You are a child of God. Your playing small does not serve the world. … We're born to make manifest the Glory of God within us … As we let our light shine, we consciously give other people permission to do the same.

So dear one, for the sake of others if not for your own sake, stand still while I pin on you a badge that says "Magnificent Being." Now look into your own eyes and tell yourself how wonderful you truly are.

Paddling Upstream

Huffing and puffing, sweating and straining, using every ounce of your strength, you are paddling upstream. Have you created in your life a habit of trying to force yourself to go against the flow? If you've ever paddled a canoe up a swiftly moving stream, you know how difficult it is. If you rest for a minute, you are right back where you started.

Are you trying to force yourself to do something you are not ready for? Perhaps it is quitting a bad habit the hard way. Let's take the example of quitting smoking. You can decide one day that you *must* do it right now, cold turkey. So you throw away all your smokes and prepare to tough it out alone. Every moment, day and night, you dream of cigarettes. You struggle and struggle and sweat and strain. You make yourself and all those around you miserable with your misery. Eventually, in a weak moment, your resolve crumbles and you go back to your old habit, feeling like a failure. That is paddling upstream.

Sure, many people have been able to make it through the agony of changing a habit by willpower alone. But there is an easier way. We need not kill ourselves attempting to make a change by sheer force of will. Our will muscles grow tired too fast. Try instead praying for Spirit to do it for you in Spirit's way and in Spirit's time and promise to do your part to follow the guidance you receive, day by day. Stop paddling against the current. Paddling with the natural course of your stream will lead you to the goal you seek.

August 2

The Rocks and Stones

Project your thoughts to the earth, the very ground beneath you, to arise, to lift its vibrations and quicken its heart to make ready for the New Age.

This day, take the earth into your loving consideration. Walk barefoot on the grass or lie on the sands of its shores. Touch the moist soil with your hands. Put your physical self directly in touch with the earth.

Take a rock in your hand, or a crystal. Hold it lovingly and thank it for its beauty. Project to it the need to raise its vibrations and help it to do so. See it as atoms of swirling energy and see its atomic activity quickening. Place it over your heart center and give it your divine love and appreciation.

Now picture the whole globe gently awakening from slumber. Picture it breathing in the light and love and life of Spirit. See it becoming joyful and starting to sing a divine song of praise. Feel deep within yourself the heartbeat of the earth as it quickens with excitement and joy. Truly, as written in the play *Jesus Christ Superstar*, "The rocks and stones themselves will start to sing!"

Stained Glass

If you walk by a cathedral on a sunny day, the stained glass windows look dark, undefined, and unappealing. Ah, but go inside. Step within, and suddenly these windows, backlit by the sun, spring to life in brilliant jewel tones, bright and beautiful.

Now think for a moment of our fellow humans as stained glass. If they have not let any of Spirit's light inside them, they have not backlit their glorious colors. To us, they seem dark, undefined, unappealing.

But look—over there is someone who has let in some light. The colors are beginning to show. The pattern is emerging. Look—there is another with even brighter colors. When we see people whose colors are still dark, we can rest assured that their beauty is there, unlighted and unseen but still there.

Picture someone who seems dark to you, someone you see in your life, or someone you see on the news who is being led away in handcuffs. Now picture Spirit's light entering this person through the top of their head and filling the person with light. Picture their colors emerging and project the greeting, "Hail to the light in thee. You are so beautiful to see."

Z - z - z - z - z

Some people wake up grouchy; some people wake up slowly; some hit the snooze button and sleep on awhile. But everyone wakes up eventually and gets up to start their day. So it is true of waking up to Spirit, to cosmic consciousness.

If you are reading this, you are one of the early risers, those who are seeking and finding their answers and their paths. Some of our brothers and sisters are yawning and starting to wake up too, and for many, it is difficult and slow. Some are grouchy about tossing aside their dreams of reality in favor of a true reality. Some are not quite ready for the day and hit the snooze button.

If you have a relationship with one of these, you know it can be frustrating that they aren't listening to the truths you are trying to tell them. Or they may even be hostile to cosmic truths. Okay. Back off. Keep the silence. You would not stand at the foot of someone's bed and try to explain things to them while they are asleep, nor would you attempt to educate someone the very moment they open their eyes. Have patience. Everyone will waken sooner or later. Our job is to improve ourselves so we can be examples of the light that will attract those who are rubbing the sleep out of their eyes and looking around. Be wise. Let people come to you and say as a woman once did to me, "I want what you have."

Signs of the New Age: Calling All Colors

I heard on TV recently that a wonderful movement has been started in a southern state. Someone with a big heart realized that children of various races would benefit from spending time together with the intention of really getting to know each other. This person, whose name I did not catch, posed the idea and got it going in her community.

On the TV show, there were interviews with several of the children involved. Their discussions about racial issues have made them really see each other as individuals. Friendships are growing, which is what always happens when people take the time to get to know each other by working together with a common purpose. Now it is rolling full blast with chapters in many different places and national conferences.

The south has much racial healing to do, much baggage still there between races. But this movement, known as Calling All Colors, is a beautiful step in the right direction. Let us add our projections of light for racial healing today, wherever it is needed.

But there is one other aspect of this movement that astounds me and convinces me that earth will fulfill its destiny to become a planet of love. And that is this: the movement was begun by one person acting all alone, convinced she was right. She was eight years old.

It's Worse Than I Thought

It is even worse than I thought. Here I sit in tears after watching an episode of *Touched by an Angel* (3/5/00). They showed me that not only do people starve in the Sudan, but … some are taken into slavery! I had no idea.

This TV show depicted a mythical US senator being inspired by her son to free some of the slaves. Her son, a young boy, had seen pictures and read a couple of the letters of some slaves, and he raised money to buy many at fifty dollars each. In the show, the cash is handed over, and the people are freed. But the show is fictional. In reality, no slaves are being freed.

Dear lightworkers, please unite with me in fervent prayer and projections of light to Sudan. May the warring factions there come to see the light of God's presence. May they see the error of their ways and the horror of all the bloodshed and slavery.

The light of truth now begins to shine so brightly into the darkness of this place that people turn from evil ways and wake up and see that they, indeed, are their brothers' and sisters' keepers. If South Africa could change as it has, then the Sudan can become a paradise of peace. Let the tears of all the nations for these suffering people rain down on the Sudan to create an oasis of the living waters of Spirit. Let the people be refreshed and strengthened by their holy water of peace. Let it wash away the years of hatred and killing and slavery. And let it bring forth a new nation, clean and free of its terrible past. Sudan, we the lightworkers call you forth to become a nation of peace.

The Delete Key

Here I sit at the computer typing a memo. As I type along, I create it as I go. Then I read over the part I finished and decide I don't like one sentence. It doesn't belong there. It doesn't fit in. So I highlight it and hit the delete key. It instantly disappears. Where did it go? Nowhere. It has been uncreated. It no longer exists.

Hmmm. I think I have some sentences in my head that need to be deleted. They are incorrect thoughts. I don't like them, and they don't fit what I want to create. Let's see, I think I'll highlight a sentence I don't like. Yes, I know what it is (I can't tell you because I don't want to say it ever again). Now instead of my old method of arguing with the idea, I'm just going to hit that delete key and uncreate it. Just a moment ... there, I deleted it. Yay! It has disappeared. Gone, gone, gone.

So tell me, do you have any sentences in your head that bring you down, say nasty things about you, lie to you, or even abuse you? If so, how about taking one sentence, getting it highlighted in your mind, and deleting it forever? Bang. It is gone. Promise to never speak or even think that sentence ever again. Now you are free of it.

August 8

The Truth about Keys

Oh No! Not again! I lost those darn keys again—and just when I need to hurry up and get going.

Have you been doing this lately? Well, I have. I find sometimes I'm not paying attention to what I'm doing, as my head is in another world. Whenever I get stressed, I lose things. It used to frustrate me to pieces. I would rush around the house, searching countertops, pockets of coats and jackets, looking under things. Then I'd give up and rush back to the car to see if they fell on the floor or were in the ignition. Nope, not there either. Then I'd frantically retrace my searching pattern, getting later and more anxious and telling myself I was stupid.

Then I realized what I was doing. I was abusing myself and creating so much stress that I could not hear my inner voice, which was trying to tell me where my keys were. So I took two actions. First, I took the anxiety off myself by duplicating all my keys and keeping them in the garage. Whew! Now, if I really need to leave right away, I just grab the other set. The second thing was to consciously realize that Spirit was trying to tell me where to look, if I could only calm down and listen. So now, instead of rushing about when I lose keys or anything else I need, I immediately sit down, close my eyes, breathe deeply, and listen. And it has been working. Now, within a minute, the idea of where to look comes to me, and it is usually right. I give thanks and go peacefully on my way. Try it.

Boundaries

Today, we celebrate boundaries. Personal boundaries define where you end and I begin. They protect us from being stepped on, and they define what we will accept and what we will not.

A person without good physical boundaries stands too close to your face while conversing. He touches us in unacceptable ways, poking us, tickling, getting in our space. It is up to us to limit physical contact to what feels comfortable to us.

A person without good mental boundaries blurts out her life story at first meeting, asks us how much money we make, how much we weigh, how often we have sex, and other intrusive questions. She seems to want to get in our heads with us and know all we know about ourselves. We have a right and a duty not to give any answers we don't want to give. And we don't need to make excuses for withholding information.

A person who has no emotional boundaries wants us to hear every emotion he has—a play-by-play of feelings. And he wants to know all of ours too. If we ask him, "How are you?" we get the awful truth of how depressed he is and why. His voice is practically a sigh, and he drags himself around melodramatically portraying all his burdens, hoping someone will innocently ask, "How are you?"

So let us send a prayer to those who have poor boundaries, that Spirit will show them a better way to relate to others and let us model good boundaries so they can learn from us how to respect one another.

August 10

God, Help Me!

Do you feel sorry for this man? He was called away from work he loved to a new job that he was forced to take against his will. He tried to get out of it, named someone he said would be better at it, to no avail. This new job was not in his field and was an exceptionally large and difficult task. He toiled, day after day, dirty and covered with sweat, and exhausted from the hard labor. His task master visited the job site often, demanding to know when the job would be done and berating him for being slow. He was not even paid for a year and was forced to live off his savings.

And as he worked, he often prayed, "God, help me! I am wasting my life away from what I am meant to do." But he received no answer, no reprieve, no relief, no removal from the torturous and hated work.

Well, do you pity him? Do you feel for him? Do you wonder why God did not help him, did not give him his wish and plea, did not release him?

Say, do you ever feel the same way about your own prayers? Do you ever wonder why God won't give you what you ask for?

Well, I'll finish the story. The poor man eventually gave up trying to be released and did his best to finish the awful job. And he did finish. It took four years. But, in the end, Michelangelo did, indeed, paint the Sistine Chapel under constant badgering from Pope Julius II. And, in so doing, he created one of the world's greatest art treasures and became one of the greatest painters who ever lived.

So why did he pray so hard against the task? In his view, painting was not his profession, as he was a sculptor. So, did God answer him?

The Fly

The Encounter: Human Version

Oh boy! Saturday! Finally a chance to take some time for myself. I gather my cold drink, sunglasses, and a book, put on suntan lotion and a bathing suit, and set out with a grin to enjoy this lovely weather. Ah, peace and quiet and the warm sun. I sip my drink, open my book, and then it happens. Buzz–zz–zzz, circling my face at close range. "Darn fly! Get away from me!" I swat wildly, but it comes right back. I feel my annoyance becoming anger, my peace disrupted. That fly is out to get me. If it comes back, I'll kill it.

The Encounter: Fly Version

Wow, what a great new flying trick I've just learned. Darting, twisting sideways at breakneck speed, skidding to a halt and backing up. Way to go! Uh oh. What's this? A monster just lumbered into my acrobatic flying zone. "Hey, monster, watch this flying!" (Monster starts wildly waving tentacles.) Gee, maybe it is applauding my grace and style. "Now for my next trick, monster ..." (Swat!) Wow, that monster is clumsy; it is applauding so hard it nearly hit me. Oh well, time for lunch. "Bye, monster."

Let us pause a moment today to consider that our interpretation of events may not be the whole story.

August 12

The Wall of Comedy

"Wow, she is so funny, just a scream," said the first. "I wonder how she thinks of all that stuff," said the second. "She keeps me rolling in the aisles." The two got into their cars to go home after an entertaining evening dining out with Gracie.

Meanwhile, Gracie headed to her car alone. *Well at least they had fun*, she thought. *I wish they would have noticed how depressed and stressed I really am. I wish they had asked me how I feel.* Tears began to roll as she unlocked the door.

Do you know a Gracie? Always up, funny, popular. Gracie is hiding her real self behind a wall of comedy. Laughing on the outside and crying on the inside, that is our Gracie. But she is so good at hiding that no one ever suspects. She doesn't think anyone wants to hear her story or get to know the real person inside her mask of fun.

If you are friends with a comedian like Gracie, think a moment: Are there subtle signs of inner pain in face or posture? Is there a silent desire to have someone really ask to know the truth?

If you are a Gracie, let me say, please take a chance with the truth. Although it may be scary, it will set you free.

The Dark Side of Fame

Wouldn't it be great to be so good at what you do that you become famous for it? People would flock to see you, would send fan mail, would applaud you.

I was reading a biography of Liberace, the great pianist and performer. I always loved his talent, his humor, his outrageous costumes, and the joy he took in showing off his jewelry in close-up on TV—"Oh look at my new ring. It is a piano made of diamonds!" His personality seemed so sweet, so happy.

Oh really? Here's what he said while in tears, complaining to a man he hardly knew about a business and personal relationship gone bad. "I hate my life," Lee said, looking through red-rimmed eyes. "Do you know what it feels like to have no one you can trust, no one you can talk to? Can you imagine how isolated I feel? I never know if people like me for me, or if they like me because I'm Liberace. I'm surrounded by takers. They've all got their hands out. Gimme, gimme, gimme!" Lee wailed.

So today, let us project some light of love to those who are famous who may be in the same boat as Liberace was. Fame is hard. We thank you for your talent. We send you hope that you will find some real friends who can love you for yourself.

August 14

Maya—Illusion

Look around you. Take in what you see. Your room or maybe the outside space you are looking at is full of things to see.

What you see is an illusion. The Hindus knew this long ago; they called it "Maya," which is Sanskrit for "illusion." Somehow, they seemed to be clued in to a greater reality than we can observe with our senses. They seemed to know there were wonders beyond what we can perceive.

In the modern day, we have discovered that everything is made up of whirling molecules with a lot of empty space between and within them. Your hand isn't solid. Neither is the table. Yet our vision persists to tell us it is. We can sit in a chair, and it seems to be solid, but it isn't, and we aren't either. Our earthly bodies are not equipped to perceive beyond this illusion through to the reality behind the illusion. If everything is just mostly empty space, then your hand should be able to go right through that table, but it can't—not yet anyway. Some of the things Jesus demonstrated showed he had control over matter, and he promised that someday the things he did, we will be able to do too.

So today, let us focus on envisioning our spirituality growing and our senses heightening so that we can see the truth behind the illusion. Once we see, we can take actions like putting our nonsolid hand through our nonsolid table and so much more. Envision yourself emerging from Maya to truth. Believe.

Too Tall

After years away, I went back to the street where I grew up. As I walked around, it didn't feel familiar. Everything seemed a little wrong. Finally, I sat down on somebody's porch steps to rest. Then I looked around—and bang, everything snapped into place. All the memories came flooding back roller skating, playing tag, sledding, jump rope, playing jacks on the porch. Now I laughed to myself. I had gotten too tall for my memories to register. I smiled to be home again, to be a young girl of nine playing with my little friends.

This reminded me that my view of everything is limited by my current circumstances. If something is on the TV news and my opinion of it doesn't match that of a friend, we may both be filtering it through our past and current circumstances.

So today, when my opinion of something contrasts with the opinion of another, I will try not to think they are wrong and I am right. We are merely looking at it differently. As we grow, we change our minds as well as our bodies. And even when grown, we still keep on growing in our thoughts and opinions, and we mellow a little. Today, I will just try to see that there is more than one way to look at things. Will you try too?

Paint Thinner

Neither do men light a candle, and put it
under a bushel, but on a candlestick; and
it giveth light unto all that are in the house.

—Matthew 5:15 King James Bible

The spiritual light of our true self is always shining brightly. It cannot ever be
dimmed or turned off. It is the permanent spark of Spirit that is our essence.
However, as the Bible quote suggests, this light can be covered up so it is not seen.
What covers light? Hatred, greed, ignorance that we are all one people, and all
the other negative thoughts and emotions.

Let's visualize a person today, someone you know or someone on the news, who
sees himself as darkness, who sees the whole world as darkness. This person has
based his life on principles of darkness, believing that he must brutally take what
he wants and beat others down, all out of fear that good things will otherwise
never come to him.

Let's visualize a lightbulb that is turned on and shining brightly. That is the
person's divine self. Now picture the bulb as having been covered with thick
black paint. We know the light is bright within, but neither we nor he can see it
at the present time.

What this person needs to make a turnaround in attitude and action is to be
shown the light within. So let's help. Get your paint thinner and a cloth and scrub
at one spot. Keep going, harder; this paint is really stuck on there. There it comes.
The paint is starting to dissolve, and now one little area we've been working on
is clean, and the light inside can now be seen. Seen by you and by the world, and
most importantly, seen by that person who didn't know it was there and didn't
know he was a part of divine light. Say to him, "Look here. You *are* light."

You Can Lead a Horse to Water

We all know the rest of that sentence, "but you cannot make him drink." Let's look at this proverb. It speaks to me of our impatience to give our good ideas to another, only to find them resistant and unready. The horse will drink when it is ready, no matter what we do.

I will take this to heart today. I often want to pass on my ideas and opinions. It does no good to try to force them on another person. For example, I am excited about my spiritual path and long to convince others of the ideas I have found. Sometimes I will send a book to someone, hoping they will read it and find treasure like I have found in it. Sometimes they drink, and sometimes they aren't interested or are even put off by my effort. So, I ask you, are you leading any horses to water? Your grown children, your coworkers, your loved ones? Are you finding resistance too? It could be philosophical or your brilliant idea for loading the dishwasher.

Well, today, let's take a patience break. For today, let's back off on spouting opinions, tips for living, brilliant ideas, and so on. We acknowledge that all people are in God's hands, and we don't have to be the one to convince someone who resists. They have a right to not listen to us. God has many messengers. Sure, we can try giving our wonderful opinion or truth but with discretion, stopping if we meet resistance or indifference. And if you are on the receiving end of someone who is trying to push you, be firm and kind. Say, "Thanks, but I am not in the market for any advice right now."

KIMBERLY CLAYTON

The Rowboat

Have you ever been in this situation? You are alone in the middle of a lake in a rowboat. You have lost your oars and are just stuck there, all alone. This, folks, is the rowboat of denial.

Denial of a problem, denial of emotions, denial of the truth leaves us in this predicament—cut off from pleasure, from progress. But what happens as the denial begins to crack, as insights crowd in? The boat develops leaks. You grow alarmed and try to mend the boat, but denial just cracks further and further. For you cannot unlearn what you have learned, cannot un-feel what you now feel. There is no return. Soon this boat sinks, leaving you cast adrift in the water.

What you have learned and felt does not lead you to instant healing. For now, you must

apply these things. You must swim or sink.

Have you been in this rowboat of denial—in the past or present? Have you felt the boat sinking? It can be a scary process, this splash into the cold water of truth. So let's help ourselves and others who are being dumped from their leaky boats. Let us stick together and help each other swim to the shore. There is no turning back. Stroke, stroke, stroke, float and rest, stroke, stroke, stroke. Look! The shore! We are almost there!

August 19

Lightwork: Prisoners

A special mission awaits our attention—prisoners. You are our focus today. You have wound up behind bars, removed from your normal life. Yes, you have done something to cause your imprisonment. But that is your past.

Today, we connect with you in your present. You have choices to make every day as you serve your time. We call on you to make good choices in this life you now have. Remember you are children of God. You have responsibilities to family, to your fellow prisoners, to society.

We encircle you with light and see you bathed in the royal blue light of the sword of truth. Find the truth in yourself, the truth that you are divine. Resist joining gangs. Resist violence. Treat others kindly. Strive to better yourself. Strive to learn how to live a life without crime, a life that honors us all. Recognize we are all one and we all must take care of each other.

If you will be released one day, prepare yourself to be a good citizen. If you are in for life, show others how to live a good life within.

Remember God forgives. We forgive. Forgive yourself and ask God to direct your life.

Books and Covers

"You can't judge a book by its cover," goes the old saying. Today, let's take this thought and apply it to people we see or meet. We humans almost automatically make judgments about people by their covers. What kind of covers do I mean? Appearance—specifically, body size, color of skin, clothing, hairstyle, and so on. And if they speak, then we also add in voice tone and accent, as well as their grammar.

It is okay to register this information, but it is only the look and sound of the person I'm seeing. I can't tell about them from this cover they present to my eyes. Often our mere observation goes further, as we generalize what we think we would find if we got to know them. We may judge their worth by these cover items, marking them as a part of a group we either like or don't like.

For example, you sit next to an obese man. What does your observation of this fact of appearance mean to you? Does it ever mean that you would prefer not to talk to this person, or, heaven forbid, actually become friends with him? What about someone with poor grammar or a foreign accent, or someone wearing dirty clothes?

Today, let's try to become aware of whether we are making any snap judgments about strangers based on their covers. And if we are, let's realize we are generalizing about a category of people we have applied to them. Let's be careful to stop those judgmental thoughts as they arise and replace them with, "I am near a child of God. Period."

KIMBERLY CLAYTON

Help the Oceans

I heard someone on TV say there is so much plastic in the oceans that its mass is more than the mass of all the fish in the sea! And even worse, it breaks down into tiny bits that are eaten by little fish, who are then eaten by bigger fish until finally the fish wind up on our tables. We can't even see the plastic bits, as they have become as small as molecules, but we are ingesting plastic along with our dinner. Ick!

So let's today wield the sword of truth and call out, "Stop polluting the oceans! Find a way and clean up the oceans." We send this thought out to everyone who is polluting the oceans. We envision all the nations recognizing that this is an urgent problem. We see them taking actions to restrict dumping and to begin cleanup efforts. We envision corporations realizing their responsibilities to be stewards of the earth. We see them discussing in their conference rooms how they are going to stop creating so many plastic products, how they are going to stop dumping, and how they are going to cooperate to clean the oceans.

More and more, I see news articles about some companies using waste products to turn the waste into energy to run their factories. Let us envision more of this going on until we succeed in this monumentally large task.

And then there is us—you and me. If you are drinking out of a plastic bottle, please recycle it. And maybe you and I could go further, using reusable containers more and making less garbage as much as possible. Okay?

August 22

Signs of the New Age: The Backpacker

I heard on CNN news that a young woman just out of college decided to backpack the world. She traveled far and came to Nepal. There she was saddened to see deep poverty, suffering, and children begging. Many people on a backpacking journey would move on, regretting there was nothing they could do. But this young woman decided that she must stay and help. She had her parents send her $5000 she had saved. With it, she built a huge home and school. She has taken in fifty street kids to live with her, and she provides schooling for a couple hundred more. What a beautiful soul she is!

Quite often, I hear about young people doing amazing things for others. Our young people are saving our world. Bless them. Send this young woman and her generation your love and gratitude. These youngsters aren't so interested in getting ahead in the corporate world. They are highly evolved souls who have come to earth to love and serve. No job seems too hard for them. They just step up and say, "I see this problem. I will help." Let's contribute our resources to their great efforts.

It is time for us, the older ones, to catch this enthusiasm. Let's project our light to our older-than-thirty generations. Get up off your couches and follow the young in serving the world. Let's all say, as the young do, "I will help."

Red Shoes

When I was young, I had a favorite pair of red cowgirl boots with fancy silver buckles and studs. Whenever I put them on, I was so proud. I would just look down and grin. I would stride about, imagining that I was riding my horse across the prairie. So I wore them and wore them, just as pleased as could be ... until disaster struck. They started getting tighter and tighter.

My mother said, "They are too small now; you can't wear them anymore." Oh no, you can't stop me! Now I heaved and tugged and stomped them on. And, oh, how they began to hurt me. But would I listen? Heck no. For I did not want my feet to betray me by growing. I was happy just where I was, thank you. I planned to just stay the size I was forever.

Well, my feet had other plans. Wiser than I, they knew they must grow. Finally, the day came when no matter how hard I heaved and stomped, I just couldn't get my heel down inside. In despair, I finally gave up and cried.

But all was not lost. Mom said, "Come on, let's go look for shoes more suitable for a young lady about to enter first grade." So we went, and what did I see? The most beautiful, bright red tie shoes. "Wow, so this is what big kids wear."

Friends, our growth happens with or without our consent. Let's let go of our old habits that are too tight. Let's look forward to picking out our new grown-up shoes.

August 24

Singing the Earth Higher

In meditation one day, I saw and felt that millions of people had joined those of us who are working to uplift the earth. They were all around me, mostly up in the sky. And together, we began to sing a note in unison. We held that note awhile, then we added harmony. I could feel the tremendous power surge of all those beings singing the earth higher. I knew then that we will continue to work this way in the future. Singing the earth into a new dimension. Singing it clean of its pollution. Singing the elements awake to a higher vibration.

I basked in the glory of this beautiful and powerful healing song. It filled my body and soul with a thrill of joy. Imagine it yourself: a note sung by millions. Feel its beauty and power. Let it fill you and change your very cells, quickening them to vibrate in harmony. Imagine the earth receiving this song and coming awake. Imagine pollution being vaporized by the power of the song. Accept the new vibration into your body and soul and join us in the singing.

Amy and Dave

(Overheard conversation)
"Amy sure has her hands full with Dave."
"No, she has her hands full with her reactions to Dave."

These two friends are discussing a typical relationship problem. The first believes that Dave is causing Amy to be upset and stressed. But the second knows better. She knows that no one can make us upset unless we allow it. The real problem is that Amy is so busy trying to fix Dave and help him live his life better that she has forgotten her own life.

Whether Dave is Amy's spouse, father, son, or friend, the problem remains the same. Trying to fix someone else (who, by the way, usually doesn't appreciate the effort) leaves Amy no time to live her own life.

If Amy were here, I would say to her, "Amy dear, don't let your life go by without living it. Don't trade your growth and your enjoyment for futile attempts to force another person to change. Only God and Dave can change Dave. If you truly love him, back off from uninvited advice. Show him the joy of your example of a life well lived."

August 26

Knocking on the Door

Are you familiar with the painting of Jesus knocking on a door, waiting to be let in? I have seen it so many times, and always I pause a moment to open my own door in my heart and warmly embrace him, inviting him in.

What does this knocking-on-the-door concept mean to me? I believe Spirit has need of us all in our unique ways. And Spirit asks for our help, knocks, and waits to be let in. Jesus said that whatever we do for the least of our fellow humans, we do for him. So who is knocking on your door these days? Who is crossing your path, needing you to help? The knock can be small and sudden—a collector for a cause standing by your car at a light. However I treat this person, I am treating my master teacher, Jesus. Or the knock can be bigger and more long term, being asked to help with a project, coaching a team, joining a movement, championing a cause, or providing some ongoing service to a neighbor, relative, or stranger. They are all Spirit knocking. Sometimes so many that it can be overwhelming. If you have turned a deaf ear to the knock, please remember who is knocking. Please do what you can. Bless you, my sister, my brother.

Peck, Peck, Peck

Peck, peck, peck. The embryo has become a chick. It is fully formed but now needs to take the next step. It needs the strength and determination to peck through the shell and emerge into the light. That is the only way the chick can continue to grow and mature. Oh, but it is so difficult, and the shell is so hard.

Has something that once nurtured you become a shell restricting you? Maybe it is an old habit or an old attitude, once needed to survive but now turned to a prison, confining you in a shell and preventing you from emerging into the light?

Perhaps it is time to look around. Is there a shell that needs to be broken through? For the chick, nature provides a special gift, a sharp shell-piercing "tooth" that helps the chick peck its way out of the shell. For us, Spirit provides gifts such as insights that let us believe we can do it, strength and comfort from people who love us, the courage to persist until we succeed. Come on! Let's crack that shell and emerge into the light!

Starsha Dawn

August 28

Sunset

Sunset! Ah, what a beautiful time of day. The sky turns to pinks and oranges, then gradually to indigo, purple, and then midnight blue. I often stop what I am doing and rush outside to see it or pull my car over to the side of the road to gaze at beauty so sweet that it almost hurts.

But sunset wouldn't be quite so sweet if the sky always looked that way. Part of the beauty is in the fleeting nature of sunset. We are treated to the color show over a short period of time. And as we watch a gorgeous, fiery fuchsia appear among paler shades of pink, we are powerless to keep it there. It appears and changes on its own hasty schedule.

Such is life—constant change, mostly not under our control, sometimes so beautiful and sweet that we may try to hold life still right there in the pink of the sunset. But we can't, nor should we try. Change *is* life. Life *is* change. Today, let us give thanks for the movement of life no matter what it brings. And let us pay full attention to its brief, sweet moments as we move along our way.

The United Nations

I visited the UN one day in 1991. I had been there once before, in the early 1970s. At that time, with the inexperienced eyes of a youth, I saw this place as a useless failure, totally ineffective in doing anything about world problems, a mere stage for Kremlin shoe banging, venomous attacks by nations on each other, a laughing stock.

What I didn't know then was that underneath these apparent failures, seeds were being planted for a New Age of sister/brotherhood. All those thousands of diplomats who refused to give up on the UN, who saw the promise I couldn't see, persisted and worked, and built, and networked. Their efforts have made a tremendous difference!

Let me take you along on my second visit in 1991. As I walk past the flags outside, my heart thrills with delight and awe. There they are, the proud banners of so many nations, standing silently side by side, none higher or larger than another. There are more countries' flags here now than before, as some nations have thrown off status as colonies and become independent countries. Some names are changed as certain countries have reclaimed their own names for themselves instead of names imposed by empires that owned them. Yet, old or new, all have freely chosen to plant their flags here together, in spite of some hating others or even being at war with another. This silent solidarity of flags gives me hope that the nations behind these flags will also one day soon stand in similar solidarity.

I go inside and breathe in the aura of this place. Yes, a new feeling is here. The UN sings a new song that reverberates deeply in my soul like a foot pedal note of a pipe organ in a great cathedral. This new song is "Peace."

Let us link together with the UN now and join hands in this meeting place of the world, adding our voices to this song, "Peace, peace, peace, peace, peace."

August 30

Laughing

It is becoming more and more widely documented that the power of laughter can actually bring about healing, even of serious physical ailments like cancer. Laughter permits us to let go of control for a while. And when we let go, Spirit can enter our open door. So let's have a laughter project today. Let's make it our goal to laugh honestly and heartily at least three times today.

Here is permission if you need it: be silly today! If you need help to get started, make goofy faces at yourself while brushing your teeth, put your shirt on backwards and take a look at yourself. If that didn't get you started, do more. Go get a video of a funny movie or stand-up comic, or get a joke book from the library.

Here's one that will take a partner. Have someone lie with their head at the bottom of the bed, face up and talk to you. You stand by their upside-down face and watch their mouth move as they speak. Picture little eyes on their chin or draw them on if they will let you. This one always cracks me up.

Or put on some really fast music like the "Flight of the Bumblebee" and try to dance to it. Be sure to look at yourself in the mirror. If others can join you, this will be even sillier.

Go get a helium balloon. Suck in some helium and talk like Minnie Mouse. Go on, I dare you. This is especially effective if you are wearing your working clothes.

I hope by now you are picturing your own ways to bring the healing power of laughter into your life today. And whatever you do, don't just limit it to today. Reclaim laughter as your right in your everyday life.

Ode to the Elements

Oh, precious calcium, strengthens our bones.
Copper so bright electrifies our homes.
Gold and silver adorn our way.
Mercury tells us the temperature today.

Radium gives us x-rays to see us inside,
And silicon makes glass so we see nature outside.
Iron makes steel for the cars we drive.
Oxygen is important to keep us alive.

Helium in balloons makes them rise up high,
And nitrogen gives the color blue to the sky.
Argon in a lightbulb makes night turn to day,
And neon glows in color to show us our way.

What are all the elements really?
All neutrons, protons, electrons each one,
But at many different vibrations.
They create all things under the sun.

Our earth and ourselves,
All the animals and plants,
All substance of our universe,
Out of elements began.

Let us salute the elements for their service today,
And let us help them to vibrate in a higher way,
For they change as we change, as we grow day by day.
Rise with us, O elements, into the New Age today.

September 1

Lingering at the Fair

There are aspects of this change of humanity from third to fourth dimension that seem like the midway of a county fair. As we walk down this midway, we look left and right and see booth after booth of people displaying their psychic wares. Fortune-teller, past-life reader, trance medium, crystal healer, hypnotist, foot reflexologist, channel. Many of these people are displaying genuine psychic or spiritual talents. It is possible to gain information and insight from some of them, but it is only a step along the path.

Many New Agers roam from one booth to the next, seeking guidance from others. It is easy to become infatuated with this guidance, substituting it for our own spiritual discernment. It is possible to linger too long at the fair, to become too dependent on the abilities of others to channel the information we ourselves have the ability to discover from our High Self and our own teachers.

We can depend on our High Self always. We are inferior to no one, for we are all one. True, if we have not learned to access our own wisdom, Spirit will set the information we need in our path in some outward fashion. It may come through a psychic, but it also could come through a friend, a stranger, a TV or newspaper article, a dream. It is our responsibility to listen always for the truth and to recognize truth from falsehood. Trust in your own higher wisdom.

King Midas

Do you remember the legend of King Midas? The king was granted a wish, and being only human, he wished for everything he touched to be turned to gold. Lo and behold, he got his wish and was filled with glee as he busily went about creating golden objects from his everyday surroundings.

But the glee soon turned to fright as he grew hungry and tried to eat. All the food he touched was turned to gold. He realized he would starve to death because of his own wish. While he was frantically bemoaning his choice of wishes, his beloved daughter arrived home and rushed to his embrace. He pulled back, but it was too late; she had touched him and was turned to gold. What he loved most in the world had become a victim of his wish.

This fable is a reminder to us that while we are confined in limited physical forms on this earth, we sometimes don't have the wisdom to know the exact things for which we should wish and pray. Praying for specifics can work once we have gained some use of our spiritual powers. But, like King Midas, we can later find to our great dismay that the wish was in error. We must not limit Spirit's plan for us to only that which our mortal minds can conceive.

When you hunger, don't limit yourself to praying for a sandwich when Spirit has a feast planned for you. Our God knows much better than we do what is in our best interests. Trust in divine wisdom and instead pray, "Thy will be done."

September 3

Signs of the New Age: A Joint Venture

I went to the post office and discovered they had just put out a commemorative set of stamps about space. As I was paying for them, the clerk said, "This is a historic stamp, the first ever issued jointly by the U.S. with another country." And guess which country? No, not Canada or England but our former enemy, once the Soviet Union and now named Russia.

"The designs portray past space achievements and envision possible future cooperation in space exploration. A designer from each of the two countries worked together to create the unique painting that is split to make four stamps in a block."

The stamps taken as a group of four show their space vehicle and ours and two astronauts floating freely in space, facing each other, each holding out a hand toward the other. It was designed in 1991, soon after the USSR split to become Russia and several other nations.

How very beautiful to see these two old enemies now working together in space. Let us envision this cooperation broadening until our two countries become allies, working together for peace.

Compost

Pee-yu! Rotten lettuce, slimy grapefruit rinds, old coffee grounds, and crushed eggshells greet you as you open the garbage can lid. Garbage. Let us contemplate it for a moment. What can we learn from garbage? As a longtime gardener, I have come to appreciate the decomposition of leftovers into that most wonderful product—compost. Nature's original recycling program. So that awful, smelly garbage, with the help of time and bacteria, becomes a nurturing gift of nutrients to flowers and vegetable plants. From death comes life. How does this apply to us?

Well, the Hindus worship Shiva, the god of destruction. They see him as part of a divine process; destruction clears away that which is no longer useful to make room for the coming of new things.

In our lives, we do not think of endings and destruction as something to worship. We see loss only as loss, final and permanent. But it is only one point in the natural cycle of the universe. The Hindus see the other two parts as represented by Brahma, the Creator, and Vishnu, the Sustainer. All things that are going on in our lives are in one of these three stages: birth or creation, sustainment, or death and destruction. Just remember that destruction is followed by creation, death by rebirth, and even garbage becomes a part of the new life of a flower.

KIMBERLY CLAYTON

Clouds' Illusions

The events in our lives are neutral, neither good nor bad; they are just occurrences that happen to us. It is our attitude toward these events that creates a meaning, an overlay of happy or sad, pleasure or pain.

Let us explore this through the example of clouds. If you have flown, perhaps you have had the pleasure of viewing fleecy cumulus clouds from above. They can become herds of sheep moving across the landscape or beautiful cities of alabaster castles. But below, a sunbather hurries home from work early to catch an hour of sun, and there it goes under a cloud, bringing goose bumps to the bare skin. With a sigh of regret, the sunbather waits for the sun's return. In another part of the city, a laborer sweats, pounding the sweltering pavement with a jackhammer. This laborer greets the arrival of the cloud with pleasure, for it has cooled the air and eliminated the sun's painful glare.

These three people, the flyer, the sunbather, and the laborer, have experienced the same cloud, but each has judged it differently. Similar are our differing attitudes toward the events that befall us. Yet no matter what attitude we each take toward a situation, our understanding on the mortal level is so limited that none of us has the 100 percent correct opinion or understanding.

I've looked at clouds from both sides now, both up and down and still, somehow, it's clouds' illusions I recall. I really don't know clouds at all.

—Judy Collins

September 6

Admiration

Webster's Collegiate Dictionary defines admiration as regarding another with esteem or affection. To further define esteem, it is setting a high value upon, judging to be worthy. Thus, admiration is both a judgment of someone's high worth or worthiness as well as a feeling of affection for the person.

Is there someone you know personally whom you admire? Usually we admire those who have accomplished worthy things, especially if they had to overcome adversity to do so. There is the unspoken thought, *I'd like to be more like this person.* And perhaps the thought, *I would like this person to be a leader and teacher for me because he or she is worthy and wise.*

Imagine now a new world order in which we all use our innate power to judge who among us is worthy and wise enough to lead, to govern. In the New Age, this very thing will happen. In the natural hierarchal way of life, those with the highest wisdom, integrity, and love will lead. Each will learn from the one beyond and will turn back and teach the one behind. All of us will grow together. The wisest and the best of us will show us the way. See it now, create it, decree it as our right.

Changing One Little Thing

It's a good time to think about one thought pattern that we would like to change. Just one little thing. Maybe it is something we say to ourselves or something we do that is not useful, or even abusive, and we'd like to stop it. Or maybe it is a new healthy thought or habit that we'd like to pick up. Think a moment and come up with your one little thing that you want to change.

Okay. Here's the plan. You can create an affirmation, using only positive words, to replace what you want to get rid of. For example, if you are late a lot, your affirmation could be something like, "I'm doing much better at being on time." If you write it and put it where you can see it a lot, its message will start to get in. And then you can decide what actions you need to take to make it come true—like leaving earlier, getting up earlier, and so on.

Okay, so what is your one little thing? (Fill in the blanks, please.)

I want to _____

_____

The affirmation is_____

_____

_____

The action plan is

_____

_____

_____

Let's all send each other thoughts of encouragement to help us all put our plans into action. Blessings to you. You can do it! We all can!

I Will Comfort You

Do you ever feel sad and lonely? Do you ever long to be comforted as a parent holds and comforts a little child? There are many who feel this way at this moment. Let us share with those who are sad, frightened, or lonely today. Think of people in communities ravaged by war or disaster or famine. Think of those in hospitals and nursing homes, those in prison, the homeless people who lie on the sidewalk. Although there are people nearby, they can feel alone and lost.

Let us unite with them to let them feel comforted by the presence of our united spirit of brotherhood and sisterhood. Say to them in your heart, "Brother, sister, I am here. You are not alone. Take my hand; I will walk with you."

United, we stand together with the lonely and lost people, showing them our light and love. Visualize Spirit coming to their rescue and supplying their needs. See them receiving Spirit's comforting hug; see them smile, knowing they are not lost. In healing their aloneness, we too feel the comfort of Spirit's healing light and love.

The Tapestry of Life

Let us picture the interrelationships we have with all the persons currently in our life. Not just our friends and family but everyone we see on a more-than-once basis: coworkers, people who serve us on a regular basis, newspaper deliverers, the people in our churches, clubs, and associations, teammates in our sports endeavors. There are so many people we recognize personally, even though we may not know their names or share any deep feeling with them.

Picture the scope of your interactions with all these people as the creation of the tapestry of your life, with the interweaving of threads of blue, red, gold—all the many hues of a beautiful tapestry. Look backward along the tapestry you have been creating all your life, see how the colors changed as different people entered and left your interactions.

Expand your thinking to your past lifetimes here and elsewhere and see your tapestry flowing out into the universe, a soul record of pleasure and pain, love and sorrow, and growth toward the High Self. Thank your soul aspect for keeping all the colors and details of this magnificent tapestry for you to look at and learn from.

Now once again expand your visualization to one grand tapestry, representing everyone's interactions with each other. See the darker, angrier colors of past problems and hatreds on earth ceasing to be part of the present and the future colors. As the future tapestry unfolds in front of you, see those colors of strife disappearing and being replaced with a new spectrum of unimaginably gorgeous new colors, breathtaking in their beauty.

Starsha Dawn

September 10

Power

I've seen an ad in the back of some magazines with an eerie, leering man staring me down with a caption, "Have Power Over Others." That concept is dead wrong and is what got the human race in this mess to begin with. Over and over, individuals and nations have flexed their muscle and might to overpower others through war, slavery, oppression, and torture.

If God grants us free will, then all people on this planet *must* learn to grant others the same. Let us concentrate on those who abuse power and decree together with all our united strength, "Stop! If you refuse to stop, then leave us and do not incarnate among us anymore!"

Power is inherently not bad. Power is one of the divine laws that we must learn to use correctly. Here's how:

First, we work to gain power and authority over our own lower natures.

Second, we will to do Spirit's will always in all ways.

Third, we call forth Spirit's power and ask it to flow through us so that we can act in this world with love and grace, so that we can keep to the right path and fulfill our missions with strength and fortitude.

Fourth, we unite the power of Spirit's light that shines through us to work together to heal the earth and heal us all.

Will you will to use divine power divinely?

September 11

Virgo—The Virgin

The astrology literature lists Virgo traits as analytical, intelligent, precise, reliable, fussy, cold, inflexible. When I think of the positive side of these traits, I picture a scientist precisely measuring, doing the math, and keeping at solving a problem, like Spock on *Star Trek*. I also think of some people I've known who displayed the negative side of Virgo—complaining if I left a spoon in the sink, coldly discussing failings of mutual friends, needing to have everything put away in its place (place designated by them of course), and being eternally frustrated by people like me who are the opposite of Virgo.

We need the analytical patience of our scientists to calculate things like how to build a bridge that holds the traffic without falling down, and how to send a rocket to Mars instead of missing the planet due to a math error. Thanks, science people. Thanks for all the wonders you give our world. And let us today send light to those who express the negative side of Virgo. Let us say to them, "Peace. Let go a little just for today. Personal relationships cannot be perfect. Add warmth of heart to your wonderful, orderly brains and relax just a bit."

Starsha Dawn

September 12

Embrace Your Future

When we are disconnected from our higher Spirit within, we can be afraid of the future. We can believe things should, even must, stay exactly as they are now, because an unknown future is scary. Even if our present circumstances are not the best we could imagine, we may find ourselves clutching tightly to them, hoping to prevent that most frightening of all events: change!

In spite of our best efforts to prevent change or stall the arrival of the future, it arrives anyway. When it comes, we may find ourselves bruised and exhausted by our struggle to prevent its coming.

On the other hand, when we become connected to our High Self, we begin to trust that our future is in the best hands, the hands of Spirit. We can let out a sigh of relief, loosening our grip on events and circumstances. We can begin to see challenges as opportunities. We can even learn that our future can bring us peace, joy, laughter, love. We can attract these positives by devoting our attention to our growth, by trying our best to make wise decisions based on cosmic law, showing love for others through acts and words of kindness. As we grow, our best future is drawn toward us as if to a magnet. See it coming. Hold open your arms to embrace your future.

HIGH School

When I was in high school, I learned some good and useful things, but, frankly, a lot of the curriculum proved almost useless to me. Geography and geometry, more and more history, American literature, and chemistry were squirmingly boring to me. I confess I don't use them much at all, yet I spent hundreds of hours on them. And things I really needed to learn to live and grow into a wise adult weren't there at all. So here's what I propose as the new high school for the future. Sure, take those courses above and give me a little, just enough to get the point and to know where to look things up. In all the time that would be saved, we can learn these things:

1. Compassion and divine love in action (a lab course with field trips)
2. Cosmic laws (harmony, balance, attraction and repulsion, karma, give and take, faith, etc.)
3. Meditation
4. Physical activities—cooperative instead of competitive to produce a healthy body and mind
5. Holistic health—learning about the needs of the body, mind, and emotions and how to fulfill those needs (includes a lab for introduction to many healing practices and modalities)
6. Art and music appreciation (including learning that all can do art and make music)
7. Personal relationships (boundaries, handling conflict, respect for self and others)
8. Massage therapy introduction
9. Prudent and creative use of money
10. Stewardship of the earth (another lab course with field trips)
11. Self-esteem
12. Introduction to addictions and codependency (how to escape them and how to recognize and deal with them in others)
13. How to think and how to express oneself
14. Personal spirituality—an independent study course

I don't know about you, but that is my concept of a *HIGH* school! I hope you like it too. Let us picture together an educational system that honors our children's need to become wise and responsible and joyful and strong adults who will respect the earth and themselves and each other and who will lead the way to a bright new day.

Pain in a Parent's Heart

Within each of us is our High Self, our divine self. This High Self loves us with the unconditional love of a parent for a child. This parent is always with us, trying to guide and protect, trying to teach us what to do. Now, picture being your own High Self. Doesn't it send a stab of pain through your heart? It does mine. Imagine your beloved child refusing to hear your words of truth and ignoring your urgings. How sad.

Now imagine the High Self of a murderer. This person's High Self must cry out to him day and night, saying, "Stop this! Turn away from darkness and toward the light." Imagine the great sorrow as this human being, beloved child of its High Self, turns his back on these words and rampages further into the darkness.

Also present with each person are guides, teachers, and angels who have pledged to stand by this soul for its lifetime and assist the High Self to guide this person on their path. So let us join in a special projection of light directly to the High Selves, guides, teachers, and angels of every person who commits acts of darkness. Let us encircle these wonderful beings and put our arms around them in compassion for their sorrow. "We unite with you to let you know that we sorrow with you for our lost ones. We appreciate your steadfast attempts to uplift, and we hear your words of mercy, peace, and love." Now let us turn directly to those souls who won't listen to their guidance and say to them, "Come to the light. Heed your highest guidance from within. Join us in love and peace."

Beach Party

A friend called me from her vacation at the beach. She said that about thirty dogs had been unleashed and were running all over the beach, jumping in and out of the water, bumping into each other, just playing and enjoying the wonders of the beach and the company of each other.

My friend said it was a beautiful sight to see all kinds and sizes and colors of dogs romping without regard for their differences. Dogs know how to have fun, and they seem to be always ready for it. They don't care what another dog looks like; they just want to play together.

How I wish and hope that people will come to accept each other as dogs accept other dogs. Let's envision a new world in which all sizes and colors of people freely mingle in friendly ways. Let's see strangers at the beach enjoying each other instead of just keeping to their little group of family or friends. Let us send Spirit's light to the nations so they may learn to see everyone as friends. Let the world's biggest beach party begin!

September 16

Progress toward a Better World

I have been taking courses on CDs and DVDs. One that has interested me was about a thousand years of European history from the Dark Ages through the Middle Ages and Renaissance, onward to the twentieth century. I had no idea how much of that thousand years was spent in warfare. City against city, prince against duke, even religious wars between Catholics and various sorts of Protestants, and Protestants with each other—Lutherans against Methodists, and so on. One war was even called the One Hundred Years War. What a lot of unnecessary carnage over power and policy.

We have moved way beyond this now, even though there are still many wars going on in many parts of the world. Some of my friends say in dismay that the world is falling apart, getting worse, hatred abounds, and so on.

But really things are very much better—enslaved peoples are freed, rights have been improved, living conditions (water, food, shelter) are much better. So many millions have been set free of daily survival to think better thoughts and do better things. Don't let the bad things you see in the media make you think things are getting worse. They truly aren't. It's just that the media brings all these negatives that have been around for centuries into our awareness. Let us instead view our world's negatives as a reason to focus our thoughts and prayers on turning away from violence and making progress toward a better world.

September 17

The Wise and Beautiful Teacher

Once upon a time, Spirit sent a wise and beautiful teacher my way. She had blonde hair, big blue eyes, and the sweet smile of an angel. This infant grew into a young girl who knew how to love without reserve, how to trust beyond measure, how to forgive, and how to live.

She knew without being taught how we should care for each other. She understood without being told about the oneness of all life, the brother and sisterhood of all humanity. She loved the animals and flowers and delighted in the sunshine and the snow, the stars, and the smell of fresh-cut grass.

How did she know so much? Where did she learn? How did she get so special, and how did I get so lucky to know her and to benefit from the sunshine of her smile and the wisdom of her ways? This beautiful one, beloved teacher and gift of Spirit, was known to the world as someone with Down's syndrome. She left this earth all too soon, in her twenties, but those of us who knew her will remember her for a lifetime. Thank you, dear teacher, for showing me what the world can be like once we all achieve your purity and grace of spirit. Help us all, Lord, to see all human beings as divine gifts from Spirit and especially those the world calls intellectually disabled. Let us realize and enjoy the gifts these wise and beautiful teachers bring.

September 18

The Berlin Wall

In the early nineties, the dismantling of the Berlin Wall was shown on television, an inspiration to the world watching and a symbol we can look to today. Remember those scenes you saw as people took their power back, climbed on the wall, held a concert on it, and finally blasted it with sledgehammers and even bulldozers, all the while smiling, cheering, laughing, embracing each other in the sweet pleasure of freedom.

Let's apply this visualization to ourselves. Is there a wall within you? One that isolates you from a truth, from other people, from a commitment? Have you placed a wall up against a skill you want to develop but are sure you can't achieve? Is your inner child walled off from you, even a little? Do you have a wall up against stopping an old, bad habit?

If you have no walls left, congratulations! Please direct your projections today to aid the rest of us. But if you have walls, pick a specific one and see it as the Berlin Wall, standing for all those years. See it now being assaulted by your spiritual forces, including all of us who project together with you today, all your guides and teachers, all those worldwide who follow a spiritual path and who are always united with us as lightworkers, and, of course, center stage, by yourself. Pick up that sledgehammer and take the first blow to begin the demolition. That gives all the rest gathered their permission to begin. Picture a rush of thousands of helpers to the wall, leaping upon it with shouts, banging at its foundations. *Bang! Bang! Bang!* Sweat beads on your brow as you lift your hammer again and again. You hear the loud sounds of your coworkers as they bang away too. Spirit within you arrives with a big bulldozer, making a tremendous din as it pushes a big hole right through the middle of the wall to the other side. The multitudes and you begin to cheer and finally to sing a song of freedom and victory. Pause and enjoy the song, laughter, and commotion as the banging continues until there is nothing left but a pile of rubble.

Now you step forth across the rubble to the other side and drop to your knees to kiss the ground on the other side. The multitudes melt away, leaving just you in a quiet reverie, savoring the victory over this wall. You turn back one more time and look at the rubble left behind. It is dissolving away, since it had no real substance except in your own mind. You smile and bless it for the lessons it taught you, and you excitedly turn forward to fully enter into the new territory ahead.

September 19

Honesty

"Honesty, it's such a lonely word. Everyone is so untrue," sings Billy Joel. He's seeking someone to tell him the truth and can't seem to find that quality in anyone. I agree. Our society has become so untrue. All around us are liars being found out—corporate liars, stock market liars, advertising liars, even priest liars. Everyone seems to be covering up the truth, as if it didn't matter anymore.

Well, they are all fooling themselves, and so are we whenever we lie and toss it off with a justification in our minds that it's no big deal. It is the biggest deal, as lying shatters our integrity and moves us farther from our spiritual selves.

The opportunity to lie or tell the truth is one of the most basic spiritual tests, tests of our growth, tests of whether we are real or just for show. Today let's undertake a two-part honesty mission. Part 1: let's very closely monitor our words and make sure there is zero lying. This doesn't mean we will blurt out ugly truths to everyone about their shortcomings. No, not that. But neither will we lie to them. Only zero lying will suffice, not a little bit. Today we vow to be the honest ones Billy Joel is seeking.

Part 2 of the mission today is to pay close attention to the lying of others. How will we know when they are lying? Well, do you really think that bottle of pills in a TV ad will make us lose forty pounds in a month with no exercise or diet changes? Certainly not. Listen for hedging, politicians changing the subject when asked a question, advertisers promising something we know is too good to be true, and so on.

I want no part of believing in liars. Let's make today the start of a higher level of honesty.

277

September 20

Honesty, the Sequel

Yesterday we embarked on a mission of checking ourselves and others for lying. Now let's go deeper on this theme. Today, let's climb into our own heads as if they were attics. In we go. There we are, inside, looking around at sentences that are stored in our attics of past thoughts. We are looking for things that we have said about ourselves. Turn around. Over there. A whole file cabinet. Open a drawer and pull out a file. Hmm, this one is from childhood. That one's from last year, and that other one is from last week.

Take a look through these files for sentences that we've said or thought. Sentences that we don't like anymore and don't want to keep. Sentences about our shortcomings, sentences predicting dire futures for ourselves, sentences that start with "I can't, I'll never be, No one will ever, I'm not ..." These are lies. They are unworthy of you. Pull these pages out of the folders and throw them in the trash. You don't have to remember the actual sentences. Just hold the vision of throwing away these old pages of lying and demeaning sentences. Visualize all the drawers in the cabinets opening and the unworthy pages flying out, swirling in a tornado as they fly into the waste basket and dissolve.

Now envision all the false things you've said or thought about other people also flying out, swirling, dissolving. All right, that was a good housecleaning of the attic. Nice job! To keep your head files tidy, don't put any more falsehoods in there.

Something You Don't Want to Do

I find that often there is a task before me that I really don't want to do. It might have something to do with sorting, filing, heavy cleaning, or organizing. Whatever it is, I have a tendency to let it go and let it go and still let it go some more. Unless it has a deadline, like I must box things before the moving truck comes, the big, ugly thing I don't want to do can stay undone.

I find that often I am making too big a deal about how bad the task is. If I can only get myself started, then I get interested in continuing the process. So today, I say to you, do you have this problem too, the problem of getting started?

Maybe you don't, and if that is true, bless you and please send your prayers to the rest of us. So, for today, think of something you have been leaving undone. Now imagine yourself doing it and being halfway done. Won't that feel great? Won't that make you want to finish it? Well, for today, let's just pretend we are halfway done and we have just taken a little lunch break. Okay, now we can go back to work (in our imagination) and make further progress.

So, sometime soon, I hope you will join me in saying, "Yes, this is the time. I am halfway done. I think it will be no big deal to finish it." And then go do it.

Fill 'Er Up

Are you running out of gas? Have you extended yourself so far with duties and obligations that you are nearly running on empty?

An important part of our development is learning to take care of the various parts of ourselves so we can operate efficiently and healthily on this planet. We must give attention to our physical need for rest and good nourishment; our emotional need for peace, comforting, and love; our mental need for stimulation; and our soul need for time to spend in the quiet, communing with our higher self.

When you are speeding down the road in your car, it tells you when you are running out of gas. As a smart driver, you heed the message and pull off the road. How much more important it is to be watchful of your earthly vehicle for signs of running out of gas. Your various parts—physical, emotional, mental, and spiritual—are signaling you when they are needy. Just listen for them.

You should feel no more guilt about taking care of your needs than you would feel about stopping your road trip to gas up. So pull over at a full-service station and ask Spirit to fill 'er up. It will make for a much smoother trip.

Forgive Them

"Forgive them, Father, for they know not what they do."

This famous line, spoken by Jesus while dying on the cross, is our marching order as lightworkers. The time has come for us to set a pattern for the earth by forgiving everyone of everything. Jesus did not say, "I forgive you." Sometimes we cannot say it either—the hurt is too great, the pain too severe. But always, always, our High Self is ready to forgive. Forgiving releases our energy from being bound by chains of pain to the one who hurt us. So for our own sake and for the future peace of earth, let us begin the work of forgiving today. Start by visualizing someone who has hurt you and whom you have not yet forgiven. If you can, say, "I forgive you, and I ask that you forgive me for any part I played in producing our conflict." If it hurts too much and you cannot say that, say instead, "Spirit within me, forgive this person, for they truly were not illumined by the light, and they did not know what they were doing." Hold the image until you feel the release of energy that comes with forgiving.

Starsha Dawn

September 24

The Hardest Forgiving

Okay. Yesterday, you began to clear up your list of people to forgive. Today is a harder challenge. Lightworker, are you up to it? Here it is. We, the lightworkers, must set a pattern of forgiveness worldwide. We must forgive everyone for everything they have ever done to anyone who ever lived on earth. This is hard. It might take us a long time to get into this super forgiving mode. But it is good to start.

As we work toward being able to forgive everything, and armed with the knowledge that Spirit can do the forgiving if we permit it, we picture a great mass of people—all those who have ever hurt anyone. That is all of us, really. Billions and billions. We see in the crowd some tough ones to forgive: Attila the Hun, Hitler, Judas, Pontius Pilate, Pol Pot, Idi Amin, mass murderers, rapists, sadistic torturers through the ages. We look again and find among this mass of people those who have hurt us the most in this lifetime. There they all are, the unforgiven.

All of them, each and every one, are our brothers and sisters in Spirit. They have ignored their light within and done negative and hurtful things; some have done horrible things. Let us, the lightworkers, those responsible for the future of this planet, join our hands with each other in a bond of light that strengthens us as we say together, "We forgive you all. The Spirit within us greets the Spirit within you with love. May this love melt the black crust of wrong that covers you and let your divine light shine through."

Jailed

Clang! The steel-barred door slams shut. We are locked in, jailed. We struggle to hold back our panic and fear at being closed into a cell. Anger arises too, and self-pity that we could have gotten ourselves into such a state—out of control, caged.

What has happened here? No, this is not a state prison. It is a much crueler prison, the prison we create for ourselves by locking ourselves into a course of action or inaction.

We feel the rage and fear so strongly; we feel the hated feeling of being trapped and powerless so strongly that we quickly forget divine law. Circumstances cannot lock us in. Others' rejections, their judgments, and disapprovals cannot lock us in. We always retain our God-given gift of free will. This realization within ourselves makes us aware of our true power, not over anyone else's life but over our own. Look! The bars are beginning to dissolve. We can see through them! We can walk straight through them, never to be jailed again.

September 26

Footsteps

I am strong! Nothing can stop me from walking my path. Step after step, I move forward, no matter how steep and rocky, no matter if it is dark and lonely, no matter if I stumble and fall back a few paces. I walk along loving, learning, living, growing, loving—always loving.

I am learning to see divine order in my steps. I am learning to find joy in the knowledge that keeps coming to me. I am revealing my true higher self to myself. And I am beautiful inside.

I peel away the layers of myself, getting ever closer to the real me, to the child of God that I am. And as I see this self more clearly, I can begin to see it inside others too. Once we all can see and relate to the spark of God within all others, our world will be at peace, will know the love of a great big family. We will then create a new heaven on a new earth.

We are strong. Nothing can stop us from loving one another. Hear the mighty sound of all those footsteps walking forward on the path of light and love.

Libra—The Scales

Libra's symbol is a set of scales. Scales weigh and balance, and because of that quality, they have come to represent justice. So let's give ourselves a little justice checkup today.

Do you give credit to others when it is due? That is just.

Do you evaluate new acquaintances impartially, regardless of color, gender, appearance, or nationality? That is just.

Do you weigh the pros and cons of how your action will affect the world before you take action? That is using the scales of justice.

In our daily lives, questions often arise about what is the just and fair thing to say and do. Sometimes we may have a tendency toward prejudice—that is, literally, prejudging someone based on some quality or affiliation (e.g., Communist, Muslim, Mexican, gender orientation, body shape, skin color) before getting to know the person.

So how did you do in our quiz? Are you being just and fair? Today, let's all reaffirm our commitment to letting go of prejudging and instead using fairness in all we say and do. And remember, if we stay silent when others in our association express prejudices, they will think we agree.

September 28

Signs of the New Age: Getting High on Life

Newsweek had an article called "The New Age of Rave." In it they describe a surprising trend in New York's club scene. This is the advent of so-called New Age raves that are clubs without drugs or alcohol. Yes, there still is hard-driving electronic music, dancing with wild abandon, and black lights, but the young people are enjoying themselves in a healthy way, getting into an altered state by wild dancing, without needing the drugs and alcohol typical of other nightclubs. These New Age clubs usually have quiet rooms for meditation or yoga too. One interviewee says she used to get high with ecstasy, but now in these new clubs, she enjoys dancing with healthy people who are not strung out, hung over, or passed out. The movement has spread to many other major cities.

This is good news for our youngsters, who need to express themselves but do it in healthier ways. Let's add our prayers to this process of turning the nightclub scene from low drug dens into places of healthy expressions of youthful energy.

Getting Unhooked from the Past

We all have a past, and its accomplishments and failures have taught us much and have made us who we are. But are we living in the present or are we hooked into the past? What does that mean? Hooked in means to me that we are dwelling on something in the past and basically living there. Maybe the thing is the failure of a relationship or a business, or failure at college, etc. Are we supposing that the future will echo the past, that if we try again, we will fail again like we failed before? The purpose of our past is to learn from our experiences, not to keep living in those old experiences.

I have heard friends say, and I'll admit I have said myself, that no, I won't try dating (or marrying or starting a business) again because it always turns out so badly, as if things were always the same and the present would always echo the past. This is being hooked to our past.

Let's review whether we are hooked into something. How can we tell? Well, do you make any statements of always and never? I never get it right, this will never work, this bad thing will always happen … Those are putting the past into the present and future instead of letting the future be undisturbed by the past. So today, can we get unhooked, at least a little? Instead of saying never, can we say maybe it will work out this time?

Brown to Silver; Green to Gold

It was visiting an old friend who lives far away. I see her only once or twice a year because of the distance. Since I had last seen her, she had made a decision to stop dying her hair and to let it go back to its natural color. I was amazed at how beautiful her long, dark brown hair was, with one quarter of it silver threads that sparkled in the sunshine.

I was awed by the significance of what she had done. She had decided to go against the cultural norm and respect her aging by revealing it instead of trying to deny it or hide it. And as I took a new look at this friend I've known for decades, I saw a new serenity and acceptance of herself as she really is.

I decided then and there that I needed to make peace with my aging process by doing the very same thing. I had been dying my hair since I was in my twenties, as I wanted it blonder than it really was. I realized that I no longer knew what color it was now, and I decided I was eager to see again the real me. So I grew my own hair color back out, which took several months. I was pleased with my decision and actually eager to see how much gray I had, since I now could see that gray as a sign of maturity, hard won over these years. So after that last hair cut that took off the last of the old hair dye, I looked at myself long and hard, getting used to the difference in what I looked like. *Gee, I actually like my real hair color.* And what do you know? I haven't missed the change from brown to white. I only have one white lock in the front that I think looks just great and a few silver threads here and there. I'll have a front-row seat for the change to come.

I'm feeling much better about being in my middle years and about acknowledging the real me. I shall enjoy the change of my hair from brown to silver as I enjoy the autumn leaves turning from green to gold.

The Lost Tribe

Have you ever gone to a party where you are friends with everyone there? Have you sung in a choir or played in a marching band? Have you ever lived in a small village where everyone was your good neighbor? In all of these settings, a sense of community is present. You feel security and a sense of togetherness. People naturally like to congregate in such settings, because we are a tribal people. We need closeness with others, and we set up society to recreate our lost tribe.

Now is our time to return to the knowledge that all on earth are of *one* tribe; we are truly family. Let us visualize the changes we will see when all of us begin to love each other as family once again. For to truly love others as part of your tribe means to value their lives, their dignity, their progress, their accomplishments, their skills. It means to celebrate their triumphs and grieve their losses with them.

Imagine your city learning this new way of loving each other. It has become a place in which you can trust and rely on everyone, in which everyone you meet greets you with a smile. No more fears of walking the streets alone at night, for there is no one who would harm you. Your children can look to all the citizens of the city as their mentors, their role models. No more would new parents be alone and struggling in a new city, because everyone would pitch in with offers of help. Now add your own spiritual visualizations of all the wonders that await us in this new way of living. Hold the picture of the new way of life. As we jointly see it and believe it, we will create it. Why not start creating this tribe today? Smile at a stranger and silently greet them as your cousin. Wave at someone to merge into traffic ahead of you, make eye contact with a nod, and silently think, *You go first*. It is a beginning.

October 2

Law and Order

The topic for today is law and order. No, not the kind with police, criminals, and jails. I'm talking about cosmic law and divine order. This kind of law and order is an absolute, a foundation for all creation for all times and all places. We can all work with law and order or try to buck against it, but law and order always prevail in the end.

Perhaps we should examine our customary behavior. Does anything we do go against cosmic law? Here is a list of some of the cosmic laws that I learned from my teacher: love (which encompasses all other laws), oneness, equality, noninterference, growth, karma, perfection, sacrifice. That is only some of them. Pick one or two today and see if your thinking or acting needs correction or upgrading to match divine law. For example, do you hold loving thoughts or divide people into those for whom you hold loving thoughts and those whom you despise. This is a hard one, loving your "enemies." How about noninterference? Do you try to interfere with others' paths or their lessons?

And what about divine order? Are you content to let Spirit's timing guide your affairs? Or are you trying to push for the future to happen on your own schedule? Maybe it is healing from an illness. Maybe it is trying to push your son into going to college. It is quite hard to let go of pushing others and trying to drag them into what you think is best for them.

If you are trying to do your best day by day and leave the rest to Spirit, you are following divine order. Maybe your son is refusing to go to college. Maybe his future is not what you are envisioning. Maybe he will go later; maybe he will do something else with his life. Whatever the circumstance is in which you are trying to push an outcome of your own desire, you are neglecting to trust in Spirit's plans in Spirit's time.

Can you say, "Thy will be done, not mine"?

An Obstacle in the Path

Is there some area in your life in which you are beating your head against a wall? Are you frustrated that the change you are desiring has not come about? Does this area of concern apply to just yourself or does it involve trying to force a change in another? Whatever it is, have you been able to make a dent in the wall or is it still there, as solid as ever? Instead, are you showing the bruises and scrapes of this regular head banging?

Let us take a cue from nature in seeing what to do with obstacles in the path. As a river flows, it encounters rocks and logs in its way. What does the water do? Does it bang up against the obstacles and bounce back, unsuccessful at getting them to move? No, it acts with the wisdom of nature. It changes its flow off to the side and goes around them, always headed to its goal, not deterred at all. The water is flexible, ready to deviate from its straight line of flow when necessary.

When a tree grows, it sends its roots spreading out underground. The roots encounter many large and small rocks and stones. What do these roots do? With that same wisdom of the nature kingdom, the roots know what to do and just do it. They change their direction and grow around the obstacle, continuing to spread out beyond it.

If the obstacle we face is just a rock in our way, can we not be flexible too and seek a way around it instead of pounding it head-on and bouncing back? Can we look to the goal beyond the obstacle and chart a path that takes us there? Can we see the obstacle as only one part of the scenery and not the whole, huge problem? Can we look over our options and find that path that leads us around and beyond? Do you have an obstacle of your own? Can you rethink your plan and use the wisdom nature shows us to slide around it?

October 4

Your Football Stadium

The power of the light you project as a lightworker affects a great many people. All those who come into contact with you can sense it deep within themselves, even if they are not aware they do. And all those you pray for or project divine light for are likewise affected. Each of us is responsible for a segment of the population who have things in common with us—our coworkers, neighbors, those of our profession, or fellow students. This applies to those who share our interests or hobbies or sports or who are of our ethnicity or who live in our city.

Let us picture the spreading of the light in this visualization today. Imagine you are in a football stadium filled with those people who have something in common with you. The stadium is totally dark. You take from your heart a candle and hold it up. You ask Spirit to channel light through you, and you feel the presence of this light within. Suddenly your candle is aglow with the flame of God's light, expressed through your unique vibration.

You realize that everyone in that stadium can see your light. It is not necessary for you to take the candle to each person and show it to them. It is enough to just hold your candle up, as everyone can see a light in the darkness. Soon you notice that another candle is glowing, and then another and another, as more people follow your example and ask God to fill them with light. Soon your stadium is filled with light.

Ignored Advice

I'll bet you've been in this situation. Someone asks for your advice on a personal matter. You provide it. But then you find that they just ignored your wonderful advice and did the opposite, with negative results that you thought would happen.

We can feel offended when someone, especially our family or close friends, do not do what we think they ought to do. This feeling comes from being tied too closely to outcomes for other people. Each person's life is their own business, and their choices are theirs to make. When we can surely see the negative that will happen, and we are ignored anyway, there is nothing we can do. Sure, if the person is our child and they are young, we may prevent them from the bad choice. But when a person is grown, it is all up to them. Badgering, complaining, and repeatedly giving the same advice won't often work. Instead, we need to follow the cosmic law of noninterference.

We must monitor ourselves so that we don't get entangled in the outcomes of other people. After we do all we can to explain the pros and cons of future choices, we need to realize that some people learn the easy way (by taking good advice), and some learn the hard way as a result of their bad choices.

Today, let's evaluate whether we are entangled in anyone's choices. If we are, let's practice letting go, letting the person be in God's hands. We are not the only choice for advice. They may read something, ask other people, or just realize the pros and cons on their own. And, for today, let's envision other entangled people releasing others into God's hands.

October 6

Your Quiet Place

Are you feeling a little tense, hurried, maybe even irritable? Let's settle down, right now. Okay. Take a deep breath and let out some tension on the exhale. Do it again ... I'll wait ...

Pick out a visual image that pleases you—a quiet scene of your choice. Now go to that place. Close your eyes and be there. Stay there awhile. I'll wait with you.

When you open your eyes, stay in your quiet place. Try to stay there every time you remember it, all day. Take refuge there. As the events of the day rush by, look at them through the wrong end of a telescope—yes, the wrong end. The end that makes them seem very tiny and far away. They can't get at you in your quiet place. Smile that you are protected and safe there, free to feel light and happy and peaceful, no matter what is swirling around over there in the world.

Today you are IN the world but not OF the world. You are detached from outcomes you cannot control. You just do your best as events flow along and things need your attention. You do your part and then release the situations to Spirit's resolution.

October 7

Posture Please

I once knew a woman who was a retired ballerina. The first thing anyone noticed about her was her perfect posture, learned in her career. She never trudged; she glided. She never sat slumped; she always sat erect. It was not only beautiful to see but uplifting to my mood too. Her body was literally uplifted; neck extended a little, head up, back straight and tall. That is a posture I'd like us all to try out today. Imagine yourself on the stage, about to perform a ballet. You are erect with the calm grace of a practiced dancer. Your head is erect with dignity and poise. Let's walk that way today, stand that way, sit that way.

This posture tells me when I use it that I'm feeling great. That I'm ready for life. That I have vim and vigor and grace. This up-ness makes me feel up. I'm ready for great things to happen.

I'm noticeable with this posture. People take a look at me, and maybe they are uplifted too. It makes me want to twirl and even skip. My mind gets the message from my body, and I begin to hum a happy tune. My whole day is looking much brighter now.

If we want to grow into higher beings, let's get used to holding ourselves higher. Gosh, that feels good!

The Shooting Gallery

When I was young, I liked to try my hand at shooting the ducks in a shooting gallery arcade machine. They would roll by and then pop up for me to shoot. In a way, the game gave me the impression at a young age that if you stick up, you can be shot down.

For a long while, I was afraid to "stick up" and show others who I was and where I stood. I feared that this bold living of my life would only get me shot down whenever I was different. Experiences in my early adulthood only served to confirm this notion. In my little town, I found myself frequently insulted for letting someone know that I was a vegetarian. So I figured whenever I was different from those around me, I would shut up about it to get along.

Fortunately, I got over that. In my thirties, I began having more and more positive experiences after sharing something of the real me. I finally realized that standing for something certainly attracts attention, but that doesn't mean I will get shot down. Oh, sometimes I do, but more often, I find acceptance or at least tolerance.

If we don't stick up, how will compatible people find us and join us on our mutual path toward enlightenment? I invite you to be yourself, even if it means being different. Stand up and let people find you. I'm glad I did, and I believe you'll be glad you did too.

A Quieter Day; A Simpler Way

After coming home from work to first retrieve my mail and scan it, then check my phone messages, and last to turn on my home computer and read my email, I found myself longing to be back in pioneer days for a respite. I realized that the amount of words I had read just today probably equaled the entire amount of written words an average person in 1820 would read in a month. They had maybe a few books in their houses, and rarely, a letter would arrive.

No wonder I feel stressed. I am overwhelmed and overstimulated by modern life to the point where I cannot function without a calendar book by my side. *Well, I thought, tough luck. The past is not coming back.*

So how do I fulfill my craving for a quieter day and a simpler way? I know only one way. I must say no to some of the overstimulation. Long ago, I took a first step that has helped. I have not subscribed to a newspaper in three decades. Not because I don't like newspapers but because I do. I don't skim well, as there are so many articles I want to read. So if I got a paper, I would be putting in an hour on it every day. I am also starting to say no to booking my week too full of duties and social activities. I've begun dumping most of my junk mail without opening it, and I've also gotten on lists to stop receiving some commercial email and even some catalogs in the mail.

What are you doing to achieve a quieter day, a simpler way?

October 10

The Lotus in the Woods

Here I stand in the soft sunshine of a warm autumn afternoon in a beautiful, peaceful place. Come and be here with me for a little respite from your busy life. We are at an overlook about twenty stories high at the top of a wooded hill that overlooks a lovely valley that goes on for fifty miles. The view is rich with many interesting sights to see. At the bottom of the hill is a quiet river that moves straight toward us and then turns to the right. The water sparkles in the sunlight. The valley sits below us, as far as the eye can see to the right and left, partly forested and partly meadows. Along the river is a train track, and farther off are more hills of the Blue Ridge Mountains of Virginia. Ridge upon ridge, the nearer ones green and the farther off ones blue, and those the farthest away shrouded in haze as if they are a mirage.

But on the left, what is this we see? A most unusual sight. It is a huge domed building, nestled in the valley below. It is the only building for miles and miles, but that is not what makes it unusual. It is in the shape of a gigantic lotus flower, with the bottom half in the shape of pink lotus petals, and the top is pale blue like the sky, with a golden crown on the very peak. This is the Lotus Shrine, a temple of peace dedicated to all religions, known and unknown, and created as a gathering place for all who seek to create world peace. It looks both beautiful and incongruous in these green Virginia mountains, yet it seems right for this peace shrine of East Indian inspiration to be here in this peaceful setting.

So there is the visual. Tomorrow we will see what is inside, but for today, just think of a giant pink flower of peace sitting in this valley. Let us be a part of this beautiful scene, partly nature, and partly human-made. Hear the river run, the tree leaves rustle in the breeze, and the occasional calls of birds. A train whistle is heard softly in the distance as a seemingly toy train goes by so far below. Take a deep breath and let tensions sink away into the earth. Let the sunshine and the breeze touch your skin and also touch your heart and soul. Sigh. isn't it lovely?

The Lotus Shrine

Come with me and let us proceed down from our overlook to the valley below to visit the beautiful Lotus Shrine. We walk through an arch, along the reflecting pool, and into the dome. A brochure tells us that LOTUS stands for Light of Truth Universal Shrine. It is a sanctuary for silent meditation and prayer for people of all faiths. Inside its ground floor hall are displays of sayings and artifacts from dozens of religions and also from the United Nations. It was constructed by the Reverend Sri Satchidananda at his ashram in Virginia. He has led worship services for clergy of all faiths for over forty years and was inspired by the peace and joy of these gatherings to construct this permanent shrine where all can come together to celebrate spiritual unity.

What a fine idea! What a beautiful and serene place! After studying the displays, we now climb a narrow, spiral staircase to the circular meditation room at the top of the dome. Above us, the lotus petals rise and come together to create the top of the dome. Many people are gathering for silent meditation. Electric bells ring to let us know it is time.

We join those who are seated on the floor and in chairs, and we link with them and with all those on this planet who pray for peace. Let us meditate together now for peace on earth and unity of all people.

October 12

Imagining a Better World

Imagine all the people
Living life in peace ...
You may say I'm a dreamer
But I'm not the only one
I hope someday you'll join us
And the world will be as one.

—John Lennon, "Imagine"

Today, let's take John's lovely words into our hearts. Let us actually see this new world, peace reigning everywhere. Everyone has enough to eat and a place to live. Everyone is helping everyone, sharing talents with joy, considering each person of the earth to be part of one family. Picture loving interactions occurring every day among strangers. "Hello, cousin. How may I be of help?"

Imagine the young and strong burning with desire to clean up debris, tidy up cities, plant gardens, tend to homeless people, help older people, help animals, and so on. Imagine no need for police or armies or courts or jails because at last we all have learned to live with love and respect for each other, for the animals, for the earth itself. Hold the visions; decree them to be happening. We, together, insist that this lovely imagining will become reality very soon. Picture millions and finally billions of people inspired by this vision and each person doing all they can to produce this new earth, and, as John says, "the world will be as one."

Have You Seen a Hero?

In movies, those who fight wars or fight against criminals are honored as heroes. Heroes have courage and determination. Heroes have a mission and devote themselves to it. Surely, those who fight to protect us are heroes. But today I am thinking about a quieter and unseen type of hero.

I'm thinking about heroes like these:

- people who work in hospitals and nursing homes, cleaning floors and listening to old people with dementia
- medical staff who leave their jobs and fly to disaster areas
- social workers who visit homeless people and try to help them access services
- volunteers who visit the lonely, the sick, the dying, the throwaways of society
- teachers who inspire as well as educate

These are the types of heroes I celebrate today. They don't think of themselves as heroes, but they surely are to me. I have met many of these wonderful people in my long career in health care.

Today, let us bless these great souls and celebrate all their quiet and unnoticed endeavors. Let us learn from them the patience and diligence they display in accepting their missions. Thank you, beautiful heroes.

Signs of the New Age: Science

As dawn approached, the scientist finally got up from the experiment she had excitedly tended all night and stretched. This was something big—a promising new discovery. She was on the right track. But there was much work to do, perhaps weeks or months. "Hmm, it is late afternoon in Tokyo and late morning in Belgrade." She grinned as she placed a conference call to the two colleagues she had met at last year's conference. "Hello, Yuri? Hello, Akinori? I want to share my progress with you. Come work with me, and together we will solve these puzzles and make this new discovery a reality." "Yes, yes, I accept!" they both say. Yuri adds, "Remember those days not so long ago when we each would have labored alone, refusing to share results because of competition? I'm so glad those days are over." And Akinori chimes in, "Such a wasteful way to work. Now we can be free to share our insights, share the tasks, and produce the results much faster."

Let us see the bitter wall of ego and competition crumbling away from scientific endeavor and research. Let us hold the vision of a new age of sharing and cooperative brainstorming by those gifted in the sciences. It is already happening much more, due to the internet's ability to help people find each other. Some scientists have left behind the prison of ego and discovered that collaboration is more effective than competition. Still, some prefer to labor in secret, sometimes unnecessarily duplicating efforts in the pursuit of the ego boost of being first. That is a waste of precious minds. Let us envision scientists realizing that their sharing instead of hoarding information will lead them much more quickly to discovering things that help us to improve our world and heal ourselves.

Road Wisdom

The car ahead of me in traffic had one of those personally designed license plates. I love looking at these and trying to figure out what they are saying, since the sentence structure is so curtailed and abbreviated by the need to say it all within only several letters.

This car's plate said UGO4IT. *Hmmm*, I thought, *Hugo 41 T. Maybe his name is Hugo. No, that can't be right. Maybe it is UG 04 IT. No, that makes no sense. Oh, I get it! It says* you go for it!

Wow, this driver cares about me! He wants me to go for it! I felt a boost, stuck in traffic, as if a friend were telling me I could do whatever it is I want to do, encouraging me not to give up but to go for it.

Whether this driver was aware of it or not, his license plate gave me a boost and made me smile. He is using his vehicle to spread encouragement wherever he goes every day. Likely, most people who get behind him won't take the time to figure it out, but for those that do, a pleasant surprise awaits them. How very nice that is.

Then I thought to myself, *Am I using my vehicle (my voice, my smile, my presence, my words, my body language) to spread encouragement? What are others seeing when they look at me today?*

Thank you for reminding me, Mr. UGO4IT that I can go for it and that I can encourage others to go for it too.

October 16

The Wine Glass

The human condition at present is like a crystal wine glass filled with mud. This mud is the errors of the lower mortal way of living. Because our sight is dim, we can see only the filth and impurity but not the crystal vessel.

We must empty our vessel of this mud by dissolving our ties to lower earthly ways and casting off all error, darkness, and impurity. Then we must cleanse the vessel and make it shine once again—transparent, empty, and pure. Only then can the High Self, the wine, pour in from above and fill this empty vessel. You then become your own true High Self while in an earth body, evolved into a higher consciousness.

The High Self cannot descend while the vessel is unclean, for the wine cannot be mixed with the mud. We must be empty of all selfishness so that we can be filled with the greater glory of Spirit, the wine that our vessel is meant to hold.

In this time of now, our human race is going through this cleansing, emptying process. Let us visualize the success of this endeavor and see the beautiful crystal vessels being poured full of the wine of Spirit.

Lightwork: Pick a World Leader

We need to inspire world leaders to carry foremost in their hearts peace and cooperation, and stewardship of the earth. We need them to let go of negative qualities and desires for power and ego gratification. So today, I ask you to pick just one world leader and focus on this person. It could be a head of a country or some other prominent person who influences world thought and who is traveling the wrong path.

Together, we unite in our lightwork projections and prayers today. "World leader (add name), I focus on you. I am watching you, and your performance is not proper. I say to you, wake up! Stop doing the wrong things. Stop acting like an ancient warlord and start acting like a spiritual person who is in a prominent place. Think about your people. Think about the world. Listen for God's guidance as to what to do with your earthly power and act on what God tells you to do. We are all children of God, and we all need to serve each other and serve the earth together in peace and love. Get the point or get out!"

Sayings from the Lotus Shrine: The Big Blue Marble

One of the postings at the Lotus Shrine was this story: The Sultan Bin Salman al-Saud traveled as an astronaut aboard the US space shuttle. Here's what he had to say about the experience: "The first day or so, we all pointed to our countries. The third or fourth day, we were pointing to our continents. By the fifth day, we were aware of only one earth."

Seeing the earth from space makes one realize that there are no national or political boundaries drawn upon it. It is whole and undivided, one big, blue marble swirled with white, with a very thin layer of essential atmosphere that makes earth livable and makes it our precious and fragile planetary home. From that distance in space, nationality fades in importance as the realization comes that our home is the whole planet. Seeing it all at once, the whole earth makes it clear that what any nation does to harm the earth or to heal it affects the whole globe and all of its inhabitants.

Let us place before our eyes the picture of the big, blue marble against the velvet black of space and contemplate it. It thrills my heart with its great beauty, so much so that for many years I had a poster of that first shot of the whole earth on my wall. It arouses in me a protective urge to help take care of it. Let us picture all people on this planet joining us now in this visual contemplation of our home. Let it set our hearts aglow with love and with desire to heal our earth, our homeland.

The Scent of Spring in the Air

There I was standing in my favorite greenhouse in October, thinking of spring. No, I had not lost my marbles. I was picking out sunny yellow daffodils to plant. The daffodils themselves were only brown bulbs, but their pictures on the bulb bin showed them in full bloom in the spring. As I gazed at these pictures, I could almost smell the scent of spring in the air.

Later that day, planting them in the cold ground, that feeling of spring came back even stronger. I was doing my part in the fall to create my spring garden. I had no trouble envisioning the end result of my labor, as I trusted those nondescript bulbs to fulfill their promise and bloom at winter's end.

Now I realize that it was my vision of the future that propelled me to buy and plant the bulbs in the first place, and so it is in my life. If I can envision the end result, I can feel the motivation and determination to take the steps I need to take to set that future into motion.

Today, join with me in using this envisioning process to see something you want in your future. Picture yourself in this future doing or having or being whatever is your desire. Trade wishing for seeing and trade hoping for doing your part to begin the process of creating your bright, sunny future.

October 20

One Thing at a Time

Once again, I'm swamped. Too many things are waiting to be done. Once my stack of work mounts up, I freeze and have a hard time beginning to tackle it. And so the pile grows into a mountain that I'm afraid to climb, feeling both guilty and lazy.

I can spend an hour figuring out how to glue the broken wing back on my angel and another hour deciding what to do with one little stack of papers. Orderliness has not been my natural gift. I have to work at it all the time, and it is hard for me.

How about you? How is your orderliness? How big is your list? How often do you take a crack at those old jobs that have been on the list for a long time?

Order is divine. It is a power to be used to organize our lives so we aren't overwhelmed and so we get things done that need to be done. Order helps us to quickly find something we suddenly need, like the receipt for the new refrigerator that just broke down. Order tells us what to do next. It gives us peace as we look around at the beauty of things done, in their place, clean and neat.

Well I'm turning over a new leaf. Instead of feeling guilt and unworthiness at the size of the stack that is left for me to organize, I'm going to concentrate on the part that I did get finished. Every time I move, file, fix, or clean one thing, I'm going to gaze at it with the pride of accomplishment. I'm going to congratulate myself and enjoy the little bit of beauty I've created.

I invite you to do the same. Tackle your stack or to-do list one thing at a time and say, "Yay, that one is done." And if you are orderly, that is so great and so rare. Please send light and encouragement to all those like me who are challenged by the concept of orderliness. Thank you.

Despair Turned to Love

People magazine had a story about a woman whose life had been shattered when her beloved daughter took LSD and went on a crime spree, leaving one person dead and one paralyzed. After her daughter wound up in prison for a thirty-five-year sentence, this grieving mother spiraled into a long depression. She would visit her daughter, but the prison was a twenty-four-hour drive away. When she visited, she could see how in despair her daughter and the other inmates were and how much family contact helped her daughter to carry on.

She finally was able to fight her way out of depression when the idea came to her of a mission to bring hope and family time to women behind bars. The program, at a prison in Oklahoma, connects parents and grandparents on the inside with their kids and grandkids. She tapes an inmate reading a bedtime story and then sends the tape and the storybook to the family members.

One inmate, a grandmother, had never seen her grandchildren due to her son's unwillingness to connect. But when the son received the package, he was so moved that, for the first time, he brought his little son to meet his grandma. The program, called Tales for the Rising Moon, had served 130 inmates by the time of the magazine article. Making inmates part of their families again gives them hope and gives the children a connection of love.

Let us thank this kind woman for accepting her mission from God and let us envision more efforts like this taking place all over the world.

October 22

Nukes Must Go

I am worried today about nuclear weapons. First used in 1945, they stopped a war due to the world's horror at their unimaginable destructive force. But since World War II, the United States and Soviet Union began a cold war in which each side feared the other side would use them to destroy their enemy. Both nations foolishly kept producing more and more weapons until each side had tens of thousands. I was raised in that time of tension, following the directives in my school to hide under our desks in mock drills. Now I see that was totally goofy, since desks cannot do anything against nuclear bombs. But the practice was done to keep the population calm, as if we were prepared to survive the end of the world. I remember the Cuban Missile Crisis in the early sixties when the Soviets were moving nukes into Cuba until Jack Kennedy faced them down. That was the closest our world came to destroying itself.

So now it is decades later. Various treaties have diminished the stockpiles, but there are still thousands left in the United States and Russia, as well as some in a few other countries, as well as some countries trying to develop them. The US weapons are getting rusted, their delivery rockets are breaking down, and they are becoming dangerous, even if they are never intentionally fired.

Let us today envision the end of nuclear weapons all over the world. Nukes must go—now, now, now, now. Our world cannot heal while the threat of total annihilation hangs over all our heads. If you feel moved to take action on this cause, write to your congressperson, discuss it on social media, join a disarmament group. Envision these weapons melting away, like the wicked witch melted away. Gone, gone, gone.

The Fiery Furnace

Times of trouble, pain, anguish, and affliction are times when Spirit is cleansing us of impurities. They are times when we dwell in a fiery furnace.

Let us turn our thoughts today to those who dwell in the furnace of affliction. If this includes you, add yourself to the group as we work together in this projection. Let us send them projections of faith and strength that good shall come of this time as Spirit purifies the vessel and makes it ready to be filled with light.

Let us hold with those who suffer and help them to endure with patience, to bless the experience, surrender to it, and keep their vision firmly fixed on the beauty that will result as impurities are burned away, leaving only that which serve Spirit.

See I have refined you like silver, tested you in the furnace of affliction.

—Isaiah 48:10

Starsha Dawn

October 24

Scorpio—The Scorpion

Scorpions are small but dangerous. They seem quite willing to use their stinger tails to kill anyone approaching too closely. In astrology literature, Scorpios can be intense, powerful, forceful, passionate, secretive, obsessive, and jealous. Jeepers, what a load of negatives!

But if we look at the positive, there is great power to accomplish major things if the power can be harnessed. Those in history who accomplished great things harnessed power and directed it into thinking, working, creating, leading movements, and inventing.

Let's claim our Scorpio power today. Let's envision ourselves striding forth along our spiritual paths, strong and determined, feeling God's power inside, driving us onward. Let's be passionate about our great missions and let that passion fuel us through hard times. Let our Scorpio nature give us the will to keep going and never give up.

Sayings from the Lotus Shrine: Little Things

Another quote on the wall of the Lotus Shrine was:

> Even in the single leaf of a tree, or a tender blade of grass,
> The awe-inspiring deity manifests itself.
>
> —Urabe-No-Kane-Kani
> [Shinto Faith]

Nature—the manifestation of the many faces of Spirit. How often I feel the urge inside of me to be in nature, to be near the grandeur of woods and mountains and deserts and the ocean. How often I sit at a pinnacle looking out at a broad swath of magnificent scenery. But how little do I consider that the magnificence of creation is apparent in the small things—a leaf, a blade of grass.

In looking always at the big picture, perhaps I fail to look in detail at the little miracles that make up that picture. So today, please join me as I contemplate little things.

The river's essence is contained in each single drop of water—individual molecules of hydrogen and oxygen united into H_2O. All these molecules blend into a drop that flows in a unison of connection with its neighboring drops to form the flowing river that I love to watch.

Each leaf on the tree knows its duties to collect sunlight and make it into food for the tree, to give off oxygen as a by-product, to turn color in the autumn, and finally to fall as a papery, dry husk merging into the forest floor.

All the little things in creation know what to do and when and how to do it. They serve a greater whole. Spirit, please guide and direct me as you direct the leaf so that I, too, will know what to do and when and how, so I may serve the greater good.

Starsha Dawn

October 26

Lending a Hand

Many have gone before us on the path. Those we think of as great in their spirituality have traveled far beyond, have struggled, and in the struggle, they have learned and grown. That makes them great. But that is not the reason we remember them and look to them as beacons. We look to them because they have not left us behind in the dust of their passage up the mountain. They have turned around, paused in their personal journeys, and have bent down with a smile to lend us a hand in the climb.

For me, the image I hold is the master Jesus. For you, it may be another. What we know of them, we know because they stopped and turned around to teach us their stories and show us how to climb the steep parts of the path.

Let us realize we have done some traveling too. Let us follow the examples of the great ones and turn around when we are needed, to hold out our hands with a smile to our fellow travelers.

Selfies

I am totally puzzled to see that so many millions of people have acquired the habit of including themselves in every photo. Here is me on vacation, me in a restaurant, me on my couch. This seems to me a newly developing focus on the self—what I do, what I see, what I want.

I am hoping that, along with this new trend to show off what one is doing, there is not also a trend toward self-centeredness, what we used to call selfishness. There is way too much of that in this modern world. So today, let's add our thoughts and prayers so that all of us, selfie takers or not, remember to consider others. Let us project the thought that rather than focusing on self, we all look around and truly see others, what they want and need, what they are doing and what they have to say. Let's for today take ourselves out of the starring role in our lives and just be one of the crowd, looking at life as a whole picture instead of "Look at me. Here I am out in the world."

October 28

First Do No Harm

Let's focus on business today. In the Western world, business, especially big business, has typically been devoid of spiritual qualities. There has been no guiding intention of service to others. Big business has been like a man raised in the wild, aggressive without a moral code and often without manners, honesty, or compassion.

Let us envision this wild man becoming educated to be a good citizen, filled with love and obeying the laws of God. Some businesses are already beginning to use principles such as ecological consciousness, use of quality materials, and fairness to employees and to those who supply raw materials. These are beacons and examples to the rest. But so many of the rest have their eyes closed to the harm they've been causing.

So let us start them on their road to change by borrowing a motto from the medical profession, "First do no harm." To business, that includes doing no harm to customers (being honest in advertising, producing a quality product, owning up to and fixing product flaws, etc.). It includes doing no harm to the earth (eliminating harmful waste products of production, recycling, cutting down on excess packaging, limiting heat and noise pollution). It includes doing no harm to employees (creating a safe and clean workplace, paying decent wages).

There, that is a good first step. Let us visualize all businesses reevaluating and changing to fulfill their new motto, "First do no harm."

The Bully

Did your neighborhood or schoolyard have a bully? When you were little, was there a mean, big kid who would taunt you, chase you, even hit you or throw stones at you? "Hey you, pipsqueak! Momma's boy! Scaredy cat!" The bully would attack and perhaps push you to the ground, stealing your ball.

"What are you crying for? I'll give you something to cry about! Na-na-na-na-na. I've got your ball. What are you going to do about it?" If you try, you get shoved or smacked again. If you just cry, you hear, "Crybaby. Why don't you run home to your mommy?" Humiliated, you do run home, minus your ball, and minus your dignity and self-esteem. You think, *When I grow up, nobody is going to push me around.*

Well, that is what I thought too. But lately I've discovered that the schoolyard bully is alive and well. The bully went home with me to lie in wait to taunt me and push me down and call me names. The bully is inside of me.

It is the voice inside that tells me I can't, that I'm not good enough, that I don't deserve any better. Well, I've got news for you, bully. I am grown. And you don't scare me anymore. In fact, you'd better get lost or I'll come after you. Beat it!

October 30

The Three Tests

When Jesus was in the desert for forty days alone, the Bible says the devil tested him three times. These tests were designed to determine if he was ready for his mission or if his powers would be used for his own gain. The tests were to turn stones to bread as he was starving, to jump off a cliff and let God save him, and to be made the king of the world. These are tests of wealth, power, and glory. He passed the tests, as he knew God's powers were not meant to be misused for self-glory.

He became the servant of us all, using power to heal, refusing to amass wealth or to become a king, even when the public demanded it. He even refused to use divine power to release himself from suffering and a terrible death, as he knew that was not God's will for him.

How does this relate to us? Well, we all have some little power. We have some money, and we have some ability to talk to and persuade others individually or through social media. So today, let's look at how our own power and money are being used. Do you try to glorify your accomplishments and make sure people know of them? Do you think yourself better than other people? Do you hold on to money while being given a mission to be generous or help a cause? These are not worthy thoughts of a lightworker.

Today, let us pass the tests of turning aside from individual power and glory and accept our missions to be the servants of the world.

Signs of the New Age: Sandwiches

I heard a story of one wonderful man who saw a need and is trying his best to help. The need—hunger among homeless people. The project—first he obtained seventeen old refrigerators. Then he recruited donations of food from businesses. What does he do with the food? Every night, he prepares sandwiches and then drives around to streets where homeless people reside to give sandwiches to these people.

This man is persistent in his mission. He has personally delivered seven hundred thousand sandwiches so far. What a beautiful soul! Here is another lightworker, seeing a need and deciding that this need must be a mission for him.

Let us send God's blessings to this man whose name I do not know. Let us envision more and more good souls hearing Spirit's call to a mission to help others. Let's envision this waking up to missions and moving beyond thinking about it to actually deciding to do something. Whether the mission is to help people, animals, the environment, refugees, people who are ill or dying, or any other cause that Spirit gives out, let the lightworkers take up their missions and do whatever they can to help out. And what about you? Are you getting an inkling of a new mission or are you already involved in one? Bless you. Carry on.

November 1

A Beautiful City

I have had the pleasure of vacationing in two places that were perfectly clean. One was an artificial setting, Disney World, a place in which there is such a horde of picker-uppers that they can keep up with the garbage-dropping customers. Disney World is kept so clean that I could not even find a single gum wrapper on the well-swept streets.

The other place was a large city of over a million people, Vienna, Austria. I could walk through the business area of this lovely city and find no litter, no cigarette butts, no graffiti, and no dirt. This city did not have a horde of paid picker-uppers, like Disney World. They did not need them. For here, there was a sense of public pride, a sense of community. There was nothing to pick up because *nobody* would be so crass as to throw garbage on the street. There was no graffiti to clean up because nobody would dream of defacing public property. Nobody would snuff out a cigarette and leave it on the street. Nobody would break off a flower from the beautiful public displays.

In America, I am pleased to see groups of civic-minded citizens out on the streets and highways picking up garbage. It is a start, but it is the Disney World solution, and frankly, there aren't enough picker-uppers to keep up with the litterers in most places in this country.

Let us project to the heart of this problem. Let us visualize those folks who litter and who disrespect their public places as having a revelation—waking up and saying, "How disgusting my actions have been! How wrong I was! I won't ever do that again." One by one, they come to their senses; they at last become moved to respect their fellow citizens and to take pride in their surroundings. Let us see all our citizens in all our cities and towns become stewards of the land. Let us see all our cities and towns becoming as beautiful and clean as Vienna.

Former Friends

It's funny. I believe that we are all one, all of us on earth. I believe we should be loving each other with divine love—even the strangers in faraway lands. Yet, in spite of this, I find to my dismay that I have had to let go of a few people whom I have loved with a personal love. It is far easier to maintain an attitude of divine love toward strangers I've never met than it is to follow cosmic laws within a personal relationship, whether friend or lover. So there have been times when the people I loved and I have had to part.

Every one of these people is still loved by me, with both a divine love for their High Self and a personal feeling of heartbreak and loss of the relationship. Even if the relationship had negative aspects, I still remember and miss the good parts of it.

If you, too, have some people still in your mind and heart with whom you have parted, please join with me in my prayer today on behalf of all broken relationships. "Thank you, Spirit, for the opportunities you gave me in those relationships. Thank you for what I have learned. I also thank each of you, my former friends, for giving me experiences I needed to grow, for the happy times and even the sad and angry times. I now send my love to each of you with a belief that we are truly one in Spirit. If we meet again, let it be in love and reconciliation. And if we do not, I surround you all with light as you go your separate ways, and I wish you Spirit's blessings all the rest of your days."

November 3

Dealer's Choice

Okay, it is your turn. I've been dealing out the thought for the day, and you've been going along with my train of thought for most of the year now. But today, you are the dealer. You are in charge of choosing your own special project for the day.

There are so many things that need to be healed here—our planet, countries, businesses, families, relationships, ecology, science, politics, and of course our own weak points.

Stop a minute and see what topic comes to your mind. Let your thoughts flit about from topic to topic like a butterfly. Wait until Spirit and you settle on your very own topic for the day.

When you have it, announce it out loud. Then project in your own words or visualizations that Spirit is working through everyone involved to bring about the highest good for everyone in the situation. If you can do it, picture what the situation will look like after it is healed and hold the image.

Meanwhile, the rest of us will be supporting you in spreading light to the area you have chosen while you support us in ours.

Good work! Rest assured that you have helped to uplift us all.

Sayings from the Lotus Shrine: Be of Good Cheer

He who cheers up a person in difficulties, Allah will
cheer him up in this world and the next.

—Mohammed
The 42 Traditions of An-Nawawi

In reading this verse at the Lotus Shrine, I am struck by two concepts. First is the obvious one, that Spirit rewards us by doing the same good to us that we do to another. But there is a second message I see in the use of the phrase "cheer up." The author did not say "fix" this person's problem; did not say "come to the rescue"; did not say "take on this person's burden." No, it says "cheer up." I take that to mean that we are to be a friend with kind words, being there, doing what we can do to give some cheer to the person who is going through a hard time. But the person's problem is theirs to go through, not ours. I find peace in that and also a duty to be cheerful ourselves, not to echo the other person's distress in ourselves.

And what are we promised from Allah? To be cheered up, not to have our problems fixed or taken away. Allah is not promising that we will have no problems but is promising to be there to cheer us when we need it.

We learn the lessons this earth teaches by experiencing all sorts of things and learning to be steady and centered in Spirit through it all. Let us give thanks to know Spirit is always there to cheer us whenever we are down. And let us give thanks that we are part of Spirit's plan to cheer others when they experience the rough spots in their lives.

The Odometer

How well do you know your subconscious or soul? Our High Self and our masters and angels try continuously to give direction, and they do it through the conduit of the soul or subconscious. Your subconscious is beautiful. It keeps the digestive system going and your circulation flowing. It keeps your to-do lists, your memories, your emotions. And it obeys your conscious just as it obeys the High Self. Your subconscious lovingly and literally works to create for you whatever you think. This obedience can cause great difficulties if you have given negative orders such as, "I'm stupid, I never do things right, I'm too [whatever]."

You can closely connect with your subconscious. How? Since I'm on the road a lot, I decided to conduct an experiment to see if I could get my subconscious to notify me each time my odometer was about to turn over one hundred miles. I commanded it out loud several times to make me look at the odometer each time I reached a ninety-nine going to one hundred. It worked wonderfully. During this period, although I very seldom looked at the odometer, I found myself being strongly drawn to look at it when the ninety-nine was going into the hundred. It happened almost every time over the few years of the experiment. I was learning to hear better this still, small voice of the subconscious that is our guide and our supplier of hunches. This experiment showed me how closely the subconscious pays attention to what I say.

Would you like to give this a try? It doesn't have to be the odometer but should be something periodic that you otherwise would not pay attention to. And by the way, it would be a good idea to stop making negative decrees and replace them with positive ones—I am healthy, I am smart, whatever is the opposite of what you are getting rid of.

Dressed for Success

What's the best price you could hope to pay for a snappy Liz Claiborne suit, secondhand? For patrons of Lublin's Dress for Success New York in Manhattan, the answer is *free*. This is not a standard thrift shop. It is a nonprofit organization devoted to helping women referred by welfare agencies to obtain designer business clothing so they can go for job interviews.

The owner, Nancy Lublin, in a *People* magazine interview said she started the store with a $5,000 inheritance from her great-grandfather, who came to the United States with nothing but the clothes on his back. She has been quite successful in obtaining donations from corporations, designers, and a host of celebrity backers like Gloria Steinem, Rosie O'Donnell, and Oprah Winfrey who turn in their own clothes to the shop.

Not only is this shop booming, but Lublin has provided consultation to two other shops now open and three others soon to open. This very special woman devotes herself full-time to this endeavor, taking only a modest living expense from the enterprise.

Bless you, Nancy Lublin! You are surely doing Spirit's work. Lightworkers, let us send light to this enterprise and others like it and to the women who come through its doors on the way to their new lives.

November 7

Hurry, before It Is Too Late!

In the biblical parable of the weeds growing in the wheat field, Matthew said that the weeds and wheat must continue to grow side by side until the harvest, at which time they will be separated. That is why we see people who love and people who hate all mixed in together here on this planet.

We are near to the harvest time now. Those who choose the light of Spirit are standing side by side with those who choose the darkness. But soon they will be separated by the Harvester. That means some of our race of humankind who persist in following the darkness will be removed from incarnating anymore among us on earth, once the vibration of this planet is raised by those who choose love. They will be lost to us, and we will proceed in our evolution without them. You may say, "Good riddance. They are evil people."

Well, unlike real weeds that cannot change their nature, these brothers and sisters of ours are actually spiritual beings like the rest of us but cloaked in darkness of their own choosing. Let us have compassion for the spirit within them and cry out to them one more time, "Leave the darkness. Take our hands and come toward the light. Hurry, before it is too late!"

Fabulous

I pass a coworker in the hall, and I say, "How are you?" "Fabulous," he answers. I'm so tickled by his gleeful, upbeat answer that I've decided to adopt it myself. I'm going to create some great answers to that standard question of greeting. I really want to be fabulous, and if I say it, I believe I will begin to feel it. So, over the next several days, I try out several of these: glorious, divine, wonderful, perfect, stupendous, delightful. Each time I say one of these, I get a surprised smile from my greeter, and yes, I really do feel that way. The more I say it, the happier I feel. And the reaction I get only serves to add even more to my upbeat mood.

Want to join me? Are you feeling fabulous? No? Say it anyway. As they say in Alcoholics Anonymous, "Fake it till you make it." Go on. I dare you. Say it and embrace it—become it. Your aches and pains don't matter to your wonderful mood. Refuse to feel awful. Refuse to feel so-so or pretty good or okay. They aren't good enough for you anymore. Okay. Here's your chance to practice in private with me before you try this on others. "So how are you today?"

"I'm _____!"

November 9

Dissolving the Mountain of Little Papers

Remember my experiment with my subconscious, having it notify me of each hundred-mile turnover on the odometer of my car? I'd like to say a little more today on this topic of giving commands to the subconscious. All day every day, we are thinking. We go over things in our heads, rehash past conversations, worry about the future, and generally have a stream of often negative talk going on. Think of all the years we have been doing this and all the sentences we said that our subconscious has heard and tried to obey.

In short, we have a lot of trash in our subconscious. And not only from things we have said or thought, but if we accepted something negative that was said to us—by a parent, a boss, a spouse, or a teacher, for example—our subconscious believed it all. We may have tried putting in positive affirmations, but they fall into the collection of everything else, like a giant mountain of little strips of paper with a sentence written on each one. That mountain of papers is sitting there, sapping our energy and our self-esteem as our subconscious tries to figure out what we really want to be, to think, to do, to become.

Today is housecleaning day for the mountain of little papers in our heads. We may know some of them if they have been routinely spoken or thought, but others are inaccessible to us. Not a problem. We can enlist our subconscious to do the job for us. "Dear subconscious, I would like you to consult with my High Self and submit *all* my sentences for review." Follow the command of our High Self to cancel or keep whatever you are directed. "And dear subconscious, this decree is permanent. Only keep things that my High Self approves. I will do my best not to say negatives, but if I do, ignore me, as I don't really mean it."

Okay, say this loudly to really make it clear to the subconscious you are serious and giving a permanent command. Then let it go and know that your mountain of little negative papers is being dissolved. What a relief! And, oh yes, make it a plan to stop saying negative things about yourself.

November 10

God's Love

God shows us love through the touch of a loved one's hand, the welcoming greeting of a dog, the pink of the sunset, and the gold of an autumn leaf. God shows us love through the song of a bird and the kiss of a summer breeze. God shows us love through the silent white blanket of new fallen snow and the blossoming of spring flowers. God shows us love through the twinkling of diamond stars against a velvet sky.

We have but to look, to listen, to notice—and there is God, all around us and in the beating of our hearts.

We show God love through our kindness to strangers, our smile at a baby, our service to each other and to the earth. Jesus said, "Feed my sheep." Can we do that? Can we truly love, without judgment of who is worthy? Just as God truly loves us all.

November 11

The Little Things

Do you ever do a slapdash, poor job of housecleaning? Such as wiping off the kitchen counter but not the sink? I sometimes do. Do you ever vacuum the floor but don't go under the tables or neglect to stoop and pick up that one piece of lint that the vacuum just can't suck up? I sometimes do. Do your children do this, and does it get you annoyed?

Well, so, who cares really? What does housecleaning have to do with spirituality? I think of it this way. If I am going to take on a menial job, I should strive to do it well, just as I would a very important job. Why? I see everything we do (and say and think) as part of our spiritual development.

I don't always get it right, but I try, when I do these tasks like cleaning or weeding or filing, to think of these efforts as metaphors for orderliness and cleanliness of mind and spirit. For instance, when I weed, I say to myself (sometimes out loud too) that I am rooting out resentment and anger. When I clean, I think, *I am cleaning up my thoughts*. If I can have integrity in the little things, it helps me grow. Would you join me?

Lightwork—Legislatures

Today, let's unite our focus to project light to all those who serve in any sort of local, state, national, or international political bodies (legislatures, school boards, Congress, etc.). Let's envision a huge group of legislators all sitting in an auditorium while we lecture them.

"We are happy you came to listen today, despite your busy schedules. We are here to remind you of some key aspects of your mission.

- You are there to serve the people.
- You are to live by the golden rule.
- You are to act with the highest level of integrity and honesty.
- You are to put aside your own personal desires (such as being reelected) in favor of doing right.
- Along with your power comes responsibility. What kind of responsibility?
    o   to be stewards of the earth, helping it heal rather than exploiting it
    o   to do all you can to ensure that people who are poor, sick, old, children are cared for
    o   to keep a humble heart and to remember that you are a servant, not a master

We thank you for listening. We encourage you to live by these precepts every day."

November 13

The Styrofoam Cup

When I was young, if I wanted a drink of water in a public building, I could pull down a tiny paper cup and fill it up. Those cups were weak and would collapse and leak. Then a big innovation came about, the discovery of Styrofoam. Gee, we loved these much better cups; they didn't leak at all. And so vendors all over the country rushed to replace paper with it. At the same time, another item was slated for the trash heap—paper drinking straws. For those of you who are too young to remember those, they were the only straws in your drink at the soda fountain. They too were weak and often got a kink and stopped working. Gee, we thought ourselves modern when we got rid of those in favor of that wonderful new thing—plastic! Soon plastic and Styrofoam were everywhere. You could no longer find a paper straw or a paper cup.

And of course, both Styrofoam and plastic are made out of petroleum oil. Back then, we didn't think about the everlasting nature of these products and how they would turn themselves into immortal mountains of trash not only in our landfills but often making their way to huge garbage piles floating on the oceans.

Now I see a new recognition coming to us all that plastic and Styrofoam are not good for the earth. I got an ice cream in a little dish recently and noticed that the dish was made out of some sort of sturdy paper. I see signs now everywhere that businesses are trying to not use so much plastic. We are migrating out of plastic and Styrofoam dependence to using products that are better for our world. Now I can get a cup of coffee in a paper cup.

And this is only one trend in the ongoing awakening of businesses that what they develop and sell us must become cleaner and better for us and for the planet. Let us envision the success of these efforts, so that one day we will be free of plastic and Styrofoam and free of the garbage mess they create.

Sayings from the Lotus Shrine: Love that Floods the River

We go back to look at another quote from the shrine today:

> Let your love be like misty rain, coming softly but flooding the river.
> —Zulu, *Madagascar*

Let us celebrate love, soft as misty rain. There are many loves—of one's spouse, one's family, one's country. There is love of beauty and music and art, love of this world, this universe, and, of course, love for the Creator of it all. For a love as soft as mist to flood the river, it must rain on and on constantly for a long time.

Can we be soft in our love, as soft as mist? Can we be constant in love, enough to flood the river?

Join me and hold the image and the feeling of your love being so soft, so tender, enveloping the objects of your love with a lovely mist. Feel the quiet peacefulness that the softness of your love brings.

Set your soft love in motion to rain down constantly on all people you hold beloved—on and on and on your love falls upon your loved ones. They feel it and absorb it even if they are not consciously aware of it.

Hold this soft, steady love for the earth and all that live upon it. This love floods over and heals all things. It is all around you too. It flows through your being and makes you smile with joy that you are beloved, that you are one with all others, bathed in the soft mist of love.

November 15

Expectations

At age twenty-two, I was a social worker for a cottage of fifty-nine teenage girls in a large institution for people with profound intellectual disabilities. Most of the fifty-nine had been dropped off at our place by their parents shortly after birth, as was the custom in those days. These girls had been raised in an institution and had never been in a house. Many were aggressive, screaming, slapping themselves, hitting others, smearing feces. Most were so disabled as to have no verbal language.

One day, the director of nursing came to our cottage to introduce a wealthy older man. He said he and his wife were recently retired and their children were grown. They were lonely for young people in the house, and they wanted to foster some of our girls. I looked at him with utter disbelief, as did other staff who heard this. He toured and met the girls. Together he and I picked out three girls who had no families. They were to have an afternoon visit that, if successful, would be followed by a weekend and then eventual permanent residence.

The day came. A nurse aide, three excited girls, and I arrived in the van. We were welcomed in, and the aide and I immediately were horrified at what the girls would do, as the house was filled with expensive breakables and fine furniture. The girls sat on the couch in front of a glass coffee table. Next the wife brought all of us iced tea in crystal stemware. The girls somehow knew how to be careful and respectful, and the visit turned out just fine. Eventually, this couple fostered the girls.

I learned a lesson of a lifetime—that beautiful expectations can develop beautiful behavior. Do our negative expectations ever keep beautiful behavior from happening?

Cruise Control

On highways, I love using my car's cruise control to keep me going at the right speed, neither too fast nor too slow. Once this is set, I can enjoy driving without constantly looking at my speed. Hmm, maybe I need a cruise control in my life, keeping me from being too fast or too slow. What do I mean? Well for me, too fast would be jumping into a decision without taking proper time to think about it. In stores, the merchandise is cleverly arranged to get us to do just that, to pick something up on an impulse without thinking if I need this or want this. Car dealers do this too, telling us once we are in their clutches that if we buy right now, we will take advantage of some special offer. I am getting better at resisting this too-fast concept. Once, I bought on impulse a time-share that wasn't even built. That was a disaster, with monthly payments on something I should not have bought, couldn't use, and surely didn't need. But I don't do things like that anymore.

So what does the too-slow concept mean to me? Well, sometimes I can be too slow in accepting an invitation so that I miss opportunities to have fun, meet new people, do interesting things that I have not done before. For example, a lady whom I barely knew through business invited me to vacation with her. I thought it odd since I didn't know her well. Usually I would say no, but this time I said yes and found we had a very good time and got to be good friends.

So I must remember to keep my cruise control on so I can be just right, not too slow or too fast. How about you?

November 17

In a Mess

"This is a real mess, and I don't know what to do."

When we hit the rough spots, it is natural to want the pain and problems to just go away. When faced with a spiritual crisis that tests our resolve and darkens our path, we should just hold tight and take no action, make no decision until we know spiritually what we should and must do. At those times, Spirit is aware of our pain, and Spirit will provide direction and courage if we allow it in. We are being tested, but we are also being guided.

Suppose you are working at a company and you know the CEO is lying about profits, or suppose you work for a building contractor and see the boss using substandard materials and techniques that endanger the building and its inhabitants. What do you do when chaos is all around, when others have dropped their integrity for material gain or someone is lying and cheating?

Or suppose you and your business partner are faced with temptation to do wrong to get yourself out of a mess. These are times when our spirituality runs smack into our messy problems. The right answer is always the same: integrity.

Corporate executives are constantly faced with the temptation to behave unethically or illegally to increase profits, hide wrongdoing, or boost egos. Sometimes they are caught red-handed and punished. Sometimes they get away with it. Or do they?

Today, let us direct our thoughts and prayers to support right action.

The Nation of God

Today, I call forth the citizens of the nation of God. It is pretty easy to be a citizen of a country, either by being born there or moving there and filling out the paperwork.

But to be citizens in the nation of God, we undertake responsibilities:

- to surrender our will to divine will
- to act toward all people with respect as equals
- to forgive everyone for everything
- to embrace cooperation instead of competition
- to acknowledge every one of us as a divine child of God, no matter our outward appearance or actions
- to act as stewards of the earth, caring for animals, plants, air, and water
- to be courteous, kind, loving, charitable, and honorable in all our thoughts, words, and interactions.

Let us all say today, "Yes, I am a citizen of the nation of God!"

November 19

Signs of the New Age: Little Homes

I saw a video on Facebook about a kind and creative man who has made it his mission to do something to help homeless people. This man was moved when he saw so many people living directly on the sidewalks, covered only with tarps or cardboard boxes as they shivered in the rain and snow. This man figured out what he could do, in spite of his limited finances.

He regularly visited the local dump, looking for discarded building materials. He gathered these materials and created out of them tiny living quarters that were up off the ground, with a floor, a roof, walls, and a door to keep out the weather and provide some privacy. When he finishes one of his creations, he locates a homeless person and gives it to them. True, these little places don't have plumbing or electricity, but they are a big step up from lying unprotected on the street corner.

And the video showed how happy it made people to trade their ramshackle setups for clean and dry dwellings. I could see not only gratitude on their faces but a sparkle of dignity in their eyes. They realized someone saw them, instead of ignoring them like most people do. The understood that a fellow human found them worthy and not a discard of society.

Today, let us thank good people who get up off their couches to serve others. These are the lightworkers, making a better world. Let's join them in our own way.

The Wisdom of the Little Ones

No wonder they don't always listen to their elders. Who? The little children, the two-year-olds. They are totally absorbed in living. We watch them and think we know what they are doing and what they are thinking. Oh really?

They see the world from near to the floor. If we sit with a little child and see her intently gazing at a framed photo, we may think she is looking at the picture. Well, maybe instead she is studying the wood frame. The truth is we don't know what is going through that two-year-old mind because we are trapped in our adult perspective of naming and judging everything.

I think of these little children as anthropologists discovering a new land. They come across many artifacts without a clue as to their purpose. Sometimes they figure out an item and learn to use it as we do, but maybe they think about an item in a new way, free of preconceptions and rules. We can learn from their freedom to just be, to just observe life without judging everything.

If you can, get down on the floor and watch a tiny child explore. Let go of naming everything—this is a couch, a rattle, a piece of lint. Just see, just experience life as this child does for a little while. Perhaps the little ones show us a different kind of wisdom, the kind that accepts life as it is, pure and simple.

November 21

Just Listen

I sat in my office cubicle just behind a hallway with a water cooler. Every day, a group of men gathered there to chat. Since they couldn't see me, they didn't know I was listening to their man conversation, since I always wondered what men talk about when it is just men. I listened to them for six months. After the first few days, I realized that I never heard them listening to each other. Instead, they seemed intent on waiting till a speaker took a breath so they could jump in with a story of their own. It was a competitive endeavor, each vying with the others for their talk time. Never did they react with further questions. Never did they ask for further information. Nor did they offer a reaction, an acknowledgment, or sympathy.

I thought to myself, *This is a bad sort of conversation. It is more like a series of announcements—my new car, my daughter graduated, I fixed the sink, on and on.* And so, I thought, perhaps I should do some listening to what I am saying in conversations. Am I conversing, reacting, or just announcing?

So I ask you this too. Are you listening or just waiting for a chance to jump in? Take note today of your style when a group conversation takes place. Do you let the talker finish? Do you use body language to encourage them along (nodding, eye contact)? Do you use the best listening tool—silence? When your conversational partner seems to be finished, they may not be really done but merely sorting their thoughts. Try keeping quiet for several seconds to see if they add more to their story. That's not easy for me in this speedy world, but I intend to try, and I invite you to try it too.

Goliath

In the Bible, David, a shepherd boy, faces a giant warrior, Goliath. David seems to be so unprepared, so small and weak, and Goliath seems so strong and confident and skilled in the arts of battle. Yet David uses a skill he gained as a shepherd of throwing a stone with a slingshot he had used to keep his sheep safe from wolves. He threw his stone and killed the giant.

And so I ask you, which sin is your Goliath? Is it greed, gluttony, anger, envy, pride, lust, or laziness? Usually one of these will stand out as the one that is the largest problem, the strongest opponent of our spirituality.

Today, let us all see ourselves as David, ready to do battle with our Goliath. Although we may seem small and weak, we are not, as God guides us on our path to become better people. Let us take up our stones and swing them to hit our Goliath right in the eye and kill him.

Let us declare, "I am no longer subject to this bad quality. I reject it and replace it with right thought and action to follow God's plan for my life."

November 23

Sagittarius—The Archer

The symbol for the astrological sign of Sagittarius is the centaur, a being half-human and half-horse, joined inseparably together. The centaur is an apt metaphor for our race on this planet after the Fall, our higher nature combined with our inhabitation of physical animal bodies. The strangeness of the combination of two different creatures connected into one shows the incongruity of our fall into the third-dimensional world of matter, leaving behind our natural state as spiritual beings and taking on an animal vehicle to function on this dense material plane.

Yet the choice of a horse for the animal part of us is a positive metaphor. We are not depicted as connected to a tiger, symbol of passions and aggressiveness, nor to a turkey, nor to a mouse, with their obvious connotations. We are connected to the horse, a noble animal of speed, grace, and power, an animal that can be domesticated to obey and to carry us swiftly along our chosen path.

Today let us all be Sagittarians. Let us see our earthly physical connection as the horse on which we ride through this earthly experience, while our higher nature, the archer, aims its bow to shoot an arrow toward heaven.

Having It Your Way

There is a hamburger commercial that says, "Have it your way." That's fine for ordering a burger, but what about wanting everything to go our way, for life to proceed as we please? Doesn't that sound great? Sure!

But it is false, a dream. Not only can't we force everything to be our way, but even if we could, we would miss out on some of Spirit's plans for an even greater outcome.

I once had a chance at two internship jobs. One was near my aging parents in a small city. The other was farther away in a big metropolis. I have always found big cities scary and not places I would ever want to live. I longed for internship job #1, but they rejected me, and #2 accepted me. I had to force myself to accept job #2, but that job has led to wonders I could not have even dreamed of. Having it my way, I would have missed the wonderful plan Spirit had for my life.

Jesus taught us, "Thy will be done." Not having it our way but surrendering to whatever Spirit has planned for us is the best way to live. Can you surrender to Spirit's way?

November 25

On the Road

The weather forecast was grim: snow, sleet, and freezing rain. It was supposed to arrive in the late afternoon, but I looked outside my window at 9 a.m., and it had started to snow hard and fast. It was sticking to the road already. I thought of a friend who had told me she planned to travel today into the mountains of West Virginia. She was planning to leave this morning, before the weather hit Maryland.

So I called her to see if she had gone on her trip. I got no answer but left a message. Suddenly, a flood of worry hit me as I pictured her driving into an unexpected storm. Then I realized that worry wouldn't do either of us any good, but prayer would help us both. So I pictured her in her car and wrapped her in light—and her car too. And I held that visualization for a while until I felt the adrenaline of worry leaving me. As it happened, my friend soon called in the middle of my prayers to tell me she had decided not to go and was home safe. She had been shoveling when I called, and she called me back as soon as she got my message, since my voice sounded worried.

This reminded me of all those who really go out on roads in bad weather. Please join with me to pray for those who are on the road when conditions are bad. Let us visualize them wrapped in light and their cars or trucks or buses too. Let us visualize them protected by angels as they complete their journeys safely.

Now let us send light to the roadways themselves, so that all who drive on the roads drive in the light of God, being careful, being polite, looking out for bad conditions, and looking after anyone who needs help. Let us see all those ribbons of roads crossing our nation as ribbons of light. Isn't that a pretty sight?

Signs of the New Age: The Guardians

In Chicago, a group of veterans were having trouble finding their purpose after military service. They talked it over and decided that the neighborhoods nearby were dangerous. There were frequent attacks, thefts, muggings, and so on. They decided that, too often, children were caught up in the violence as they tried to walk to and from school.

So the nonprofit organization Leave No Veteran Behind developed the Safe Passage Program to provide assistance for veterans while protecting children and reducing youth violence. Group members stake out dangerous blocks and stand on the street corners to guard the kids and keep them safe from harm. They use walkie-talkies to call each other for help when violence is breaking out, and together they put a stop to it.

These guardians serve our nation, one block at a time. Let's bless these noble souls and send them our prayers that they find their way in society and our thanks that they protect the next generation.

Turn Around

Once you have grown, you cannot un-grow;
Once you have known, you cannot un-know.

There is no turning back to past days,
No picking up again past ways.

The self you've outgrown
You must discard.
Or else there's no room for new you,
And your path would be too hard.

Say farewell to your past;
It is over and done.
Your great leap to the future
Has already begun.

Never can another
Do your thinking for you,
For you are finding for yourself
What is right and true.

Do not stand with your eyes on your past.
It is autumn leaves on the ground.
All you need to go forward
Is ... turn around, turn around.

Gratitude

Today, let's look back along our spiritual path. Let us remember those who assisted us, taught us, and inspired us. Let us for a moment review what they did for us, and let us express our gratitude. They might include those who actually were in our lives, and they might also include those whose lives inspired us from afar. They might include authors of books that meant so much to us or even movies or TV shows that showed us how to progress on our path to greater spirituality and greater acceptance of our role as healers of the earth.

We are who we are because of what we have received from these wonderful people. We don't walk the path alone. Many go before us, leaving us wisdom. Many go along with us, growing and learning together, even if they are not physically present. One inspiration for me is Kahlil Gibran and his book *The Prophet*. That book and its wisdom is something I recall again and again when his words match a situation in my life or the life of a friend. I'll bet you have your inspirations too.

Today, let us thank the wise ones and express to them our gratitude for helping us move forward on our paths.

November 29

Responsibility

Why do the CEOs of major corporations make so much money? Are they smarter than most people? Are they more gifted? Braver? Stronger? Perhaps they may be, but the reason for the pay is not their abilities but the fact that they have been entrusted with very big and complex responsibilities—to manage present operations and forge bright futures, making critical decisions that will guide the actions of many and result in large gains if they choose right, or losses if they are wrong.

How does that apply to any of us non-CEOs? Well, let's look at the responsibilities in our lives. Being a good student, a good citizen, a good worker, a good parent, a good person. These are major responsibilities. They are complex, and they require diligence, character, determination, an eye for details and a view of the big picture, courage to act in accordance with cherished beliefs, and patience to hear opposing viewpoints with an open mind.

Sometimes the complexity of what is required of us can feel burdensome. But let us turn that feeling around and give thanks that we have been given responsibilities that will help us grow, learn, and achieve worthwhile goals.

The master Jesus has set forth some complex and difficult responsibilities for us. He has told us, "Feed my sheep, obey the commandments, and most important, love one another as I have loved you." Whatever your belief system, these are beautiful goals. Let us accept these commands and all our personal responsibilities with joy and determination to do them wholeheartedly, day by day.

November 30

How Fast He Grows!

I've had the privilege of watching a young boy change from an infant to a toddler to a school boy. Always, I marveled, "Look how fast he grows!" It astounded me how many things he learned in such a short time—crawling, walking, running, talking, counting, using a sharp knife and a hammer, drawing, singing, and on and on.

Why does he grow so fast while I grow so slowly? Here's what I see in him:

1. He is completely open to growth.
2. He has no fear of trying, missing the mark, and trying again and again.
3. It never occurs to him to stop where he is.
4. He has a boisterous joy in accomplishing his mission of growing.
5. He doesn't need to read books to learn what to do next. He just knows.

I think you and I can learn a few things from this youngster—don't you?

December 1

The Mountainside

Today, I sit in the early morning at a beautiful, peaceful place. Let me share it with you. Come with me to this place to start your day in peace.

I am on top of a small cliff about five stories high, overlooking a glassy blue lake about two miles wide. Across the lake are three gentle peaks of a mountain, fully forested with majestic firs. A cloud has floated in from the right and has gotten itself nestled up against the right flank of the first peak. The sky overhead is rows and rows of cirrus clouds, fluffy as sheep. A small wisp of a cloud has gotten itself snagged on the middle peak. At my feet, wild daisies dot the edge of the cliff. Many birds are singing. In the distance, a goose honks as it flies by.

Sit here with me awhile in this beautiful place. Take this grandeur and peace and install it in your heart. Center yourself with this vision. Now bring a loved one mentally into this place with you, then some others, until finally the whole world stands here with us, silent and awestruck with the peace that flows into our hearts.

God's Waldos

When I was in college, I toured its nuclear reactor. Since things were so dangerous down under the deep pool of water, humans couldn't get near it. Instead they used mechanical hands that sensed what a pair of real human hands in special gloves were doing in a safe space. The mechanical hands mimicked the action down in the reactor that the human was performing in the protected zone. Grasping and removing spent rods and replacing them with new ones as a remote-control operation was fascinating for me to watch.

Later, I learned that scientists working with dangerous materials often sat behind glass and used similar mechanical hands to perform tasks in the danger area. I was told that these mechanical hands are called Waldos, after a disabled character in a Robert Heinlein science fiction novel who invented mechanical hands to assist his own weak hands.

This might seem an odd topic for us, but consider this. God does the same thing in creating a physical being—us—to use as God's hands to operate in this world. If I think of myself as one of God's Waldos, then I realize that I can act as God's hands in the world. But only if I give over my mortal will to God's will and surrender these hands to be used. Sounds like a great idea to me. Will you join me and be a Waldo too?

December 3

The Chocolate-Chip Cookie

I was once offered just one bite of a friend's extra-large chocolate-chip cookie. As a joke, I opened my mouth wide and took my one bite all the way up to her finger. Well, was that ever a mistake! In addition to my friend being peeved, I had another issue. My mouth was full all the way to the back of my throat, and I could hardly chew without choking myself. That is a classic example of biting off more than I could chew, a habit I once had that applied to much of my life, not just to eating cookies.

Here was my pattern. If I had a nice three-day weekend coming up, I would develop a list of chores as long as my arm, like painting a room, filing the whole pile of unfiled receipts, ironing everything, weeding the whole garden, and so on. I would start off with gusto, digging into the first task. After a couple hours, it would become apparent to me that one of these big tasks could easily take the whole three days. I would quickly get discouraged but would persevere with my list until I was exhausted.

Now I don't do that anymore. I have a better grasp of how long things take and a better understanding that I need rest and recreation as much as accomplishment of my to-do list.

Think over your own pattern. Are you biting off more than you can chew?

Nemesis

Today, it is time to do a little work on coming closer to unconditional love. Sounds good, right? We can do that, right? It is not the easiest thing to do, but here we go. Pick a person in your life whom you dislike—your nemesis. (If there is absolutely no one in your life whom you dislike, congratulations. You are more advanced than most of us. You can instead pick a public figure whom you dislike, or who is disliked by many on earth.)

Here's what we are going to do in this meditative exercise. Picture yourself and this person sitting at a large conference table, across from each other. Perhaps you squirm a little as you look into this person's eyes. Now, more people are coming into the room. Your High Self and the other person's High Self enter first, look at each other with love, embrace, then proceed to sit down—yours next to you and theirs next to them. Now, in come the angels, teachers, and guides of both of you. They likewise greet all others with loving embraces and then stand behind each of you—yours behind you and theirs behind them.

Hmmm, all these beings seem to love one another. They beam with the joy of Spirit. Look at them watching you to see what happens. They are sending you and the other person streams of light of beautiful colors. You feel the peace and joy this light brings, and you smile at the other person.

Hold this feeling and image a little while. Forgive the individual you are envisioning. Now when you see them the next time, let the images and feelings come back to memory. Realize you are being watched by many higher beings as you encounter the person. No matter what the other person says or does, try your best to hold to a steadfast vision of their High Self, guides, and angels, present and watching with love. Hold love in your heart for the High Self of this person and hold hope that the lower, conscious self that is facing you can feel the love and now or someday respond with a softening toward you. As the person departs from you, send peace and smile at their back. Maybe, just maybe, they will smile someday too.

December 5

Stored Energy

A car's battery is a form of stored energy. It just sits there until you turn the key in the ignition. Then it transforms its stored energy into active energy, providing power to start the engine.

Money is also a form of stored energy. It just sits there waiting for someone to take action and use it. Today, let's look at money in this new way as stored energy we use, not only to get by in this world but to heal and uplift the world and its people.

First, let's concentrate on large sums of money that rich people are holding in storage, in investments or banks. They have more stored money than is needed for them to have food and shelter and fun and security about the future. Let's unite with those people who are storing more money than they will ever need and shine Spirit's light on them. Let's picture them being inspired with ideas for using more of their money for the public good than they do now.

Now we can turn our attention to ourselves. We acknowledge that all we have belongs to Spirit, loaned to us to be used for our needs and for good works. All that we give lifts the world to a higher place. Let us renew our commitment to give all we can to help others. Let this stored energy of money become active, as people who are storing it start using it to help others and to heal the earth.

The Itch

My right shin has an itch. It calls for help. My right hand asks the torso to bend over so it can reach the shin. Ah—scratch, scratch, scratch. Relief!

As I observe this, it seems so simple and elegant how my body parts cooperate to get the job done. So does my shin feel guilty at asking for help? Does it feel unworthy? Does it make plans to repay my right hand? What could my shin do to help my hand anyway?

We know the answers. No, my shin just accepts the pleasure of the scratch as something it needs and deserves. No need for thanks, for repayment. Why? Because I am one body, not separate parts.

Well, guess what? We are all one. We are part of Spirit. So let us be truly one. Let us act as one. How?

Whoever cries out to us has been placed in our path for a reason. Let us truly practice the philosophy of helping each other as effortlessly as my hand helps my shin.

To each according to need, from each according to ability is a thought I associate with Marxist philosophy. They preached that concept but failed to enact it because it takes a spiritual awakening, not government edicts. So let us be the ones to enact this noble concept. And when we are on the receiving end, let us be as innocently grateful as my shin and not indebted or feeling unworthy of the help. Spirit sends us to each other so we can help and be helped.

December 7

All People Are Our Teachers

I settled in to a long cross-country flight with a promise to myself to write three pages of this book before I relaxed and did other things, such as sleeping, reading, or doing puzzles. The man in my row noticed I was busy writing and asked about the book. I let him read a few pages to get the flavor of it.

Pretty soon, he started offering me stories he uses in the business training he provides. I found his stories to be great ideas, and I busily took notes for future pages while he talked.

And, to boot, there was still enough time to complete my task of writing three pages. If I had been silent and distant in order to complete my task, I would have missed out not only on his ideas but on the opportunity to connect with a great guy and to receive some encouragement from him about the book.

I realized what a gift we humans can be to each other when we give each other a chance. And I realized that opportunities to learn from another can come at unexpected times and places. Thank you, fellow traveler, for teaching me this. Now I can keep an eye out for future opportunities to connect and learn. I hope you can too.

Sayings from the Lotus Shrine: Soft Strength

Practice yielding and develop strength.
—Lao Tzu

I look at this saying, and at first, it seems almost incomprehensible. If he is talking about physical strength, that's not how I've been taught to develop it. At my health club, the trainers encourage lifting weights, heaving, straining, and sweating.

So what is this about? A friend of mine who studies martial arts tells me that they are taught to roll with a blow and let the person's blow meet not resistance but their turning and yielding. This throws the attacker off balance and their own momentum, then knocks them down.

But is this what Lao Tzu meant? Or is he also talking about moral strength, strength of character that flows with the changes in life's flow and, as we Westerners say, doesn't sweat the small stuff?

Then again, maybe it means still other things. Maybe it carries a different message for each of us. Think it over. What does it mean to you?

December 9

Pronouncements of Doom

Some people I know have a habit of thinking the worst about the future. For them, worry is an art form. Give them any set of circumstances, and they can immediately find some aspect of that situation to worry about. For those really top-notch worriers, they can simultaneously worry about several dozen possible future scenarios for different people, even for people they've never met.

They have a library of pronouncements of doom:

- Get back; you'll fall off the ledge.
- You'll drown if you go in the water now.
- Stay off the road on holidays; a drunk could hit you.

And so many other worried pronouncements. These pronouncements have power over their thinking. They are pretty sure the dire event really will happen, and it drives them nuts with worry. They also have the result of being afraid and making their children afraid to live life.

Think back over the conversations you had yesterday—even ones in your head. Were there any pronouncements of doom, however small? If you had any, it is time to start working on replacing worry with faith that we are in God's hands and with a prayer for safety instead of the worried response.

One good way to start the change is to catch yourself as you are making a pronouncement of doom. First, cancel the thought by saying or thinking, "No, I don't know that to be true." Then replace the thought with a positive statement that thanks Spirit for taking care of the situation and for helping you not to worry so much.

December 10

Signs of the New Age: "Forgive Us"

On TV, I watched a story about the Roman Catholic Church in France. During World War II, France was occupied by the Nazis. The French Vichy government was responsible for sending many French Jews to the death camps. In the show I was watching, the French Catholic Church spokesman admitted the Church knew of this atrocity but did nothing. The spokesman said, "Because of our silent complicity, innocents were killed. We ask to be pardoned."

I believe this is an extraordinary example of the desire to cleanse the past by being sorry and asking forgiveness. In this case, different people are in charge from those who were silent, but because they represent the same organization, they decided they were responsible to ask for forgiveness. It is true that this asking for forgiveness doesn't take away the tragedy, but it indeed is a public acknowledgment of wrong action, and as such, I believe it is a good sign that this world is uplifting its consciousness and realizing the wrongness of what has been done.

I expect to see more of this as members of various organizations and even governments come to realize that members of their group have committed grave errors in the past. Let us send light to strengthen those who turn back to take stock of the past and of actions that members of their group have done. And let us send light to the descendants of those people who were wronged, that they can find it in their hearts to do the forgiving and letting go of the errors that have been committed so many times in so many eras in our long and bloody history.

December 11

Your Real Job

Let's talk about the place where you are employed. If you are not employed, concentrate on a place where you go to school or where you spend time as a volunteer. Picture yourself entering this place. Close your eyes and feel the vibrations of the other people individually and collectively as a group.

You, as a lightworker, have a real job here—to bring more light to this place. Please make these affirmations with me:

I project light to uplift these people:

1. So that all lying is replaced with the truth;
2. So that all cheating is replaced with honest work;
3. So that all bickering is replaced with cooperation and helpfulness;
4. So that hatreds and dislikes are replaced with tolerance and respect.

I pledge to be a shining example of all these affirmations today and every day.

Now envision the changed place. See and hear and feel and know how wonderful it has become—pats on the back instead of stabs in the back, laughter instead of nastiness, service to others instead of attempts to cheat or deceive, excellent products instead of shabby ones.

This image may be far from the truth today, but it will come true if you hold the light. Will you?

Sayings from the Lotus Shrine: Trip to the Market

> We are on a market trip on Earth, whether we fill our
> baskets or not, once the time is up, we go home.
> —Ibo People of Nigeria

What a lovely concept—our lifetime on earth pictured as a trip to a bountiful market with much to look at and much to select. In we come at birth with empty baskets to be filled with whatever we choose to purchase. We can walk along just looking and looking, or we can stop and decide we want something and pay for it and put it in our basket. We can't carry everything the earth has to offer, but we can fill our life's baskets with things gained—patience, love, beauty, compassion, knowledge and wisdom, strength, growth, varied experiences, and lessons learned. Or we can just look and not get anything. Or we can be so enamored with all the treasures on display that we run from booth to booth, wanting it all but stuck in confusion, not knowing what to buy and what to leave behind.

And how do we pay for what we select? Not with money but with the very days of our lives. We pay years to learn, years to grow, years to experience the results of our choices. But even if we make no choices and move through the market in a fog, our time is eventually up, and our life is over. How are you participating in the marketplace of life?

December 13

Five-Year Plan

I was sitting next to a stranger at a business conference luncheon. After pleasantries, he said to me, "So what's your five-year plan?" I think it was a popular thought in the business world, and maybe still is, to arrange your career and maybe your life by making your five-year plans and accomplishing them. I'm not one of those people. Instead, long ago I turned over my life to Spirit. "Here is my life. You gave it to me, and I give it back to you. Do what you want with me." This was not easy to do. It took me fifteen years of thinking about it to actually surrender my life. I had worried, *What if I surrender and Spirit makes me do something I hate?* Finally, I realized that Spirit will direct us to what we love and make things happen that fulfill Spirit's plan and also make us happier than when we guided our lives ourselves. And it has been much more wonderful than anything I could have thought of or planned.

Spirit always wanted to guide my life but would not do so unless invited. I have lived in the comfort that I don't need a five-year or any type of plan to chart my progress. I instead have learned that Spirit will give me guidance and messages as to what to do next, and I don't need to worry about what is farther around the next bend of my path, because I am not the one planning my life.

So that is basically what I said to this man at the conference, that Spirit guides my life, and I don't need to make plans or worry about it. I believe he thought I was nuts or just stupid and I would never amount to anything. Only Spirit knows.

Lightwork: Dangerous Jobs

We continue our lightwork projections, thinking today about those whose jobs are dangerous. I am thinking about roofers up on the pinnacle of the tower and skyscraper riveters, walking the narrow beams high in the air and counting on their good balance to keep them from falling. I am thinking of miners who labor in semidarkness, hoping there is not a cave-in. I imagine you can think of more people who work in danger.

We, the lightworkers, send you Spirit's light to surround you and protect you from harm, to guard your safety and your health. We thank you for doing these needed jobs to benefit us all. We keep you in the light and wish you a safe and happy life.

December 15

A Long Winter's Nap

"And mama in her 'kerchief and I in my cap
Have just settled our brains for a long winter's nap ..."

This passage from "The Night Before Christmas" echoes in my head as the Christmas season approaches. But these lines of the poem always confused me when I was a child. I couldn't figure out why anyone would wear hats to bed. But now I get what the author meant. He lived in a time when there was no central heat, no electricity. The only heat in the freezing months was from the fireplace. And as the night went on, the fire would die down lower and lower, and the bedroom would get colder and colder. That's why the hats were needed. And in the middle of the night, someone had to get up and put more wood on the fire. Brrr. It chills me to even think of those old days.

But those days are not over for everyone all over the earth. So today, let us think about poor people freezing in cities, rural areas, and third world countries, and let us wrap them in fuzzy blankets of Spirit's white light. See them feeling the warmth of God encircling them so they can survive.

And, on the more mundane level, let's take a look in our closets. Are there warm coats and sweaters we no longer wear? If so, let's make a plan to donate them so they can be of use to keep people warm.

Practicing Divine Love

Today, I invite us to think about how we are all one and how we must recognize this and love everyone. Picture yourself at the mall. Visualize all the people who pass you by. In your mind, say, "I love you," to all of them at once—no need to repeat it for each one.

Now expand your vision. See your whole city. See it as if you are on a hill above it. In your mind say, "I love you," to everyone in the city.

Broaden your focus again. Now you float above the world. You look around and see the thousands and millions of fellow lightworkers, all floating above the earth. A sense of excitement and joy fills you to see all of us, working together in the light. See us linked in a web of light, encircling the whole planet. Today, lightworkers, let us join the mighty chorus of the millions who shout, "We love you, all people of the earth. God loves you. We are truly one."

December 17

The American Dream

All my life, I have heard this term, the American dream. To have a good job and enough money to buy a house. To have a family and provide for them. These are all good things. People around the world who don't have a chance to have these things yearn for them.

But the American dream is lacking something. It is too personalized—my job, my house, my family, my new car. What is lacking is a sense of community, of helping other people who aren't in the family, of giving, of sharing, of being humbly thankful for what we do have.

Life should not be a game of accumulation. It should be a spiritual path toward being a better person, with lessons to learn and pitfalls to negotiate that teach us something if we let the lessons and pitfalls be our teachers.

We hear often that people who have "made it," either through fame or fortune, are unhappy. Some turn to drugs, some to suicide. The dream is empty unless it includes kindness, charity, caring, and sharing. Today, let's see those who are striving to make it realizing what is truly important in their American dream.

The Burning Bowl

Long ago, I encountered the practice of the burning bowl, and I have done this ceremony ever since. I spend the last weeks of the year thinking over things that I say or think that are outdated and unworthy of the spiritual soul I am trying to become. To dramatize the letting go of these old words, I write or type them on paper. For me, they could be things I say about my shortcomings (too old, too ugly, too tired, etc.) or condemnations of groups of people (those awful Wall Street brokers).

I write the actual sentences I want to get rid of, and then I cut the paper into strips, one strip for each thought. I get a bowl or can that I can use as a burning vessel and put some sand in it so the flames go out safely.

Then I pick a day for the ceremony. After lighting a candle and meditating, asking Spirit to cleanse me of outworn thought patterns, I begin. For each strip of wrongful thought (such as, *I don't have enough money,*) I say it out loud and say something like, "I banish this." And then I set it on fire. As I do this, I say an opposite sentence that is intended to replace it, such as "I have all I need to do what I want." I throw it in the bowl and move on until I do this with all of them. After all is said and done, I have a little pile of ashes, representing my determination to rid my mind of wrong thoughts and to replace them in the new year.

I invite you to join me and many other lightworkers in this practice. It's time now to work on your list and then, before the year ends, do your own burning bowl ceremony.

December 19

Leave Your Egos at the Door

What a great event it was for global unity, the writing of the song "We Are the World" and the worldwide broadcast of the We Are the World concert. I've always appreciated the emotional impact it had on me, both its words and its enthusiastic adoption by millions of people. But I didn't know this part of the story that makes me appreciate it even more.

A man told me this story. Lionel Ritchie wrote the song and came up with the idea of gathering a horde of famous singers to record it together. I remember the music video of all those stars crammed together on risers, singing as a choir instead of individuals.

Mr. Ritchie was a little worried at the prospect of all these superstars cooperating to sing the song. He posted a sign at the entrance to the studio, "Leave Your Egos at the Door." He realized that he had invited over one hundred singers but had solo parts for only a handful. Since he did not want jealousy and competitiveness to enter the process, he assigned the solos himself. And he pulled it off. All these singers realized that they were showing the example of "We Are the World" by blending together to heal the world.

I congratulate those singers for understanding the value of cooperation and harmony over individual glory. And, since that event, there have been many other events around the world that have accomplished a similar gathering of individual stars for good purposes.

Let us hold the thought that this type of group harmony catches on all over, not only for singers and songs but for all sorts of cooperation projects in many other fields, companies, neighborhoods and cities, all for good purposes.

Tangled Lights

Well, it was that time again, time to put up the Christmas tree. After I got it put together, no easy task with over thirty branches of six different sizes, I faced the task that I dreaded the most—putting on the lights. I had carefully wound them on a frame last year, and now I began taking them off and testing each set. Although I laid each set of one hundred carefully down in its own pile, when I attempted to pick the sets up and arrange them on the tree, inevitably, some got tangled, extremely tangled. With a deep sigh of self-pity, I sank to the floor to get them untangled.

"What is my lesson here?" I said out loud to no one. "I guess it is patience and perseverance. Okay, let go of being angry about it and concentrate on calmness and gentleness." And it worked. Sooner or later, each string made its way onto my beautiful tree, considerably brightening both the room and my spirits.

Hmm, I wondered, was this a subtle spiritual message that my own inner light can get tangled in negatives—anger, resentment, worry, self-pity? Those can make a mess of my spiritual path until I sit with patience and gentleness and get myself untangled. Are you tangled too?

December 21

Winter Solstice

Today is the shortest day of the year, winter solstice. It is becoming popular to have a ceremony at this time to honor the cycle of the earth that signifies nature is resting between growing seasons.

Let's have a winter solstice commemoration right now, you and I. Close your eyes a moment and feel within yourself the echo of this time of dark stillness that is filled with the silent promise of spring. Visualize plant bulbs resting under the ground, sleeping until warmth comes. Visualize trees with no leaves that have their sap stored safely underground.

Now turn your attention to your mind. Visualize the many thoughts and memories that are resting inside. Some don't belong; they are artifacts of the past, emotions and reactions to things that happened long ago. Without naming any of them, become a winter gardener. Ask Spirit to help you pull out all thoughts and feelings that don't belong. Picture it as if you are really gardening inside your head.

Now that your "soil" inside of you is weeded, envision yourself planting new bulbs of wonderful thoughts. And just like our certainty in the coming of spring, we await the blossoming within ourselves of our new thoughts.

Capricorn—The Goat

When I think of the meaning of Capricorn, I think of the hardy mountain goat who climbs the mountain peaks. Surefooted on treacherous rocks, the goat slowly and carefully picks her way up to the top.

On our paths to greater spirituality, we are faced with slippery boulders that we must cross. They can be laziness (I am spiritual enough), distractions (I need a vacation in Vegas, the carnal city), lack of commitment (Do I really want to try so hard? Why not live it up?).

To climb, we must leave some things and some people behind, which is not easy. It is easier to coast along with the crowd. It is easier to accept the prejudices of the mob, to sit back and indulge our senses. But that is not what I want. I want to climb higher, to be a better and better person. I want to leave behind the dark parts of myself and of the world. I want to be like a Capricorn. Do you?

December 23

Signs of the New Age: The Five-Year-Old Girl

Here's a story I heard on the news. A five-year-old girl saw a story about homeless people in her city on her local news. The story said they were cold and needed hats and gloves. She decided she had to help. She emptied out her piggy bank of the money she had been saving for two years. And she sold her toys and dolls door-to-door around her neighborhood to make more money.

Then her mom took her to a store where she, eagle-eyed for a bargain, purchased three bags full of hats and gloves. Her mom then took her to the shelter where she handed out her merchandise to the homeless people there. She talked to each person and wished them a merry Christmas. The news station had heard of this project, and they sent a crew along to the shelter to film it. They saw how moved the people were that this little child was helping them.

This saintly little girl is one of a generation of highly evolved souls coming to this earth now to help us move the planet to a higher vibration of peace and love. They see injustice or a need, and they go right out and do something. Think about it. This girl did not tithe (give 10 percent). She instead gave *all* her money, plus sold her own toys and beloved dolls to help total strangers. That is awesome! Who among us adults have that much compassion to give everything?

Goodness moves others to goodness. As she was leaving the store, one of the clerks was so moved he bought and gave to her three new Barbies. Let us today give thanks for this girl and all of her generation—the wise children who will save us if we will listen to them.

Stepping Up

Many of the stories I've told about signs of the New Age have something in common. It seems that suddenly the people in these stories have awakened from the dream state of status quo to realize something was very wrong that they didn't notice or think about before. And along with the awakening came an almost desperate urge to fix the problem themselves since no one else was fixing it. So they stepped up to the plate no matter how impossible their mission seemed. It doesn't matter how many people thought they were nutty for trying something so big or something that had not been done before.

You know, they remind me of Noah. Noah was an ordinary person who awakened to a strange mission, a mission that was hard and long and one that was seen as nutty by others who were nearby. But he persisted against all odds. He was driven by that same sense of urgency that drove some of those whose stories I've told. Let's thank Spirit for them all. They are blessings to our world.

Let's hold in light all those, known and unknown, who are stepping up to create a better world. Let us help however we can, both through our encouraging thoughts and by actually, physically or financially, lending a helping hand. Let's help make their visions come true. Let's step up too.

December 25

Lights on the Tree

This is a time for lighting the Christmas tree in those households where this custom is practiced. Whether or not you participate, you have surely seen many lighted trees as symbols of the Christmas season.

Today, create your own tree in your thoughts or gaze at the one before you. Whether you are Christian or not doesn't matter much for this visualization. You can think of the lighted tree as a sign of the higher light from higher realms, no matter what you believe.

The lighted tree represents eternal life. Now think of all those people who have been lights of love and kindness in your own life. Place these people on your tree as lights, since you see them as shining examples. Think of each one as you place it on the tree and thank each one for the contributions they have made to your life.

Expand your thinking to all those whom you want to honor as lights from the larger world. For my group, I would add Gandhi, Martin Luther King, Eleanor Roosevelt, and many others who have been lights in my life and whom I admire for serving this planet. You pick whomever you like. Add these lights to your tree and thank them for adding light to this earth.

Now add the finishing touch, the light of Spirit at the top of the tree.

There! What a masterpiece! Enjoy.

The Gift

Every now and then, but not too often,
We are blessed with a gift from God.
This special gift outshines mountains and lakes and clouds and stars;
This gift is remembered always.

What is this gift so special and rare?
It is the gift of meeting a person who has an open heart.
Caring, sharing, listening, and laughing
Are the signs of the open heart.

Those who enter the company of the person with the open heart
Are truly blessed to see
The light of God within that open door,
Shining for you and me.

December 27

The Trade

When I was in grade school, I had a neighbor, Bert, who was my age. Bert and I became friends and often played together, riding our sleds in winter, bikes in summer. Sometimes we played house under the lace tableclothed dining room table of a lady in the neighborhood who was in her seventies. Bert would even play jacks with me, which was unusual for a boy.

One Christmas when we were maybe eight or nine, our families each got us a Christmas present we didn't like. The day after Christmas, Bert and I talked over our mutual problem and decided to trade our gifts. I took home his bright orange basketball, and he took my doll, both of us happy to have something we preferred and both of us eager to play with our new presents.

Well, both of our parents freaked out. Maybe they thought we were both failing our gender role development. But being good friends, my mom and dad and his mom and dad talked it over and decided to respect our trade and leave us alone.

I had so much fun with that basketball, and I know Bert just loved his doll, which was usually forbidden to boys in the 1950s. And I felt so good to have my decision respected. I'd like to thank both sets of parents belatedly for allowing Bert and me to be our own true selves, not somebody's image of the proper little boy and girl. Nowadays, parents seem so much more enlightened about their children's choices. At least that's the way it seems to me, here in the United States. But even here, there are parents who have not gotten this message. Please project with me to parents around the world to respect their children and let them be themselves.

December 28

Theme for the New Year

I don't make New Year's resolutions anymore. Why? I never kept most of them. They were too hard, too big, and by February, I'd give up and consider myself a failure. Then I got a better idea. I now pick a theme for the year. Actually, the theme picks me. I get into a meditative state, usually the week between Christmas and New Year's Eve, and poof, the word arrives on its own. I recognize it is the right one by my standard reaction, "Oh no, not that word!"

Here's what I mean. One year I picked the theme "boundaries." That meant I wanted to learn more about good boundaries in relating to others and to practice what I learned whenever needed. A theme word is not a command like a resolution to exercise every day. It is more of a project that can be picked up and worked on whenever I want. My goal for a particular year is to make some progress on my theme, as it is something I want to learn to do better.

So how did I begin the boundary theme year? I got a couple books on boundaries and learned a lot. I went to a lecture and learned more. For example, I learned that there are three types of boundaries problems: 1) people who violate others' boundaries; 2) people who are doormats for the boundary violators; and 3) people whose boundaries are so heavy and tight that no one can get in at all.

Then I began to apply my new knowledge. Whenever I thought of my theme, I thought over the interactions of my day in terms of the boundaries involved. Did I encroach upon another or let them encroach upon me? Did I refrain from nosy questions? Did I stand up for myself if needed? I talked to friends who were also learning about boundaries, and we practiced good boundary conversation, clearly stating what we meant without manipulation. Then, after I learned so much, I realized Spirit was placing situations of disagreement in my path so I could practice good boundary talking in real settings—and it worked pretty well too.

Think about the concept of picking a word for yourself today, and I'll tell you some more about my theme words tomorrow.

December 29

More on Theme Words for the New Year

Another year, two words arrived in my head, and I thought they represented two different projects. The words were *rules* and *flexibility*. I found out during that year that for me they are two sides of the same coin, but it took me nearly the whole year to see that light. The rules I looked at were ones like "I never do that, I don't like this, I always do it that way." These are patterns of responses that were so habitual in my thinking that I no longer even consciously thought about their value or lack of it. I looked over many of my rules for living, like which sock I put on first, what I eat for breakfast, how I feel about parties (never much liked them). The goal was to discover if I wanted to keep or drop the particular rule, or perhaps just be flexible with it.

Some rules proved to be almost unconscious, as they seemed to be culturally based, such as my hair style, what clothes I wear, makeup choices, having a Christmas tree. I made some changes. I decided to stop dying my hair. I had not seen the color of my hair for more than twenty years. Turns out I like it the way it really is—brown with a white stripe that sparkles like metallic silver in the sunlight.

As simple as these things are, they run deep and represent the portion of my life that I had let get into the rut of unconscious habit. The practice I did that year of looking at rules seems to have attuned me to a new habit of looking at my rules pretty often, deciding on their merits.

So, my friend, would you like to join me in picking out a theme word for next year? What will it be?

World Healing Day

Tomorrow, December 31, has been declared internationally to be World Healing Day. On this day, please join with millions, and perhaps billions, who unite their thoughts in prayers and visualizations of world peace. If you are able, meditate on this at noon Greenwich mean time, which is 7: a.m. eastern, 6 a.m. central, 5 a.m. mountain, and 4 a.m. Pacific time. But even if you miss the joint meditation time, join in sometime today, for many will be meditating and praying for world peace throughout the day until the new year comes.

In meditation, reach out your hands to link with all, holding hands in a great chain around the earth. Link also with those on higher planes and with the angel kingdom who hold the vision with us all of a great new world of peace and love.

Let us tomorrow end this year working in the light, as we began this year. This chain of so many of us, united in light, creating the new world, will help it to be born.

December 31

I Thank You

My Dear Lightworker,

I thank you for making this journey with me through this year. Your diligence and working in the light is leading us all to a glorious new world—a heaven on earth.

Thank you for:
> your loving kindness to people;
> your caring for the other kingdoms of mineral, plant, animal;
> your personal struggles to grow;
> your acceptance of your stewardship of earth.

Your efforts are bringing about a whole new day of:
> peace and oneness for all;
> planetary healing;
> one world united in love.

Together, we have walked along, lightening each other's loads, enjoying each other's company, knowing we are not alone. We are creating, day by day:
> a new world
>> of the people,
>>> by the people,
>>>> and for the people.

You have gladdened my heart and made this earth a better place for me, for you, for us all. Here's to a bright new year, with holy light growing brighter, day by day, with a golden age coming ever closer for us all. Thank you for joining me in this year of working in the light. I hope you will turn the page tomorrow to January 1 and begin anew, uplifting yourself, your loved ones, your nation, and your world with me. May it be your best year ever!

Alphabetical List of Titles

Printed in the United States
by Bookmasters

Printed in the United States
By Bookmasters